JUSTICE IN THE AGE OF JUDGMENT

JUSTICE IN THE AGE OF JUDGMENT

FROM AMANDA KNOX TO KYLE RITTENHOUSE AND THE BATTLE FOR DUE PROCESS IN THE DIGITAL AGE

ANNE BREMNER, JD
AND DOUG BREMNER, MD

Skyhorse Publishing

Skyhorse Publishing books may be purchased in bulk at special discounts for sales promotion, corporate gifts, fund-raising, or educational purposes. Special editions can also be created to specifications. For details, contact the Special Sales Department, Skyhorse Publishing, 307 West 36th Street, 11th Floor, New York, NY 10018 or info@skyhorsepublishing.com.

Skyhorse® and Skyhorse Publishing® are registered trademarks of Skyhorse Publishing, Inc.®, a Delaware corporation.

Visit our website at www.skyhorsepublishing.com.

10 9 8 7 6 5 4 3 2 1

Library of Congress Cataloging-in-Publication Data is available on file.

Cover design by Brian Peterson

Print ISBN: 978-1-5107-5136-1
Ebook ISBN: 978-1-5107-5137-8

Printed in the United States of America

CONTENTS

PREFACE

My name is Anne Bremner. I'm a lawyer from Seattle. In 2008, I was asked by an esteemed judge and his longtime colleague if I would be willing to help defend a Seattle college student accused of the brutal murder of her roommate while studying abroad in Italy.

Amanda Knox had become a household name, and her case drew a maelstrom of front page and television coverage around the world. But her friends and family insisted she was wrongly accused and innocent. When they told me the horrifying details, which involved a forced confession, a prejudiced and compromised investigation, and a seemingly irrational prosecutor hell-bent on convicting Amanda regardless of the facts, I more than willingly jumped in and agreed to help.

Little did I know it would take years and thousands of hours for our team in the United States and Italy to help win her exoneration. We battled a constant onslaught of lies and disinformation from an army of tabloid media that would breathlessly trumpet every false leak from the prosecution, not to mention the new world of social media where every mistruth would spread like wildfire.

It would become one of the most important cases of my life and test all my skills, which I had honed over decades of work as a prosecutor, defense attorney, and legal analyst. When the dust settled and I had a chance to reflect, I decided to write this book about the experience. I soon realized Amanda's case ushered in a new era, in which the media and the public, through social media, have become a powerful force in the justice system, unduly influencing judicial outcomes. (It was already a factor even before social media. Just look at the big part media played in O. J. Simpson's acquittal and other high-profile trials I've reported on as a network TV analyst over the years.)

With the advent of smartphones, everybody became a potential crime scene videographer, and the fact that footage can be loaded onto Facebook and Twitter and immediately go viral has turned the judicial world on its head. Although this type of footage can be a game changer and hold people accountable, it also holds the potential for harm, allowing viewers to make snap judgements and take things out of context before there has been a careful analysis of all of the facts. That's why we have a judicial system, and not Facebook polls, to ultimately decide guilt or innocence.

My reflections on the effects of media and social media on Amanda's case led me to go further: to some of the most high-profile cases I've worked on and covered over the years. That, in turn, led me to take a deep dive into the media influence on the prosecution, and sometimes the outcome, of some of the most watched cases and legal proceedings of our era. As a result, I expanded the scope of the book.

Michael Jackson, the West Memphis Three, Harvey Weinstein and the rise of the #MeToo movement, the Duke Lacrosse rape case, Brett Kavanaugh's Supreme Court nomination, the trials surrounding the deaths of George Floyd and Ahmaud Arbery, and the prosecution of Kyle Rittenhouse are just a few of the many cases I've spent considerable time analyzing and pondering.

This book is an exploration of the evolution of our judicial system, as well as an autobiography of sorts, chronicling my unique upbringing, my legal education, and my decades-long career as an attorney and media analyst, all of which have influenced the person I am now.

I wrote this book with my brother, Doug Bremner, MD, a noted author and physician. His medical and psychiatric perspectives bring invaluable insight to the cases, and he's also a great writer.

I can't thank my cousin, Kristine Erickson, enough for her help on this book. Her expertise and incomparable skills as a writer and editor have been critical in the completion of this manuscript. I am forever indebted to her for her selfless contribution and dedication. Finally, I would like to thanks my amazing paralegal, Joan Stapleton, who passed away too soon ten years ago from melanoma.

1
TAKING THE CASE

It was that rare day in the Pacific Northwest—sun and blue skies with just the right temperature—the kind of day most Washingtonians savor, as they know it won't be long before the summer ends and it's the start of the "Seattle Rain Festival: October through May." It was July 2008, and I was at the Semiahmoo Resort, on a spit of land jutting out into the Strait of Georgia—the body of water separating Canada and the United States on the far western coast of both countries—near Blaine, Washington. Semiahmoo, which appropriately means "water all around" or "hole in the sky" in the original North Straits Salish native language, has beautiful views of mountains in all directions—Mount Baker, the Twin Sisters, and Canadian mountains rising up behind White Rock, British Columbia.

Semiahmoo is only a couple of stone throws away from Birch Bay, which my grandparents used to visit from their home in Lynden, Washington, and the Peace Arch at the border, where past generations of my family posed for photographs. This was the "other" part of western Washington, a remote area where the Nooksack and Skagit rivers periodically flooded the land, depositing sediments that created flat plains and fertile black soil perfect for farming. It was a magnet for immigrants from The Netherlands for which the landscape was a reminder of home. My family lived there for four generations. Semiahmoo was a respite from the pressures and push of Seattle, my day-to-day location, that also felt like coming home.

Presenting itself as the Capital of Cool, Seattle was in fact a city of contradictions. Haunted by the ghosts of the musicians Kurt Cobain and Jimi Hendrix, dead by suicide and overdose, respectively, Seattle may be the most progressive city in America. It tolerates open-air drug dealing and homeless encampments throughout the city, while it is also home of the richest man in the world, Jeff Bezos, founder, current executive chairman, and former chief executive officer of Amazon, the world's largest and fastest growing retail organization. Bezos isn't actually from Seattle, though, although Bill Gates, founder of Microsoft and another one of the richest men in the world, is. The Seattle area was also the birthplace of Costco and Starbucks. The city was seemingly all about looking mellow and laid back, while maintaining a steady level of stress and drive on the inside. So, when I got a chance to make an exit to a place like Semiahmoo, even if it was doing the biz (i.e., the business, or working, as a lawyer in my case), I took it. And, hey, it was summertime.

In fact, that weekend the biz was attending the 2008 Northwest Regional Meeting of the American College of Trial Lawyers (ACTL) at the Semiahmoo Resort. The ACTL was a mostly white male kind of place, which was typical of the lawyering profession. Because it wasn't always easy for a woman who isn't into golfing to make headway in the boys' club atmosphere of the legal world, I took advantage of opportunities offered by groups like the ACTL whenever I could.

Getting to stay in places like Semiahmoo is one of the perks of my job as a successful Seattle lawyer, although I usually don't have time to kick back and relax at such events. It was during a coffee break that I saw a call coming in from Mike Heavey. Mike was a judge for the King County Superior Court, where I had presented cases many times, so I figured I'd better take his call. I picked up as I walked out to my car to talk in private.

"Anne, you probably heard about this Amanda Knox case, right?" he asked.

"You mean the student from Seattle who was charged with murdering her roommate in Italy?" I replied.

The case had already been in the media for a couple of months.

"I think there's been a real travesty of justice here. You're a lawyer who has a lot of exposure in the media. I think you can really help us."

Mike went on to explain how there was no evidence against Amanda, how it was improbable that someone whose life had been exemplary could—out of the blue—commit such a horrible crime, and how the police and prosecutors in Perugia, Italy—where she was undergoing hearings that were under seal—were leaking false information and mistreating her. Thus far, they had:

- Subjected her to hours of abusive interrogation, even hitting her on the head to coerce a confession;
- Leaked her diary;
- Lied to her by saying she had been infected with the Human Immunodeficiency Virus (HIV);
- Used that false medical information to get her to make a list of men she had slept with; and
- Used that list to try to paint her as a wicked slut, a siren who used sex to lure men to their demise.

Hearing all this, I had an overwhelming feeling that this was a travesty of justice and an outrage. I felt that, given my role in the media analyzing and commenting on high-profile cases like those of O. J. Simpson and Scott Peterson, I really was in a position to help. I agreed because this was not a case being tried in a fair and impartial courtroom. It was being tried in the media and, as I was later to learn, on the internet, in private chat rooms where like-minded individuals posted conspiracy theories and spent hours scouring the internet for "clues" they thought would be evidence of guilt.

I thought the case would go on for a couple of years, but that turned into a decade.

Along the way, I would be trailed and attacked by hacks and trolls. They plastered social media with lies and contacted every media organization where I appeared and every organization I spoke with or that gave me an award. They defamed me by saying I was "vile" and a felon who had been disbarred (an obvious lie).

In retrospect, I realize Amanda's case was a forerunner of things to come. Her trial was not a trial of law, but a trial by media, convicted by the internet, before she even had a chance to present evidence or hear witnesses. Her guilt was not decided by a jury of her peers, but by her facial expressions and calisthenics.

The Amanda Knox case was also a forerunner of our current era of "fake news," and the 2020 United States presidential election, in terms of polarization of opinion and the influence of both traditional and non-traditional media.[1] In fact, pro-Putin bloggers capitalized on the case as a way to drive a wedge between

Europe and America.[2,3] Their involvement was also a forerunner of things to come for American politics.[4] The Amanda Knox bloggers, with their conspiracy theories and confirmation biases, looked a lot like the QAnon folks that would appear just around the pike.[5]

I called Amanda's case "a conviction based on kisses and cartwheels." That is what this book is about. It's about Amanda Knox, but it is also about our present state of affairs, where courtrooms and juries are thrown out the window and are replaced by the story of the moment, where convictions are delivered by internet chat rooms instead of physical evidence, where people spend hours "doing their own research" on the internet to find information that confirms their own biases. We live in an era where everyone is an "expert" and the *real* experts are discounted and dismissed, where everyone considers themselves a journalist, yet discounts any journalist they disagree with. Justice is thrown out the window.

A central theme of this book is how the media (including what I would call citizen's media, or social media) has grown to have an oversized effect on high-profile criminal cases in our current era. The media has negative effects, in splashing scandalous news across the front pages of newspapers that turn out to be untrue and that have prejudicial effects on ongoing court cases, as in the case of Amanda Knox. That's why lawyers like me have to get out ahead of the news so we can shape the story to help our clients. The media, however, can have negative effects in other ways.

Although the jury in the trial of O. J. Simpson, accused of murdering his ex-wife and her boyfriend, were sequestered away from the media for 265 days, the media turned it into a story about race, tapping into Black peoples' grievances about past injustices and polarizing opinions about the case along racial lines. This was a story where his lawyers got out ahead of the media and created a story they felt was beneficial to their client. Although proven true, based on the fact they reached their goal of an innocent verdict, the long-term effects can only be seen as negative for justice in the future.

Scott Peterson, convicted of murdering his pregnant wife, had many similarities to Amanda Knox's case, including the fact that the press concluded from the start that he "looked guilty." The West Memphis Three, like Amanda Knox, were damaged by newspaper reports, leaked by detectives in the case, that they were involved in a Satanic cult. All of these cases are covered in this book, including the role of newspapers and the media, which are quick to scrutinize and judge people accused of crimes in high-profile cases, and the snap judgments that media consumers form based on what they see in their social media feeds or read on online forums, or the misinformation they glean from the internet. But when hard facts come to light that go against snap-judgment headlines and the lies of biased bloggers and forum posters, all that fades into the background. In this book, we are going to chase them out of the shadows and take a hard look at their impact on the proper execution of justice: not only newspaper reporters and television interviewers, but tabloid writers, citizen journalists, bloggers, Tweeters, and forum posters writing under anonymous fake names.

About eight hundred years before the birth of Christ, an elaborate and sophisticated civilization developed in what is now central Italy. The Etruscans, by their own description, were composed of twelve cities, the "Dodecapoli," which predated Rome. One of those cities was Perugia, which is now the capital of the Italian region of Umbria. The Etruscans absorbed the culture of the ancient Greeks, with whom they traded, and had a lavish culture of feasting and art where women appeared to be the equal of men. They created beautiful paintings of their domestic life in tombs for their loved ones, buried deep below the earth, and in carvings on the local cliffsides.

But the Etruscans also had a dark side. They were highly superstitious. They hung on the words of their priests, who sacrificed sheep and examined the shape of their livers to predict the future. Most of the ancient churches of modern Umbria and Tuscany are built on the foundations of ancient Etruscan temples that were oriented to be able to identify patterns of stars in the sky to aid in the prediction of future events.

Two thousand years later, the ancestors of the Etruscans are now the citizens of Perugia and other cities and towns across the modern-day Italian provinces of Lazio, Umbria, and Tuscany. Perugia itself is beautifully perched on its hilltop, a perfect Goldilocks city—not too big and not too small—that is a magnet for thousands of students from around the world seeking education in the culture of Italy, with its multiple languages and cultural education programs. They mill about in the *Piazza Novembre* and frequent bars and cafes in the narrow city streets. Although not as extreme as their Etruscan ancestors, many modern day Perugians, like many Italians in general, have superstitious beliefs. They may go to various extremes to avoid situations that they think will bring them bad luck. They won't sit with their backs to the door in a restaurant, or else they will never get married. They won't walk under a ladder, or it will give them bad luck. God forbid a black cat should cross their path. Hovering over all of this malaise is the omnipresent evil eye. In some individuals, however, irrational beliefs can be taken to extremes, just like in the United States.

Perugia is a sister city of Seattle, although the two cities don't have much in common, apart from one or two statues celebrating their sisterhood. Most natives of the cities were probably unaware of that fact until the Amanda Knox case burst on the scene.

Giuliano Mignini, the lead prosecutor in Amanda's case, was a native of Perugia. He held superstitious, irrational beliefs that weren't far afield from his Etruscan ancestors, and were way outside the norm even for superstitious Italians. He followed a conservative version of Catholicism and endorsed conspiracy theories, not unknown to many Italians, that the Masons conduct secret activities, including ritual sacrifice.[6] Amanda was dropped into this landscape naïve and unaware, and, on a fateful Perugian night at a music event, locked eyes with Raffaele Sollecito. They rarely left each other's side during the next six days.

On Halloween night, October 31, 2007, while most students were roaming the streets of Perugia and crowding into nightclubs and bars, Amanda and Raffaele were holed up in his apartment, smoking weed and making love. Amanda was scheduled to go to work at a bar owned by Patrick Lumumba, a native of Africa who had worked hard to start a business in the city, but she got a text saying he didn't need her that night. Relieved, she spent the rest of the night at Raffaele's.

The next morning, she returned home and took a shower. Finding the door of her roommate, Meredith Kercher, locked, and not getting a response to her knocking on the door, she called Raffaele, who came over and tried to break the door down without success. They called the police, who arrived and broke it down. That's when they found the body of Meredith, whose throat had been brutally slit. Prosecutor Giuliano Mignini eventually arrived on the scene and immediately formed his own opinion of what had happened. The body was covered with a blanket, which led him to the questionable conclusion that the murder had been committed by a woman. At the initial investigation of the crime scene, Raffaele was hugging and comforting Amanda, which led Mignini to decide she was a sex-obsessed sociopath who didn't care about Meredith's death. Amanda and Raffaele were brought to the police station separately. The police found a text message to Patrick on Amanda's phone, which led Mignini to conclude Patrick was involved. What followed was forty-three hours of tag-team police interrogation in Italian (in which Amanda was far from fluent), where she was hit on the head and yelled at to "remember!" She was asked to *imagine* what it would have been like to be there with Patrick and Raffaele and hear the screams of the dying Meredith. In a daze, she put her hands over her ears and described what that might have been like. Then the Italian police transcribed her imagined scenario as a factual confession. They told Raffaele the game was up and that his American girlfriend had fingered him in the murder.

What followed was a tsunami of media insanity. The English tabloids jumped on the story, fueled by the fact that the father of the murder victim, John Kercher, was one of their own (a freelance writer for the tabloids). Front page on the English tabloids was a picture of what looked like a sink covered in blood. The photo was leaked by the prosecution. How had Amanda blithely walked past this on the way to the shower? In fact, it was *not* blood; it was red dye from the chemical luminol, which had been used later by investigators to illuminate blood not visible to the naked eye. During the sealed hearings of Amanda and Raffaele, a story that they had bought bleach to clean up the crime scene leaked to the press. When a vaunted "receipt" for the bleach was finally produced, it turned out to be for pizza.

After getting back to Seattle from my weekend conference, I had breakfast with Mike and a local screenwriter named Tom Wright. Both Mike and Tom had daughters who were in the same class with Amanda at Seattle Prep, a prestigious local private high school. They all lived near each other in the West Seattle neighborhood, which would turn out to be a bulwark of support for Amanda over the next four years. They gave me more background about the case, and a few days later I met her family at Mike's house: Edda Mellas and Amanda's stepfather, Chris Mellas, Amanda's biological father, Curt Knox, and his wife, Cassandra.

I would soon obtain videotapes of investigators working the crime scene. What I saw floored me. The Italian investigators were not properly wearing protective clothing. Their hair was hanging out everywhere. The video of the crime scene investigation had frequent stops and starts, with gaps that had no explanation. At one point, a large woman mysteriously crashed through a window. Investigators were leaning up against a wall talking on their cell phones. They posed the body for photos, moving it and poking gloved fingers into the stab wounds on the neck. They were constantly talking while collecting evidence, which could have caused contamination from their saliva. They scrubbed away bloody shoeprints and footprints instead of properly collecting them as evidence.

They stopped by Raffaele's place, grabbed the first knife they found in a kitchen drawer, transported it in a shoebox, and sent it off to the lab for DNA analysis. When they decided they didn't have enough evidence connecting him to the crime scene, they went back a month and a half after the murder and picked up a bra clasp off the floor of Meredith's bedroom. It had been kicked around so much it had turned from white to black. They had failed to collect that clasp for forty-six days. They sent it to the police lab, which subsequently claimed Raffaele's DNA was on the clasp.[7]

My experience as a lawyer told me this was compromised, contaminated evidence that should not be admissible. I felt the world would be shocked to see that this was the Amanda Knox crime scene. Unfortunately, it would take four years for the Italian courts to bring in forensics experts from La Sapienza, the premier Italian university, to pronounce that the only two pieces of physical evidence the Perugia prosecutors had, the bra clasp and the knife, were unreliable due to contamination and shoddy police lab procedures, and were totally worthless in a court of law. Other than that, the prosecution had nothing but cartwheels and kisses. However, Amanda and Raffaele would sit in jail (with Raffaele spending considerable time in solitary confinement) until the final verdict of complete exoneration was reached. That would take years and three trials—not just double jeopardy, but triple jeopardy.

Many people don't think about the criminal justice system until something goes wrong—someone we KNOW to be guilty goes free or we see a headline about someone who was wrongly convicted and spent the best years of their life in prison. We want more of the bad guys convicted and none of the good guys put behind bars. And that's the way it should be.

But it never is.

There will always be guilty people who go free—some rich, well resourced, seemingly immune to punishment. Odds are that we're never going to be a country where the innocent—especially the poor, people who can't afford the best lawyers, who were in the wrong place at the wrong time, who don't look like everyone else, but look like *the kind of person who did it*—always avoid prison. But I believe it's more important to protect the innocent than to get all the bad guys. Our founders believed this, too.

Benjamin Franklin said: "That it is better 100 guilty persons should escape than that one innocent person should suffer, is a maxim that has been long and generally approved."[8]

Today, that maxim feels radical. We have access to more information than at any time in human history, yet we are increasingly less informed and more certain of our opinion, more convinced of the morality of our convictions. There are few things the public is more certain of than the innocence or guilt of a man or woman accused of something they believe to be true—a man raping a woman, a cop accused of racism, a hero turned to villain.

The Amanda Knox story is about what happens when we search for proof of what we believe at the expense of the facts, when "innocent until proven guilty" is replaced by guilty if we can't prove otherwise, and when reparations for the victim come before fidelity to the facts. When the media—including social media—acts as an accelerant to all of the above, and premature judgment overrides justice.

I've seen quite a bit. I've seen mothers who have killed their children. I've seen rapists walk free. I've cried with women who, even though I knew they were victims of domestic abuse, I didn't think I could *prove* they were. I've been in enough courtrooms and jail cells, hospitals, churches, kitchens, and funeral homes—and seen enough of the worst that humankind is capable of—to have a good idea whether someone is probably guilty or probably innocent.

When I first heard about Amanda Knox, I "knew" she was guilty.

A radio station called the first week of November in 2007, a few days after the murder had captured the world's attention, and asked me to chime in. At the time, I "knew" what everyone else knew from the salacious media reports out of Italy. I heard that she'd confessed, that she'd explained to the Italians that she'd had ritualistic, satanic sex with the roommate she'd been fighting with, that she and her boyfriend had removed Meredith Kercher's clothes and done unspeakable things to her and viciously murdered her with a kitchen knife.

I'd seen the way she'd been acting. I'd heard she was doing cartwheels at the precinct after the murder but before she was arrested. I read the same stories and watched the same cable television as everyone else.

I saw the video of her making out with her boyfriend outside the crime scene after the cold-blooded murder but before she'd been fingered by the Perugia police. I read that the two of them had lived it up and gone out for pizza while their friend's body was being parked at the morgue. I read that, in the midst of her grief, she'd gone out and bought lingerie.

All my experience told me this is not the way innocent people act. This isn't the way people in grief act. I'd seen hundreds of victims, murderers, and wrongly accused, innocent bystanders. The innocent ones don't think about their next pizza slice or the next sexy thong they're going to wear for their boyfriend. That's not the way they act. They're horrified. They're in tears. They can't function. I knew it in my gut. But I didn't need to rely on my gut.

I was assured repeatedly by the media reports that there was forensic evidence to back me up—gobs of it. On the murder weapon. On Meredith's clothes. And I knew what that meant. I knew all I needed to know. Amanda Knox did it. She was a killer. And she was never coming home.

On the radio, I said I thought the best thing her family could do was get in touch with the State Department and ask them to try and convince their Italian counterparts to extend Amanda some leniency, some compassion—the kind of things she refused to give that beautiful British girl. The evidence was all there. She did it. She was going to be convicted. And I knew her only chance was to employ as much of the weight of the United States government as possible, cooperate early, and hope for a chance to see the light of day. Someday.

I didn't give much thought to the case after that.

Until I got the call from Judge Michael Heavey.

He made his pitch. He told me what the media hadn't told me about the case. And I was in.

Amanda Knox was represented in Italy by Carlo Dalla Vedova. The lawyer for the family of Meredith Kercher, Francesco Maresca, was a classic Italian *bella figura*. Meaning that he looked smart in that courtroom in his tailored Italian suits. Too bad he didn't spend as much effort on getting the facts of the Amanda Knox case straight as he did on his suits. He walked out in the middle of one of Amanda Knox's court presentations in 2010, saying she "bored him." Since she was completely exonerated in a later court hearing, that seems like a limited approach to the pursuit of justice.

The real villain of the Amanda Knox fiasco was Giuliano Mignini. He was a member of a right-wing Catholic sect and believed the Masons were controlling the world and conducting ritual sacrifices involving babies. His beliefs had previously led him to make a complete mess of the investigation of a serial killer in Florence. That case was covered by the writer Douglas Preston in a book called *The Monster of Florence*,[9] which he co-wrote with a local Italian journalist named Mario Spezi. Young people in Italy are plagued by a lack of jobs that means they often live with their families for many years after they graduate from high school or college, and since that typically means living in apartments in cities, they have no privacy. It is not uncommon for young people, therefore, to drive off to rural areas to make love to their partners. The Monster of Florence killer was preying on these young couples, lying in wait in rural areas outside Florence and shooting them in their cars while they were in the act of making love. He would often cut off the genitals of the women after their deaths. Mignini pursued a harebrained idea that it was the work of the Masons and never caught the actual killer. When Preston and Spezi started closing in on who the real killer was in the course of researching their book, Mignini responded by having Spezi arrested and put in jail.[10] He allowed his conspiracy theories about satanic cults and ritual sacrifices to blind him to the facts of the case and lose sight of the true killer, both in the Monster of Florence and Amanda Knox cases. He was obsessed with sex and rigid, moralistic ideas.[11] He was eventually convicted for abuse of office, yet he was allowed to continue prosecuting cases.

On the ground covering the Amanda Knox trial in Italy were hundreds of journalists, but there were three English-speaking freelancers who stood out as particularly pro-prosecution. They included the Americans Andrea Vogt, a writer from Idaho, and Barbie Latza Nadeau, who always seemed to be looking at something above the skyline. Then there was Nick Pisa, a writer from the underbelly of the English tabloids, who worked for the *Daily Mail*. Pisa would later prematurely and wrongly report Amanda was found guilty, which the *Daily Mail* (or, as I like to call it, the Daily Fail) plastered on the front page, despite the fact Amanda was found not guilty just moments later.

The lawyers working with Amanda in Perugia had little experience in how to handle a case with such international implications. They didn't speak to the press, as talking to the press was frowned upon in Italy, and many felt it could actually harm a case. That's why we mobilized a group of American lawyers and others with relevant expertise (we called ourselves Friends of Amanda Knox, or FOAK) to take the case of an innocent abroad to the media instead of the courtroom. The reason? Big cases often aren't decided in the courtroom. They're determined in the press. The court of public opinion, inevitably, dictates what happens in the courtroom.

It's impossible for jurors not to be swayed by what they hear in the press and on social media, even if they don't think they are. Even if they can't remember a salacious story they read or an ignorant, easily disproven tweet, the narrative set forth in the press and social media works its way in. That's why good trial lawyers know they've got to get as many of the facts out in the press as soon as possible. You're playing to your audience. That was even more important in this case because of differences in how Italian criminal cases are prosecuted.

US law is based on common law, where findings of particular judges become precedent, and are used to form opinions for subsequent cases. After an arrest for a serious crime like murder, defendants can usually pay a fine, or "bail," which allows them to stay out of jail pending trial, unless a judge deems them to be a serious threat to the community. Defendants have the right to be tried by a jury of their peers. A judge oversees the trial, and jury members are picked randomly from the community. Lawyers for both the defense and the prosecution get to interview potential jury members and weed out those who may have particular biases and prejudices that might go against the client or the prosecution. The judge gives instructions to the jury on how they are to interpret the law in making their decisions, how to remain neutral, and how to render judgment. If convicted, they have the right to appeal, but judgment by the highest court is final.

Italian law is based on civil law, which are laws passed by the parliament and written in a judicial code. Unlike the common law, which comes from England, civil law is basically an outgrowth of the legal codes established by Napoleon, and extends to countries formerly under Napoleon like France, Spain, Portugal, and Italy. Defendants remain in jail pending the outcome of the trial. Most trials are overseen by a panel of three judges, but for crimes like murder they are conducted in the *Corte d'Assise* or Court of Assizes. The evidence is heard and verdict rendered by a combination of two professional judges, *giudici togati,* and usually six *giudici popolari*, or "popular judges."[12] These latter are randomly drawn from a local registry of persons who are eligible based on being between the ages of thirty and sixty-five, not having criminal records, having minimal education requirements, and not being in certain positions, including judges, police, and clergy.[13] Service is obligatory for all eligible citizens. Potential members are vetted in advance for biases and prejudices relevant to the case at hand, and the *giudici popolari* get instruction on how to participate in the trial. During the trial, the *giudici togati* sit in black robes at a panel flanked on either side by (usually) six *giudici popolari* wearing a sash with the Italian tricolors of green, white, and red. Although journalists writing about the case call them the "jury," this actually confuses the issue, since a more accurate translation is "panel of appointed and popular judges." After evidence is heard, the *giudici* are sequestered in the *Camera di Consiglio,* where there are beds, eating facilities, and showers for as long as it takes for them to reach a verdict. They vote with the youngest *giudici popolari* going first and the *giudici togati* going last so as not to have undue influence. They only need a majority to determine the verdict. A tie goes to the accused. If the verdict is innocence, the defendant is released and compensated monetarily for the time they spent in prison, as well as their court costs. The verdict can be appealed to the *Corte d'Assise d'Appello* where, based on an administrative review, the case can be sent back for a retrial, which occurs *de novo*.[14]

One of the sticking points of the Amanda Knox trial was the lack of sequestration of the jury during the period of the trial itself.[15] Many Italians felt unfairly criticized by people like Senator Maria Cantwell of Washington State, who pointed out lack of sequestration of the jury and the potential for bias of the Italian "jury" by sensationalized reports in the media.[16] Most juries in the United States, however, are not sequestered, and similar efforts to vet and instruct juries to avoid biases occur in both countries. Only high-profile cases, like that of Michael Jackson and O. J. Simpson, which are covered later, have sequestered juries, and even then, it's unclear how effective or enforceable that has been. Some argue that sequestering juries causes them to try to return verdicts more quickly in order to return to their normal life.

The media frenzy surrounding the Amanda Knox case was allowed to happen by prosecutor Mignini, who had his judgment fixed on a sex-crazed female murderer as his explanation of the case. He fed the press a steady stream of tabloid headlines, which made their way into tweets and stories on Facebook. The salacious stuff, the stuff that wasn't true—it was having no trouble spreading across the globe. The truth in this case, as it usually is, was much more boring and thus had a much harder time spreading. The story of a prosecutor out of control isn't limited to Italy, however. The story of the out-of-control prosecutor in the Duke lacrosse case is told later in this book, as is the creation of a myth of a satanic cult in the case of the West Memphis Three by police and prosecutors. In those cases, creating prejudice through leaks to the press had many parallels with Mignini.

In highly publicized cases, jury candidates often come in with preconceived notions based on what they've previously heard. That's why we vet juries so carefully, because jurors have often already made up their minds. I'll often ask the jury pool to write down everything they know about the case—everything they've heard and where they heard it. You can get a good idea what their view of the case is just from that exercise.

In a cop case, I'll ask questions to the group like: "Who here wanted to be a cop when you were a kid?" Nobody raises their hand. So, I'll ask why: "Because you get shot at." "Because everyone hates you." It tells you about their biases, which we all have. I'm not looking for people who aren't biased. In cases where I'm representing police, I'm looking for people who can set those biases aside.

When we pick juries, we ask every prospective juror: "What do you think about the case? Do you think you'll be able to put your personal bias aside?" If they are unable to do so, or if they consume news about the case or discuss it, the judge can declare a mistrial.

Think about that for a second. On social media, we make up our minds as we read tweets and headlines, or look for "facts" on online forums that are often biased, not properly sourced, and/or filled with misinformation. We gravitate toward news sources and social media posts that align with our preexisting biases. Our criminal justice system is set up to keep erroneous, misleading, and ill-gotten information out of view of juries so they can better determine guilt and better protect the innocent. As anyone who read about the last two presidential elections on Facebook or Twitter knows, not all information is true. Not every source is credible. When facts are a matter of life and death, information is vetted by a judge, not an algorithm.

I was uniquely qualified to deal with the Amanda Knox case because I was a high-profile lawyer with experience dealing with the media. I could go on television and talk to the camera and make a convincing argument. I was well spoken and articulate. I could deal with the muck and sewer of the tabloids, which this case entailed. Judge Heavey knew me, and right away he thought of me to help address this travesty of justice.

But the other reason I was "uniquely qualified" to work the Knox case wasn't so obvious. In spite of my outward confident persona, I've always seen myself as an underdog person. This may be hard to believe for a girl who grew up in relative privilege. I also endured tragedy at an early age and understood what it was like to be different.

But that's a longer story I'll deal with later. Right now, let's move on to the trial of a lifetime.

2
THE TRIAL OF A LIFETIME

MEREDITH "TOOK TWO PAINFUL HOURS TO DIE AFTER REFUSING
TO TAKE PART IN EXTREME SEXUAL EXPERIENCES"
Nov. 10, 2007: Meredith Kercher died slowly and in agony at the hands of three friends, an Italian judge said yesterday, as police revealed that they are able to identify a fourth suspect involved in the Briton's brutal murder.

The British student was slashed three times with a knife during a sickening drug-fueled attack which lasted up to two hours.

Miss Kercher, 21, was killed because she refused to participate in "extreme sexual experiences" with her female flatmate, the flatmate's boyfriend and a bar owner in the town of Perugia.[1]

Amanda Knox was a nineteen-year-old student at the University of Washington in Seattle when she decided to study abroad in Italy. She wanted to learn to speak Italian.

Her parents were divorced. Her mom was a kindergarten teacher, and her dad worked for a department store. They were middle class but not wealthy. To pay her way to Italy, she worked three jobs. For all kinds of reasons, she was thrilled to be going.

It's not unheard of for single teenagers traveling abroad—or to a coffee shop, for that matter—to think of meeting someone. Amanda was a kid, and she acted like it. Before she left, her sister videotaped her talking about how she wanted to be with different guys. It was the kind of mildly salacious, ultimately innocent slumber-party banter that could be humorlessly taken as being rather telling, even damning. But it is not a crime to be young, and to be interested in romance and sex. It was ultimately just sisters talking, with excitement, before Amanda left the country.

She chose Perugia, the sister city of her hometown, Seattle, for the same reason that thousands of other international students choose to study there. First, it is singularly beautiful, picturesque, the kind of medieval city that's splashed on brochures handed out from tables on college campuses worldwide preaching the opportunities, joys, and enlightenment of studying abroad. Second, it's full of kids like her: smart, curious, adventurous, and away from home for a year or so.

In Perugia, she was paired up with two other young women, one a twenty-one-year-old British student from the University of Leeds named Meredith Kercher. Their house was big, tucked into the hillside. They each had their own room. And their living quarters sat on top of a separate space that was occupied by some young men.

Amanda moved in in the fall of 2007, and she'd only known the girls a few weeks before their house made headlines around the world. She got along well enough with her roommates. But, again, it had only been a few weeks.

Toward the end of October, she met a young man her age named Raffaele Sollecito at a classical music concert. She thought he looked like Harry Potter. They hit it off fast, the way college kids on exchange have a habit of doing.

She got a job at a local bar called Le Chic as a waitress. She was scheduled to work on Halloween, but her boss, Patrick Lumumba, texted her to say she wasn't needed. She texted him back: "Ci vediamo più tardi"—her attempt at what we say in English: "see you later" or goodbye. But for Italians, her phrase would be interpreted as literally making plans to meet up again later that night. This was the first of many lost-in-translation moments that would later have disastrous implications for her.

Amanda spent the night at Raffaele's. The couple watched *Amélie* on Raffaele's laptop, smoked some weed, and spent the rest of the night at his house.

Meredith went to a Halloween party dressed as a vampire. While she was there, she ran into Rudy Guede, a local drifter and small-time criminal who was known to carry a knife. Rudy had a thing for Meredith. After leaving the party, she stopped off at the apartment of some British girlfriends, watched TV, and ate some apple crumble. She went home around 9:00 p.m.

The next morning Amanda went home to take a shower, and she noticed the front door was open a little bit. This wasn't too surprising. They'd had trouble latching the door, so Amanda didn't think much of it. In the bathroom, she saw a little blood. Again, she wasn't concerned. One of the girls had just had her ears pierced, and she thought it may have been that. But she was startled to see feces left in the toilet, which seemed completely out of character.

Amanda went to Meredith's door and knocked. There was no answer. She tried to open it, but it was locked. She called Raffaele, and he came over.

They both tried the door again. Meredith didn't answer and the door wouldn't open, so they called the police.

The police got the door open and found Meredith's body, mostly covered, with just one foot sticking out from underneath a blanket. There was blood on the wall. The bed was stripped. Her bra was on the ground. She was almost completely naked. There was a gaping wound on the side of her neck. It was clear she'd been murdered.

From then until they took her into custody, in the eyes of the police, everything Amanda did made her more and more of a primary suspect. She and Raffaele were kissing. She was reportedly doing cartwheels (something Amanda would later deny). The two went out for dinner, shopping for "skimpy lingerie," whispering sweet nothings to each other in the store. She was also making strange faces at Raffaele, which nobody could understand. Amanda wasn't doubled over in grief like her roommate, like you would expect someone to be when their friend has just been brutally murdered, with the killer at large. It made the police suspicious.

Convinced of the pair's guilt, the police took Amanda and Raffaele into custody, then separated and interrogated them in ways that likely violated international law.

Over the next five days, Amanda was interrogated for forty-three hours in a language she barely understood. They asked her to imagine it, just imagine what she would have done if she'd been there, if she'd heard the screams? She said she would have covered her ears. They translated that into meaning she *was* there, that she had heard the screams. To them, that put her at the crime scene the moment

Meredith was murdered. But when Amanda told them she did not know who killed Meredith, one of them slapped her across the back of her head and commanded her to remember.

The police found what they thought was the hair of a Black man at the scene, and they wanted to know who it belonged to. Amanda didn't know. But she told them her boss was black.

Maybe, somehow, she'd brought something back from work that had his hair on it. That's when the text message of an American girl trying to translate the simplest phrase—"see you later" *(ci vediamo più tardi)*—became fodder for a life sentence. The police didn't read it as her telling her boss, "see you later," as in . . . see you whenever. They saw it as an Italian would see it, literally: "We will see each other later." The police were convinced she had been confirming a rendezvous with Patrick Lumumba to rape and murder her roommate.

Here's how Amanda later recounted what happened next:

The Perugian investigators refused to believe me when I told them I had not met Patrick that night. They painted a story for me, about how I had witnessed Patrick killing Meredith. They told me I was traumatized by the incident and had amnesia. When I told them that wasn't true, they said I was lying, or confused. They bombarded me with questions and scenarios, over and over again, into the morning.

I trusted these people. They were adults. They were authorities. And they lied to me. They lied to me that there was physical evidence of my presence at the crime scene. They lied to me that Raffaele said I went out that night. They threatened me with thirty years in prison if I didn't remember what they wanted me to remember. Finally, in the delirium they put me through, I didn't know what to believe. I thought, for a brief moment, maybe they were right. Maybe I did have amnesia. I told them I could see blurred flashes of Patrick, like they said. I told them I could imagine hearing Meredith screaming, like they said. They wrote the statements; I signed them. Then they rushed out to arrest Patrick Lumumba.

Within hours, I retracted those statements. I told them I had not met Patrick that night. They didn't care. Patrick had a rock-solid alibi. They didn't care.

They locked him up, upending his life. And they didn't release him until two weeks later, when DNA from the crime scene came back and identified the actual killer: Rudy Guede.[2]

While Guede became a suspect, the police would never let go of the idea that Amanda was the killer, the leader of some kind of satanic sex slaying that she roped Rudy and Raffaele into. They wouldn't let it go.

Meanwhile, Rudy Guede had fled to Germany and confessed to the crime over a taped Skype call with a friend. The police picked him up and, after a short trial, he was convicted of the murder of Meredith Kercher. Again, they weren't satisfied to have the murderer in custody and convicted. They had to have Amanda, too. They were sure she was involved.

To the Italian authorities, Amanda was the symbol of something for which they had disdain: the American vixen, in the country to corrupt Italian men. She was the devil with the angel face, the thing Italian mothers feared. It was too good a story not to be true. Don't mind the evidence or admission that Meredith had been robbed and raped before being killed by a drifter. That's too easy, too convenient of a story. You want it to be the American whore.

The news of this case was dominated by European tabloids—somewhat by necessity. The language barrier and distance meant it was hard for American news outlets to dominate coverage the way they do with so many other trials that have captured the world's attention.

The British tabloids were far more interested in the murderer of one of their brethren being this beautiful, sex-crazed American girl. They delightfully printed every lie and fanned every rumor. Chief among them was her supposedly twisted sexual proclivities.

Amanda had Carlo Dalla Vedova to represent her in the courtroom, but as her case was playing out in the media—and on social media—worldwide, she needed someone representing her in the court of public opinion.

By then, I'd been working on national television for over a decade, albeit not nearly fulltime. I'd learned how to make a case in front of a national audience and felt confident I could bring the truth about her case to a larger audience by reaching out to network anchors like Nancy Grace and Anderson Cooper.

This was a case that instantly became a national sensation, so it wasn't hard to get it covered. But it was hard getting the facts above the roar of the nonstop sensationalism pedaled by the prosecution. Our team had the facts. And I needed to get them out.

Another reason I was able to assist is that I'm from Seattle. I knew the people who were telling her story locally, the people with whom she went to elementary school and with whom her parents worked. A local TV station may have only reached three hundred thousand people a night, but those were the three hundred thousand people most important to Amanda and her family.

I was born in McAlester, Oklahoma, in 1958, while my doctor father was working as a resident at a local hospital. My parents met at the University of Washington while my mother was studying business and my father was in medical school. She was a year older, because he skipped a few grades and was a teenager when he started medical school.

In lieu of military service, my dad interned at Wounded Knee in South Dakota and moved our family to the Native American reservation. Some of my earliest memories are from the reservation—my brother dancing in ceremonies; playing with turtles; digging a hole in the ground with a dog. But my first real memories are from our home in Olympia, Washington, where my father moved to set up his psychiatric practice. We lived out on Fishtrap Road, way out on the water, in a Japanese-style home with boardwalks and little bridges, a stable for horses, and a big field, all surrounded by woods for lots of play. We boarded horses, made forts in the woods, waterskied, and generally ran wild with our cats and dogs.

Our neighbors lived far away. One had a bear. Another kept an ape. And we'd ride our bikes to visit them. It was an incredible place to grow up.

I was very independent and preferred playing with animals over girls. My dad always called me "princess," but I told him to call me "sport." I was ambitious and adventurous. I had a vivid imagination and got in trouble for exaggerating.

From the time I was in grade school, I loved reading books. At school, I would brag about winning the award for reading the most books in a month. From a young age, I was reading about women, strong women. There was a series of books written for readers my age about women who had done extraordinary things, like Dolly Madison and Narcissa Whitman.

And my sister and I read true crime books and stories of murder. Everything we could.

Dad was a history buff. The house was filled with books about art and war. There was more conversation about the most recent biography one of us was reading than about politics.

Mom was an active member of the Governor's Festival of the Arts and was friends with people like Giovanni Costigan, a professor of history at the University of Washington in Seattle who once had a debate with the conservative William F. Buckley that drew more spectators than that night's Seattle SuperSonics basketball game.[3] (Granted, they were a pretty crummy team back then.) She was kind of a bohemian, beatnik type. And she was a beauty.

She looked just like Jackie Kennedy and was vivacious and active. She stayed home with me, my sister, and our two brothers. She could have worked outside the home doing anything she wanted. But when we grew up in the 1960s, you just didn't do that.

But our perfect life soon got destroyed.

One day mom got sick and died in the ambulance on the way to Seattle.

It was around Valentine's Day. I remember because I was embarrassed that mom made my box for my classroom Valentine's party using turquoise crepe paper fringe, which I didn't think looked as cute as the conventional heart-decorated Valentine's boxes the other children had.

I was seven. She was thirty-one. It was spinal meningitis.

For a while afterward, the house was full of people and casseroles. Then we kids went to live with relatives who had eleven kids of their own.

Losing your mother at a young age is a tragedy that changes you for life. It is one of the worst things that can happen to you, equivalent to losing your own child. But that event gave me a different perspective on life. It made me into a fighter for the underdogs of the world. The Amanda Knoxes, when everyone else has given up on them. If I could come back from that dark place, I could help them do it, too.

Though there were four of us under the age of eleven, my father was very sought after, as any handsome, newly single doctor in the 1960s would be. Three months after my mother died, my father remarried—on June 4, 1966, my eighth birthday.

Our new stepmother had a degree from the University of Oregon and worked as a social worker in the community mental health center. She was just like Mary Tyler Moore—now, with a husband and four kids. She had a million pairs of shoes. The hair. And a very cool place on the beach that all of us loved. She was only twenty-four at the time. After my father remarried, we didn't talk about my mother too much. I went through a lot of angst over the years because of that. It was a different time.

When I was in high school, I wanted to be an actress. I liked the idea of being up on the silver screen. It seemed so glamorous! I started out college at the University of Puget Sound, my father and uncle's alma mater.

For my major in college, I picked medieval history. I'd always loved the Middle Ages, and my grades were good, so after my second year I was able to transfer to Stanford.

After finishing my bachelor's degree at Stanford, it was only going to take another year to get a master's, so I decided to stay on and get a master's degree in medieval history and then go teach somewhere or at least work at a university. My father disagreed.

"Not on my dime!" he said. "You'd be a good lawyer. Why don't you go to law school?"

He liked the idea so much that he bribed me. He said: "I'll tell you what. I'll pay for it. You can have your car from high school. And I'll pay for your rent, and I'll give you thirty bucks a month for mad money." I thought: *What the hell?*

I took the LSATs, but I didn't study for them. In fact, I stayed up late the night before—going to a Bonnie Raitt concert in San Francisco. The next morning, I rode my ten-speed bike to take the test on campus at Stanford.

My scores were fine—great, considering I didn't study—and plenty good for me to get into law school at Seattle University. In a rather bizarre twist, a friend I went to Stanford with freaked out on her first day, so I took over the lease on her apartment and bought her books.

I worked all through law school. Sometimes I was paid, but it was never about the money—Dad took care of that. I enjoyed being in the courtroom whenever I could. I clerked for the Tacoma City attorney's office. I also took summer jobs at law firms in Seattle. (At the time, the Seattle University Law School was actually in Tacoma, an hour away.) Looking back, Seattle was a small city. Just a few high-rises and a jail. But I took the bus into Pioneer Square and felt like I was in the big city.

I wasn't even on the totem pole at that point. I washed the boss's car and catered lunch for his clients and the board of directors. I wrote letters, took dictation. The grunt stuff. But I soaked it all up.

During law school I clerked for the Tacoma City attorney, where I had a fabulous mentor, a hysterical woman who helped me understand the basics of law in ways that the self-serious law school types couldn't. She used to say things like: "Go watch this guy in court today. He's a piece of shit. Never do anything like he does." Or she'd say: "Watch this guy. He knows his stuff. That's how you perform at trial."

Those summer jobs are where I learned how lawsuits really worked, how to put forth a case and to plan litigation—the kinds of things you don't learn about in law school. One of the attorneys I worked under, Peter Buck, taught me how to treat clients.

Peter treated everyone like they were a million bucks. He was generous and kind, philanthropic. What a local lawyer should be. He was also energetic, engaged, and wickedly smart. He let me follow him around, and I just loved it. He also valued my opinion and let me write some legal memos and letters about land use and constitutional law. He worked on each one with me. It was the blocking and tackling of law work—practical and, for me, a young law student, invaluable.

I was so excited to start my legal career that I decided to graduate early. So, I'd get up at four and take the early bus to Seattle. Then I'd bring work with me for the bus ride home and take classes at night. I didn't have any time for myself, but that was OK. I loved my job and was desperate to finish school.

I've always said that I've lucked out career-wise every step of the way—often in spite of myself. This started right out of law school, when I was offered a job by Judge Robert Dixon—whom I will forever know as "my judge."

Judge Dixon was everyone's favorite ex-prosecutor. He was the smartest and most wonderful judge in King County. He was funny, and certainly the only judge in town who drove a yellow Trans Am with flames down the side. When he sent me to the bank to deposit his paycheck, he always told me to "run like the wind."

My judge had close to an eidetic memory and could quote Shakespeare from the bench. I was so lucky that I worked for him. It was the luck of the draw to work for the kind of "Renaissance man" that everybody loves, even the other judges, who would come back to his chambers and ask him questions about their own trials. He was like a sage. He knew everything.

A fabulous trial lawyer before he became a judge, he was always giving me pointers. After a day in court, he'd say things to me like: "Did you see what the prosecutor did there? *Never* do it like that!" Or, after jury selection, he'd second-guess the attorney's decisions with me, and let me know which ones he would have kept in and why. It was a master class that you can't get in law school.

Judge Dixon only hired women bailiffs because he liked encouraging young women in the field. When two of his previous bailiffs, Ava and Joanne, heard I'd been offered the job but hadn't yet taken it, they both found me and told me the best thing I could do for my career was to take the job. I'm so lucky they did. It wasn't until I started clerking for my judge that I committed to the idea that I wanted to be a lawyer.

Being a bailiff isn't glamorous work, but you get to see how the entire operation runs—in the courtroom and behind the scenes. I helped Judge Dixon with legal research. I kept his chambers ship shape. I handled his scheduling. I brought him lunch. I mailed his Christmas cards. I made sure prosecutors and counselors were getting all their questions answered. And I spent a lot of time watching trials.

Before court was in session, the judge would stand in his office, smoke a cigarette, and look out the window. Then he'd look at me and say: "Bailiff, announce me!" And he'd throw his cigarette into the garbage can.

I'd step into court and say: "Department No. 107 session, the Honorable Robert E. Dixon presiding!" Then I'd run back into chambers—"Where'd it go?!?!?"—and dig for his cigarette. I never thought it was demeaning or degrading. It was hilarious. He took care of me. I took care of him.

I took the bar exam early and passed, which, serendipitously, was a boon to my career. An inordinate number of my peers flunked the bar that year. Some of them already had jobs in the prosecutor's office and had to quit.

I hadn't been working for my judge for a year when, one day, the prosecutors' supervisor came into court and motioned me toward her with one finger.

"How'd you like to work in the prosecutor's office?"

It was an incredible opportunity. But I loved my judge.

"I like where I am, working for my judge," I told her. But it was too late.

"We've already made the arrangement," she said.

"What are you talking about?"

"We've made a swap."

One of my peers who flunked the bar had to leave her job in the prosecutor's office.

"She's going to become the judge's bailiff, and you're going to work for us."

There were female lawyers when I was in law school and there were women supervisors in my office when I eventually became a prosecutor. But there weren't that many women who were truly great trial lawyers—seasoned and spectacular.

I liked what I saw in court. I started to like the idea of putting on a trial. I liked the idea of helping people who had been victimized. And I liked the idea of being a good trial lawyer. I knew I could be a good one.

I thought being a trial lawyer meant you got to be both the composer and the performer—writing and performing your own sonata. It seemed like the perfect way for me to combine my book smarts with what I liked about the idea of being an actress in a very compelling way.

I could also see that very few people were good at it. To this day, a lot of lawyers aren't great in trials—or ever even go to trial. They're good at writing and researching. But not the performing and case building that I found so fascinating. I thought I could be good at it and that, over the years, I might be able to do some good, as well.

My first big case in the prosecutor's office was the case of a serial, violent rapist in Seattle. The year was 1987. A young man was attacking women around Harborview Medical Center while they were walking to work, robbing them, and raping—or attempting to rape—them, while threatening them with a steak knife. He was terrorizing the city.

During one of his attacks, he pulled a woman out of her car, hit her across the head with a board, and dragged her into an empty apartment near the freeway. A neighbor saw what happened and held him at gunpoint. But he escaped. We charged a young man—a young Black man, which will matter in a second—named Tyrone Briggs. He lived in the same apartments and all the women identified him, as did the man who held him for a time at gunpoint.

But here's the twist: Briggs is a stutterer. None of the women mentioned a stutter. It's pretty well known that people who have a stutter don't *always* stutter. Some don't stutter when they sing. Some don't stutter when they yell "fire!"

His defense claimed the cops got the wrong guy on account of the stutter, but I thought that was nonsense, as did our speech experts. I told the jury: Marilyn Monroe doesn't stutter when she acts, Mel Tillis doesn't stutter when he sings, and Tyrone Briggs doesn't stutter when he rapes.

The jury was convinced, and Briggs was convicted. But after the fact, the defense got to one of the jurors, who volunteered: "You know, I did talk to the other jurors about a stuttering problem I have." Based on that, the judge declared a mistrial.

Was that justice? Hard to say. But remember, our system is designed to protect the innocent. That means the guilty sometimes walk.

The fact that the juror himself was a stutterer was a potential source of bias. It should have been revealed during jury selection, as it would have been grounds for dismissing the juror. Briggs had the right to a fair trial, and that meant an unbiased jury.

What's to be done? Let's try and prevent it from happening again. It's time for you to become a part of the process. We want to make sure that you don't make the same mistake that juror did, not disclosing his condition beforehand, wasting a lot of time and money, and putting justice at risk in the process. But for that you've got to be prepared. So let's get to it. It's time for your education.

For you, the jury.

3

YOU, THE JURY

There are many different kinds of courts in this world, each with its own rules, setup, and personality.

But "court" doesn't always mean a physical place: it can mean the site of hearings for justice, like impeachment trials in the United States Senate, where partisan, elected officials are the jurors. Their roles are established in the Constitution to find fact and truth. Many times, these "courts" don't truly embody our fundamental belief in the concept of justice for all, and in practice, they are entirely about supporting the party line.

There is also the omnipresent court of public opinion, in which we are all members of the jury.

And, yes, there are real trials, the kind that those of us who live in the United States are reminded of every time we hear about one in the media or receive a jury summons in the mail.

Let's pretend, for a second, that you're sitting in the venire, the entire panel from which a jury is drawn, in a courtroom in Seattle. You're being considered to serve on a jury.

Some potential jurors haven't read the US Constitution, which is a shame. But I can confidently guarantee that unless you have sat on a jury, none of you are aware of the instructions a judge gives to a potential jury. Over time, a set of instructions has been developed that appears to be the best we've got for finding people who are qualified jurors.

Qualifications for a jury are not like qualifications for a job. It doesn't take a degree or even a diploma to sit on a jury. But it takes a mindset. Here's how the judge would start:

This is a criminal case brought by the state of Washington . . . The defendant is charged with the crime of murder. Keep in mind that a charge is only an accusation. The filing of a charge is not evidence that the charge is true. Your decisions as jurors must be made solely upon the evidence presented during these proceedings.

The defendant is presumed to be innocent. The presumption of innocence continues throughout the entire trial. The presumption means that you must find the defendant not guilty unless you conclude at the end of your deliberations that the evidence has established the defendant's guilt beyond a reasonable doubt.[1]

The judge wants you to consider the accused innocent until after all of the information has been presented and all of the trial has concluded. This means that in a sexual assault case, the judge wants you to consider the accused attacker innocent after a woman explains the unspeakable things he did to her; after a witness explains the accused was in a different city at the time of the alleged assault; after the father of a son murdered in his baseball jersey cannot account for where he was on a Saturday afternoon; after the father's best friend confesses they had been on a bender for two days.

Have you ever done this before? When was the last time you heard some damning information on Twitter about someone you didn't like and said to yourself: OK, but I really need to hear two more days of vetted information about this before I make up my mind.

The State has the burden of proving every element beyond a reasonable doubt. The defendant has no burden of proving that a reasonable doubt exists. The defendant has no duty to call witnesses, produce evidence, or testify. A reasonable doubt is one for which a reason exists. It may arise from the evidence or lack of evidence. A reasonable doubt is a doubt that would exist in the mind of a reasonable person after fully, fairly, and carefully considering all of the evidence or lack of evidence. If, from such consideration, you have an abiding belief in the truth of the charge, you are satisfied beyond a reasonable doubt.[2]

Here's a question: do you even believe in reasonable doubt? Do you believe doubt is reasonable? Do you have doubt about anything? Or do you hold fast to beliefs in things about which you know nothing more than the headlines in your Facebook feed? After British voters resoundingly chose to approve the country leaving the European Union in what was known as "Brexit," the number one search term in the United Kingdom was "what is Brexit?"

The purpose of this process is to make sure we select a jury that is free from any outside or preexisting bias that might interfere with its ability to fairly decide the case based on the evidence and the law as received in the courtroom. People aren't very good at being jurors. Mostly because it goes against all our natural impulses and asks us to set aside much of what we are most proud of: what we believe and what we stand for. When you're sitting in a jury box, you're supposed to be a blank slate. And few people want to do that. Lately, fewer see the value.

> *It is important that you discharge your duties without discrimination, meaning that bias regarding the race, color, religious beliefs, national origin, sexual orientation, gender, or disability of any party, any witnesses, and the lawyers should play no part in the exercise of your judgment throughout the trial. These are called "conscious biases"—and, when answering questions, it is important, even if uncomfortable for you, to share these views with the lawyers.*[3]

That's easy, though, right? Who among us isn't willing to agree not to pass judgment based on race, color, religion, sexuality, etc.?

However, there is another, more subtle, tendency at work about which we must all be aware. This part of human nature is understandable but must play no role in your service as jurors. In our daily lives, there are many issues that require us to make quick decisions and then move on. In making these daily decisions, we may well rely upon generalities, even what might be called biases or prejudices. That may be appropriate as a coping mechanism in our busy daily lives, but bias and prejudice can play no part in any decisions you might make as a juror. Your decisions as jurors must be based solely upon an open-minded, fair consideration of the evidence that comes before you during trial.

We rely on generalities, biases, and prejudices as a coping mechanism. Is it even possible to expect jurors to provide open-minded, fair consideration on *only the evidence that comes in during the trial?*

Here's the thing about having an open mind: it's losing currency. Debate is up for debate. When was the last time you felt comfortable learning something publicly? Being willing to admit you didn't know something, you didn't have an opinion about something, or you weren't willing to take a stand until you had more information? It's not fashionable. But it's your duty as a juror.

In a moment, I am going to ask you some background questions and the lawyers will also have a chance to follow up with some questions of their own. Most importantly, you are to look within yourselves and see if there is anything there in your life experiences or your personal beliefs that might be such a strong influence that it would overcome your ability to serve as a fair and impartial juror. These questions may sometimes involve issues that are sensitive for you.[4]

What the judge is saying here is that, just as having *more* information will not necessarily make it easier to parse innocence and guilt, having more life experiences will not necessarily make you better suited to impartially consider the evidence in a case. For example, if your brother just died in a drunk-driving accident, you might not be able to impartially decide the fate of a bartender who overserved a regular right before he got behind the wheel of a car and killed three teenagers. Sure, you probably know a lot more about what those teenagers' families are going through, and you might make a great advocate for them, but does that mean you'll be able to consider only the facts presented inside a courtroom better than someone who has not had that experience? Probably not.

It is essential to a fair trial that everything you learn about this case comes to you in this courtroom, and only in this courtroom. You must not allow yourself to be exposed to any outside information about this case, including from your family and friends. Do not permit anyone to discuss or comment about it in your presence, and do not remain within hearing of such conversations. You must keep your mind free of outside influences so that your decision will be based entirely on the evidence presented during the trial and on my instructions to you about the law.[5]

Here's the thing: everyone involved with a trial knows this rule isn't always followed. Avoid outside information about the case? Please. Jurors violate this rule all the time. We know this.

Even though the rules are broken, that doesn't mean they're not important. It stops jurors from introducing new material when they're considering the facts. It prevents jurors from going rogue, from becoming prosecutor and defense attorney, or trying to make a case to their fellow jurors that the information they've found on their own is more important than the information they were presented with in the courtroom. Having said that, knowing this rule is broken is an important part of mounting a defense.

Until you are dismissed at the end of this trial, you must avoid outside sources such as newspapers, magazines, blogs, the internet, or radio or television broadcasts which may discuss this case or issues involved in this trial. If you start to hear or read information about anything related to this case, you must act immediately so that you no longer hear or see it.[6]

Why do you think it is that judges—and the American criminal justice system—believe you are better able to make a fair decision in the case if you have *less* information than is available? You're getting days and days and days of it in the courtroom. So, why would it matter if you got *more* information about this?

We'll get to that in a little bit, but let me ask you another question: how many times have you felt that you were better able to make a judgment on a case because you weren't in a jury box? Because you were privy to information—damning, gruesome, and obvious proof of guilt—that you read on the internet, but that wasn't allowed to be shown to the jury? That makes you better suited to determine guilt and innocence, doesn't it?

During the trial, do not try to determine on your own what the law is. Do not seek out any evidence on your own. Do not consult dictionaries or other reference materials. Do not conduct any research into the facts, the issues, or the people involved in this case. This means you may not use Google or other internet search engines to look into anything at all related to this case.

I want to emphasize that the rules prohibiting discussions include your electronic communications. You must not send or receive information about anything related to the case by any means, including by text messages, email, telephone, internet chat, blogs, or social networking websites. Do not even mention being on a jury when using social media, such as updating your status on Facebook or sending a message on Twitter.[7]

The United States judicial system is . . . imperfect at best. Does it sometimes send innocent people to jail? Yes. Does it let some guilty people go free? Also yes. The test of time has shown, however, that it holds up pretty well. And a cornerstone of the system—why it works as well as it does—is that it demands that you the juror stay away from the places where people get their information: newspapers and social media, including Google, Facebook, Twitter, etc.

If you become exposed to any information other than what you learn in the courtroom, it could be grounds for a mistrial. A mistrial would mean that all of the work that you and your fellow jurors put into this trial will be wasted. Retrials are costly and burdensome to the parties and the public. Also, if you communicate with others in violation of my orders, you could be fined or held in contempt of court.[8]

The judge is serious. Hopefully you've understood their point: The best chance the world's premier judicial system has to distinguish between innocence and guilt is if you stay away from the place that you have come to rely on for the truth. Because—and this may come as a shock—Google, Facebook, and Twitter aren't very good at sussing out the truth.

Throughout the trial, you must maintain an open mind. You must not form any firm and fixed opinion about any issue in the case until the entire case has been submitted to you for deliberation.

As jurors, you are officers of this court. As such, you must not let your emotions overcome your rational thought process. You must reach your decision based on the facts proved to you and on the law given to you, not on sympathy, prejudice, or personal preference. To assure that all parties receive a fair trial, you must act impartially with an earnest desire to reach a just and proper verdict.[9]

To accomplish a fair trial takes work, commitment, and cooperation. A fair trial is possible only with a serious and continuous effort by each one of us. Thank you for your willingness to serve this court and our system of justice.[10]

Now you're ready. You, the jury. Prepped, educated, and ready to go.

Buckle up, because we've got a lot of cases to cover.

And this is the most important part.

The opening statement.

4

FIRST IMPRESSIONS ARE LASTING

The opening statement is the most important part of the trial.

Let me say that again. *The opening statement is the most important part of the trial.*

It's taught that 80 percent of jurors make up their minds during opening statements. They filter the rest of the information that comes at them during the trial through the prism of what they've decided during the opening statements. And they never change.

I can see it in the way jurors look at me. The nodding. The physical cues. Once you know, you know. There are very few surprises. Very few juries don't do what you expect them to. They rarely change their mind. Why would they? The rest of us don't. That's why you've got to get it right the first time, in the opening statement.

We hate to change our minds. We hate to admit we're wrong. And we hate to think that a story isn't working out the way we believed it would. Or the way we want it to.

It's human nature. It's how our minds work.

Furthermore, we want things to work out a certain way. We don't want to think people will make false accusations or that fathers will assault their sons. But it happens. We want things to work out the way we have it pictured in our minds. We focus on what fits and discard the rest. Once we make up our minds, we look for evidence to confirm our beliefs. It's a well-established phenomenon that's been studied by psychologists. It's called confirmation bias.[1]

Most of the time, we don't know we're doing it.

In the early 1970s, a group of researchers at Stanford University placed advertisements in a newspaper offering two dollars to people who would participate in an "experiment in decision-making." Sixty women were presented with twenty-five cards containing suicide notes and asked to determine which ones were fake and which ones were real. Before they started, an administrator told them "the average score was about sixteen correct out of twenty-five." After examining each card, they were told whether they had been right or wrong. Each woman kept track of her own score.

Here's the catch: unbeknownst to the women, the results were predetermined. At random, the sixty women were preassigned to be told they had either gotten twenty-four right (a successful score), seventeen right (an average score), or ten right (failure, sorry). After the test was over, the researcher left the room for a few minutes, allowing the women to consider the results.

When the researcher returned to the room, he told the women what had happened: that the results were selected at random, that the score they wrote down had nothing to do with how they'd actually performed, and that the deception was necessary because they were actually studying "the effects of success and failure on physiological measures":

> To emphasize that the subject's score had been determined randomly prior to her arrival and that it could not have been influenced by her performance, (the administrator) showed the subject the actual schedule that determined her assignment to experimental condition and her initial score. The (administrator) specifically stressed that this score contained absolutely no information about the subject's actual task performance. Every subject was explicitly asked to acknowledge her understanding of the nature and purpose of the deception before the experimenter proceeded to the next phase of the study.[2]

With that, the researcher got up, explained that he was going to fetch the participant her two dollars, and, by the way, "while I'm gone, would you mind filling out this questionnaire?"

The questionnaire asked the women three questions:

1. How many answers do you think you actually got right?

2. How many answers do you think the average student would have gotten right?

3. How many answers do you think you'd get right if you took the test again?

The results were fascinating.

The higher score they'd been told they had gotten—that is, the higher the random score they had been assigned—the higher they assumed they would score on the test if they took it again. In other words, the "success" group thought of themselves as better than average, and likely to perform well again in the future, while the "failure" group thought they did worse than average, and that in the future they would continue to do poorly. They still, basically, believed the scores, even though they'd been told they had been assigned completely at random.

Even after debriefing procedures that led subjects to say that they understood the decisive invalidation of initial test results, the subjects continued to assess their performances and abilities as if these test results still possessed some validity.[3]

Think about that: even after people were told the results were totally random, it still gave them a false sense of how well they did at the task and how well they'd do in the future. They had been given information that was completely made up, then given concrete information to the contrary—told that they had been given completely false information—and yet they still believed what they'd first heard.

The researchers then did a second study, where they repeated what they did before, but this time they had some observers watch. They did a regular "debriefing" where the researchers told both the test subjects and the observers that they had faked the subjects out in telling them how they did, then they gave a "process" debriefing where the researchers told the subjects and observers the real purpose of the study.

This time, after the "regular debriefing," both test subjects and observers continued to believe in their initial results. In other words, both believed that the "success" group would do better in the future and the "failure" group would do worse, even though they were told that the results were faked.

The group that had the "process" debriefing had mixed results. The test takers and the observers who knew the "real" purpose of the study, that both the scores were completely artificial and the true purpose of the experiment was to see how well impressions persevered even when false information was corrected, were split. The test takers mostly got it. They filled out the questionnaire and the results were less determined by how well they'd been told they had done. But for the observers, the perception persisted:

Observers, who overheard this process debriefing, however, were less dramatically influenced. Their estimates of the actor's initial performance . . . continued to show clear perseverance effects.[4]

Let's think about that for a second. Let's say someone was asked to watch you play poker, and to keep track of how well you played. You lost every hand and, understandably, when asked how well you played in the game and how well they thought you'd play in your next game, the person watching you thought you played lousy and you'd keep losing your money. Then the person watching you was told the deck was stacked. That you had no chance. That even the best poker player in the world would have gotten the exact same lousy score and gone home without any money. Furthermore, the person watching you play was told this wasn't about poker at all. It was a study. A study looking at how much the impression of someone else perseveres even when presented with conflicting, accurate information, and told that what they used to know was false. The person was told they believe that "when you see someone play poker, and they play lousy, even if *I tell you that it was a setup*, that they had no chance of playing anything other than lousy, we're guessing that the initial impression will persevere, that you'll still think they're a lousy poker player. That's what this is about. Not poker!"

What this study shows is that, even after all that, they're still going to think you're a lousy poker player.

In other words, your first impression is the most important, even if it is based on false information, and even if you are shown evidence that the original information you were shown was false.

The study authors found two important takeaways in their experiments. The first, basically, is that once we've had our first impression, we want to stick with it. When presented with information to the contrary, we tend to dismiss it. Information that supports it, however, we tend to embrace. So jurors make up their mind during the opening statement. After that, it's almost impossible to change their minds.

Like I said before, it's called confirmation bias.[5]

Or to put it another way, trials are won and lost in the opening statement.

When I was a kid, if there was a piano in the room, I was playing it.

I played for all the singing groups, orchestras, some of the plays. I took classical piano lessons and gave local recitals and competed nationally. I practiced four hours a day and could play all the movements of my favorite Chopin and Beethoven pieces from memory. Nothing I did growing up or in college, not even law school, prepared me for presenting a case in front of a jury like playing piano did.

Giving a piano recital and presenting an opening statement to a jury are almost identical experiences. The preparation, pacing, pauses: putting together a case for a jury is the same as putting together a piece of music for an audience.

Preparing for a competition, I practiced. And practiced. And then practiced some more. For me, there was no substitute for spending time at the piano. To mentally prepare for a competition, I'd go over the music in my head and spend time alone.

It's the same way I prepare for a trial today. I spend time with the material—alone—and get ready to perform. I follow my training. The senior attorneys in the prosecutor's office would tell us to simply tell a story. I focus on how I'm going to make my opening statement. What is the story I am going to tell? Is it compelling? Will it grab the jurors' interest? Is it too long? Do they care? In my days alone, away from friends, TV, and email, leading up to the trial, I let the opening argument unfold inside my head. I let the story bounce around in my head until it's lost its rough edges and I'm only left with what's most important.

My best opening statements come together on sticky notes, the back side of grocery lists, and those random pieces of paper that come at the end of a checkbook. But I don't bring the notes—much less a projector—into the court-room. I want them all in my head. I want to play from memory. The less I have to look at my notes, the more I can focus on my performance.

Most civil lawyers drag out their opening statements for hours. I think anything over an hour is a waste of time. If you can't make your case in forty-five minutes, you probably don't know how to make your case. If you can make your case in thirty minutes, the jury will have the patience to sit and listen without losing their concentration, and you're golden.

I've gone up against teams that have been over the top with visuals and PowerPoints. In those cases, I go the other direction. I bring in nothing. I tell them a story that grabs them by the throat and makes them sit up and listen. The story wins every time.

Over the years I've gone from exclusively making my cases to juries to going in front of the camera as a TV commentator or correspondent on high-profile crimi-nal cases. I'd grow to realize that talking to a television audience was a lot like addressing a jury. You've got to be concise; you've got to be clear; you've got to be convincing. While I don't buy into the dramatics you often see on TV and in mov-ies, you've got to be able to perform.

Just like a piano recital, in which playing the notes is only a portion of the per-formance, I would learn that it wasn't just the message I brought in front of the camera, but the way I relayed it. The way I greeted the audience, engaged with the host, and stimulated the debate.

In the end, it's all about being a great storyteller.

The best opening statement I ever made was when I was defending local police in the Mary Kay Letourneau case—the teacher from the Seattle area who had an affair with her sixth-grade student—and it came down to five words: "nothing could keep them apart." That case was also the one where I hit my stride standing in front of a TV camera, presenting the facts to the public in a way that made sense.

Mary Kay was the centerpiece of a media feeding frenzy, scorned and dispar-aged for her transgressions of social boundaries by some and snickered at by oth-ers. But in our legal system you are innocent until proven guilty in a court of law, and in spite of the disgust that her actions evoked in many, she still had the right to be represented in court. My job was defending the police. I didn't represent

Mary Kay. But it just so happened that my best defense for the police was making arguments that were essentially like arguing on her behalf.

In arguing for the police in their case, I was arguing for Mary Kay.

Mary Kay wasn't the first woman whom I gave voice to in court, and she wouldn't be the last. As time went on, my opening statements got better, and I became a stronger advocate.

But there was one Seattle woman I couldn't help. That's because she came before my time.

THE TRAGIC TALE
OF FRANCES FARMER

Amanda Knox is hardly the first woman from West Seattle who was locked up for not acting right. Perhaps you've heard of Frances Farmer, or at least the Nirvana song in which she was immortalized by Seattle's own Kurt Cobain: "Frances Farmer Will Have Her Revenge on Seattle."

In her false witness,
Hope you're still with us,
To see if they float or drown.
Our favorite patient,
A display of patience,
Disease-covered Puget Sound.
She'll come back as fire
To burn all the liars,
Leave a blanket of ash on the ground.
I miss the comfort in being sad,
I miss the comfort in being sad,
I miss the comfort in being sad.

By all accounts, she was smart. And nobody who ever saw her could deny she was pretty. From the time she was a girl, she didn't act the way she was expected to. In 1931, when she was a senior in high school, she won an essay contest with her piece, "God Dies."

The essay started like this:

No one ever came to me and said, "You're a fool. There isn't such a thing as God. Somebody's been stuffing you." It wasn't a murder. I think God just died of old age. And when I realized that he wasn't any more, it didn't shock me. It seemed natural and right.

    Maybe it was because I was never properly impressed with a religion. I went to Sunday school and liked the stories about Christ and the Christmas star. They were beautiful. They made you warm and happy to think about. But I didn't believe them. The Sunday School teacher talked too much in the way our grade school teacher used to when she told us about George Washington. Pleasant, pretty stories, but not true.[1]

The essay shocked the nation. An article headlined "Seattle Girl Denies God and Wins Prize" reverberated around newspapers across the country.[2] Farmer was flooded with letters. "If the young people of this city are going to hell," one Baptist minister reportedly told his congregation, "Frances Farmer is surely leading them there."[3]

Women are the corrupting ones.

But the fallout from the essay was merely a warning shot in what would be a brief, sometimes celebrated, highly controversial, impossibly tragic life.

She ended up in Hollywood opposite stars like Bing Crosby in *Rhythm on the Range*. But she was uncomfortable with the Hollywood system and the trappings of fame. She also may have struggled with alcoholism. She might have been bipolar.[4]

One night she was pulled over for driving with her high beams on—which the police tended to make a big deal of on the West Coast during the war years. What followed was a tragic case of over-escalation. There was a fine, and some of it was unpaid. Somehow, this became reason for her to be dragged from her hotel room—naked, allegedly—and hauled into court, where she lashed out at the cops, the judge, and anyone else within earshot. She fought like a hellcat, and the pictures lit up the pages of newspapers.

FRANCES FARMER TO GET HEARING

Hollywood, Jan. 15, 1943 (U.P.)—A complaint was filed in superior court today asking a hearing to determine the sanity of Frances Farmer, blond screen actress, jailed yesterday after a 24-hour spree. Dr. Thomas Leonard, a psychiatrist, filed the complaint, and Miss Farmer was ordered removed immediately to general hospital pending a hearing next Wednesday.[5]

How could a woman act like this? This is not the way women are supposed to behave.

Frances ended up in the custody of her mother, who had her committed to the Western State Psychiatric Hospital in Lakewood, Washington. There she said she was gnawed by rats and raped by doctors and orderlies. By some accounts she was lobotomized. She lost years of her life behind those walls.

After she got out of the mental hospital, Frances Farmer worked menial jobs. She acted in community theater. And eventually, she ended up back on the screen. But she never achieved the stardom that was her potential.

She died in 1970, at the age of fifty-six.

She had so much going for her, and she was torpedoed by the authorities who didn't understand why she was behaving the way she did and didn't care to understand. Doctors, lawyers, psychiatrists, parents. But the knockout punch was delivered by the news media. They painted her as an out-of-control nut case who deserved what she got.

As a child, suffering after my mother's death, I mentally gravitated toward Farmer's case. Years later I wondered if her outcome would have been different if there were a strong voice like mine to advocate for her. Back then, Frances Farmer didn't have an advocate.

And I was too late for another woman who was discredited and denigrated by men who were doctors and lawyers. But in her case, it was just one man, who was both a doctor and a lawyer. Her husband.

That woman was Betty Broderick.

6
BETTY BRODERICK:
A WIFE SCORNED

Betty Broderick was a dutiful wife who raised her children and worked to put her husband, Dan Broderick, through both medical school and law school. Their first child, Kim, was born in 1970, one year after their marriage. She slept in a bureau drawer in their dorm room. Over the next few years she gave birth to four more children: Lett (b. 1971), Daniel (b. 1976), and Rhett (b. 1979). An unnamed child died soon after birth. Betty was a loving mother who sold Tupperware door to door with more than one child on her hip to support the family in Dan's early years, while he attended Notre Dame, Harvard, and Princeton.

Betty and Dan were both Catholic, and they promised to love each other (like from the old Johnny Mathis song) until "The Twelfth of Never." But Dan wasn't faithful, and he dumped her for an alternative version of Betty who was seventeen years younger. If you put Betty's wedding picture from 1969 next to the wedding picture of Dan's new wife, Linda, twenty years later, they could be the same beautiful woman.

He filed for divorce in 1985. By that time Dan was a powerful lawyer who dragged her through court and got custody of the kids, the house, and all the money. Betty felt she couldn't get proper legal representation because none of the other lawyers in the county wanted to cross Dan. She likened his scorched-earth emotional and litigation tactics to "putting a housewife in the ring with Muhammad Ali."[1]

The divorce was finalized four years later.

Betty had raised four kids, and she drove an RV with the license plate "LOADEMUP." One time, she drove that RV straight through Dan Broderick's front door.

Later she got a key to the house from one of the kids. On November 5, 1989, she snuck into the house before dawn, and shot and killed Dan and Linda in bed.

Betty's case was portrayed in the Netflix series *Dirty John: The Betty Broderick Story*. Meredith Baxter Birney played Betty in *A Woman Scorned*, and Oprah's show with Betty was the highest rated at the time. She became instantly recognizable, a household name.

Opinion on Betty's guilt was divided. Her first jury hung, and one juror said after the trial, "All I want to know is what took her so long."

A second trial in 1991 sentenced her to thirty-two years to life in prison. But for most of the public the judgment was definitive and merciless. One man interviewed on the street in La Jolla, California, said "I think she should have gotten the electric chair."[2] That was a typical reaction. Not everyone felt the same way, though, especially women. One woman said, "I think I can understand . . . the rage she must have felt."[3]

I remember when I first saw Betty at the Chico Prison for Women in Riverside, California. The year was 2015. As I sat in the waiting area, I picked up a magazine. Flipping through the pages, I came upon a prominently displayed ad reading "The Daniel T. Broderick Award for Excellence in Ethics," which was being bestowed on a worthy recipient twenty-five years after the crime. When Betty entered the room, I was struck by how tall she was and how intense her blue eyes were. Betty and I sat down in a large cafeteria where Leslie Van Houten—one of the Manson girls—sat nearby. I was struck by how many women wanted to bring their babies for Betty to hold. Betty had been in prison for more than twenty-five years. Betty told me that women who committed arguably more serious crimes had long since been released.

I was there to represent Betty in connection with her parole issues. She had been granted few parole hearings (even Charles Manson had far more opportunities for such hearings) and was serving a long sentence. Her previous parole request had been denied.

Women have always been fascinated with Betty. I know I was. What made her "snap?"

I don't think it's surprising that Betty has fascinated so many people for decades. I think it is because many identified with her. She "snapped" under pressure. And like so many women of her generation, she supported her husband and expected to be a part of the anticipated "upside" of both of their efforts.

So why the fascination and identification with Betty then, now, and presumably in the future? There are certain cases that resonate with our collective, most basic instincts. The pain of separation and loss of identity is something with which many can identify. Some have experienced this and more have feared the potential experience. The fear of "aging out" of our phase of attractiveness was part of the fear that consumed Betty and others who identified with her.

Or maybe it was just that Betty got screwed.

As she said, "Everybody wants a kitten, but nobody wants a cat."[4]

While so much has changed in the coverage and the perception of criminal cases during the internet and social media age, nothing in the view and coverage of Betty's case has changed. The media played an outside role, just as it did in other cases discussed in this book, like Michael Jackson and Amanda Knox. And it appears she will never be released. Perhaps all of this is because we fear what we see in ourselves, and therefore don't want to see her released.

The fascination with people like Betty—seemingly ordinary people who just snap—has fueled a true-crime craze. These people aren't much different than us; we see ourselves in them. This is also true of the victims of the killers. In the back of our heads, we're left thinking, *Wow, that could have been me.* We care about their stories because we don't want to be them but know we could have been.

Dan Broderick gets the ethics award attached to his name. Betty Broderick gets life in prison with fewer chances at parole than Charles Manson. He's a role model. She's Medea. Lock her up and throw away the key.

What is it about these women that terrify people so much? Why is it when women veer outside the normal bounds of behavior, even when they've been driven to extremes, that society not only has to punish them but crush them? When men pick up arms, we often call them valiant heroes. When woman do the same, we call them crazy nut jobs and throw them in mental institutions or jail.

Among the tragic figures in this book, the women (as you will see) all got screwed, whereas the men were more likely to get off. They weren't able to put O. J. in jail until they caught him red-handed stealing back his old football trophies. As described later, the prosecution of Michael Jackson failed, and he overdosed and died before they were able (or willing?) to catch up with him for his many crimes against children.

Bottom line? Many men have money and good lawyers and stay out of jail. Women generally have neither and suffer.

THE WEST MEMPHIS THREE

On May 5, 1993, three eight-year-old boys (Steve Branch, Michael Moore, and Christopher Byers) were reported missing in West Memphis, Arkansas, a city across the Mississippi River from Memphis, Tennessee. They were last seen playing together that evening around 6:30 p.m. A comprehensive search the next day found the bodies of the boys in a nearby creek. They were naked and hog-tied, with the right arm tied to the right ankle and left arm tied to the left ankle. Their clothes were found nearby, turned inside out. The boys had multiple injuries with one of them sustaining injuries to the penis and scrotum. The cause of death was "multiple injuries" in one of the boys and combined multiple injuries and drowning in the other two.[1] Whether or not the boys had been raped, whether the deaths occurred at the site where they were found, and whether the genital mutilation occurred at the time of death or was related to postmortem animal predation were all disputed.[2]

Three teenagers, who came to be known as the West Memphis Three, were accused of killing the boys as part of a satanic ritual. Damien Echols, age eighteen, had a history of mental illness, including hallucinations, delusions, and mood swings. He'd been previously arrested for shoplifting and had spent several months in a mental institution in Arkansas. He received disability payments from Social Security.[3] Jason Baldwin, age sixteen, had been arrested for vandalism. Jessie Misskelley Jr., age seventeen, had a borderline low IQ and violent temper and frequently got into fights. Echols and Baldwin were close friends and bonded over shared tastes in heavy metal music. They were only somewhat acquainted with Misskelley. Echols and Misskelley were high school dropouts, but Baldwin did well in school and was planning on going to college.[4]

THREE TEENS ARE ARRESTED IN MURDER OF 8-YEAR-OLDS
West Memphis, Ark. June 5, 1993 (The Baxter Bulletin):
Emotions have boiled over Friday as three teen-agers
appeared in court on capital murder charges in the slay-
ings of three 8-year-old boys who vanished while riding
their bicycles . . .

Their court hearing was interrupted Friday after the
father of the slain boys bolted from his seat and threat-
ened Echols, the first of the suspects brought before the
judge.

"I'll chase you all the way to hell," shouted the father,
Steven Branch, who later said, "I'll see you dead," before
officers restrained him and led him and Echols out of the
courtroom.[5]

The West Memphis Police thought the murders had cult overtones and decided to interview Echols because he had an interest in occultism. A polygraph examiner claimed he showed signs of deception. They also interviewed Misskelley alone for twelve hours, but only recorded a total of forty-six minutes. He confessed to the murders but later recanted, saying he was afraid of the police.[6] His statements were leaked to the press and published on the front page of the Memphis *Commercial Appeal* before the start of the trial. Misskelley later implicated Echols and Baldwin in the murders.[7] Lead investigator Gary Gitchell said he suspected Echols and Baldwin from the beginning. "It was like a big puzzle. The pieces started to fall together to make a big picture."[8] Asked by a reporter to state how confident on a scale of 0 to 10 he was in their guilt, he nodded and said: "An 11."[9]

Vicki Hutcheson was at the West Memphis police station taking a polygraph test related to charges that she had stolen from her employer the day the boys' bodies were discovered. The police had difficulty administering the test because her eight-year-old son, Aaron Hutcheson, was there with her and he was squirming around too much. Aaron told the police officer that he was a playmate of the murdered boys and claimed he had seen the murders committed by Satanists who spoke Spanish. In spite of the fact that his statements were inconsistent, and he could not identify any of the West Memphis Three, the police leaked his statements to the press. This furthered the idea that the murders were tied to a satanic cult. Vicki also said she had attended a Wiccan meeting with Echols and Misskelley. She said Echols was drunk and bragged about murdering three boys. Hutcheson could not recall the location of the meeting. The police put a wire on her and arranged for her to have Echols come over to her home. The police later claimed the recording was inaudible and couldn't be used in court.[10]

The West Memphis Three all pleaded innocent to murder. On February 5, 1994, Jessie Misskelley Jr. was convicted of murder and sentenced to life imprisonment plus two twenty-year sentences. In a second and separate trial of Damien Echols and Jason Baldwin, even though Misskelley's coerced confession was not admissible, the jury was already biased by the leaked news reports. Both were found guilty of murder. Echols was given a death sentence, and Baldwin was sentenced to life imprisonment.

Misskelley's former attorney, Dan Stidham, noted multiple defects with the police investigation. The bodies were moved before the arrival of the coroner, who wasn't called until two hours after the bodies were found. Blood at the scene of the crime was never tested. The local police were under investigation for theft, which might have been the reason they refused assistance from the Arkansas State Police. Physical evidence was stored in paper sacks bought at the supermarket—with the supermarket's name on the bags—rather than in proper containers for evidence.[11]

Reexamination of photographs of the bodies showed bite marks on one of the boys. The pattern of marks did not match the teeth of any of the West Memphis Three.

John Mark Byers was the adoptive father of Christopher Byers. He gave a folding knife to documentary filmmakers, which he said had never been used. The knife was later found to have blood on the blade. He claimed he had used it for a deer hunt. The blood was later tested and found to have a human blood type that could be either his or Christopher's. He didn't have an explanation but thought he might have cut his thumb.[12] He also had his teeth removed in 1997 after the first trial, the reasons for which were inconsistent. Because of this, his teeth could not be compared to the bite marks on the forensic photographs.[13]

In an interview Vicki Hutcheson gave to the *Arkansas Times* in 2004, she said her previous statements about the case were "complete fabrication."[14] This lead witness said she had been coerced by the police to make her prior statements and was afraid her child would be taken away:

> *Victoria (Vicki) Hutcheson says she was told what to say by West Memphis Police Department detectives, and that if she did not testify as instructed they could take her child away from her and implicate her in the slayings.*[15]

She further said that the recording the police made of Echols—which they had claimed was incomprehensible and was later lost—was clearly recorded and contained no incriminating statements.[16] She said the police hid her away from defense attorneys after she testified in the first of two trials, and that police destroyed evidence.

Vicki Hutcheson's son, Aaron, also said he was "tricked" by the police into making his statements about seeing the murders, and that the trauma of the murders might have affected his recall.[17] Years later he no longer knew whether he had actually seen the murders. The police didn't take account of the fact that Aaron's story changed, or that he could have gotten information from news reports and neighborhood gossip. His story illustrates many aspects of false memories, including the source of a memory not being able to be recalled. A number of research studies have illustrated this effect, as in studies of "flashbulb memories," or memories of historical events.[18, 19, 20]

When the space shuttle *Challenger* exploded shortly after liftoff, it was observed live on television by thousands of school children. They were watching because one of the crew was a teacher.[21] Years later, subjects were asked to recall how they learned about the disaster. Many people would state that they were in a particular place or with certain people, but those statements were shown to be false. Typically, what occurred is that someone told them about a particular detail, and later they forgot where they got that piece of information.[22, 23] As we cover in more detail later in this book, they felt it was their memory, and with subsequent reporting to other people it became more real to them. This is not deliberate lying or falsification—it's just how the mind works.

Echols's former lawyer, Dan Stidham, noted that the case was entirely built around Misskelley's false confession and Hutcheson's testimony in Misskelley's trial, which he said he always knew to be false. But those stories had been leaked to the press and influenced the opinions of jurors in the trial against Echols and Baldwin. (Remember what I said about first impressions?) "Hutcheson's recantation of her trial testimony was not all that shocking to me, in that I have always known she was lying," Stidham said. "The real shocking thing to me about her recantation is the level of misconduct on the part of the West Memphis police. It obviously knew no boundaries."[24]

"I lied, instead of trusting in God," Hutcheson said. "I was raised in a Pentecostal home, and I knew to do right but instead I let the West Memphis Police Department scare me to death."[25]

The case sparked wide controversy and was the subject of several books and documentaries.[26] A reexamination of the DNA evidence in 2007 showed that none of it could be attributed to the defendants. In 2010, the case reached the Arkansas Supreme Court, where the court cited lack of DNA evidence and juror misconduct in the original trial. The West Memphis Three entered Alford pleas, which allowed them to maintain innocence while acknowledging there was enough evidence to convict them. The judge accepted the pleas, and they were released based on time served, having spent eighteen years behind bars for crimes they didn't commit.[27]

Attorneys for the West Memphis Three filed a motion for declarative and injunctive relief in Crittenden County, Arkansas, on July 16, 2021, seeking DNA evidence in the case with the goal of exoneration. They were told the DNA evidence was lost or no longer exists.[28]

The West Memphis Three is a case study in the maladministration of justice, misconduct on the part of prosecutors and the police, and the potentially malevolent influence of the media. Like the Amanda Knox case, the West Memphis Three involved a high-profile, gruesome and grisly case of murder that was catnip for the press. In both cases, a small and overwhelmed police force, and prosecutors who were in over their heads, were driven by the pressure to find the killer and wrap up the case. They cut corners, contaminated the crime scenes, and botched the collection of evidence. Both cases were based on false and coerced confessions that were later recanted and testimony from witnesses who were patently unreliable. Police misconduct and suppression of evidence were rife. Both cases also highlighted the detrimental effect of poor media coverage, with leaks to the press about satanic ritual killings. The West Memphis Three case, like the Amanda Knox case, had its own plethora of blogs and forum postings, where conspiracy theories and confirmation biases ran rife. Unfortunately, if anything was learned in the case of the West Memphis Three, those lessons were not passed on to the future.

The West Memphis Three were the victims of poor backgrounds and lack of privilege. In the case of Misskelley, he lacked the intellectual abilities to avoid getting steamrolled by the system. I wasn't involved with the West Memphis Three but a few months later I got involved in a case that was the opposite of the West Memphis Three in terms of the wealth and influence of the accused and the way the media responded to the case. It also, not coincidentally, had the opposite outcome for the accused. That case boils down to two letters:

O. J.

8

O. J.: SPRINTING TO ACQUITTAL IN COURT AND ON TV

"Ever need to rent a car fast?"

Those were the words of former star running back for the Buffalo Bills football team, O. J. "The Juice" Simpson, as he raced through an airport with his briefcase and overcoat, leaping over barriers and showing his world-class sprinting style.

"Nobody has what it takes to rent you a Fairmont, Mustang, LTD, or other fine car faster."

Attractive white female agents tossed back their blonde hair as they handed over rental agreements without batting an eye, speeding him along his way as he jetted out to his rental car, jumped in, and gave the thumbs up, while "Hertz, the superstar in rent-a-car" flashed on the screen.

The year was 1978. O. J. was the good-looking Black guy with the positive attitude, whom everyone loved, and who had broken through—or more literally leapt over the hurdles—of ongoing prejudice and discrimination in the wake of the civil rights movement of the 1960s. True to form, he went on to get the super-hot blonde wife in Nicole Brown Simpson, the nice house, minor movie roles, TV endorsements, and the good life.

Fast forward two decades later, and O. J. was off racing again. This time it was on a freeway in Southern California, and O. J. was in his white Ford Bronco SUV, leading cops on a low-speed chase with a TV news helicopter overhead. They interrupted the NBA Finals to broadcast live coverage of the action.

O. J. was the primary suspect in the brutal murder of his former wife, Nicole, and her friend Ron Goldman, who were found stabbed to death on June 12, 1994, outside Nicole's condo in the Brentwood section of Los Angeles.

O. J. SIMPSON WHITE BRONCO CHASE MESMERIZES NATION
June 17, 1994: It started with a murder warrant. It ended with O. J. Simpson, a football superstar turned celebrity, in a Los Angeles jail cell under a 24-hour suicide watch . . . Simpson was supposed to surrender on June 17, 1994, after being charged for the brutal murder of his ex-wife Nicole Brown Simpson and her friend Ron Goldman. But instead of turning himself in, he fled.[1]

I remember seeing an image of Nicole Brown Simpson's driver's license on the news when I heard about her murder. The first thing that went through my mind was *Wow, he must have killed her.* It's a natural—if unfair—reaction to the news that a beautiful young wife was found dead with a male friend.

A few days later, when I was preparing a fancy rack of lamb for my girlfriends, I heard about O. J.'s low-speed chase on the radio. My friends—also lawyers—were already on the way over, so we spent the evening watching the Bronco and taking bets about whether or not he did it. I didn't know if we'd get to a trial. I thought he was going to kill himself. They read parts of his note on the radio: "Don't feel sorry for me. I've had a great life, great friends. Please think of the real O. J. and not this lost person."

After his arrest, O. J. got his orange juice and got to call his mom. Meanwhile, I thought, *you're kidding me, right? This man is wanted in the killing of his wife. He's a murder suspect. Why are they treating him with kid gloves?*

O. J.'s was the "Trial of the Century," with a dream team of lawyers on both sides, and a hundred million tuning in to hear the verdict. Opinions about the case were sharply split down racial lines.

As the trial got closer, my friend Emily, who was working as a weekend anchor at a Seattle TV station, suggested something that had never occurred to me: "Why don't you try getting on the air to talk about this case?" I'd never thought about going on TV like that, but when she said, "Why don't you see what happens?" I decided to give it a go.

To prepare for my unpaid weekly appearances on regional television, I had the biggest TV with the biggest screen I could find set up in my office. Like everyone else who could, I watched all day. When I had to be in court, I had a young paralegal sit in front of the TV and watch for me, updating me when I returned.

I don't remember the specifics of my first few times in front of the camera. I could hardly get a coherent sentence out of my mouth. I was brought onto the set, ushered to the weatherman's chair, and told to look at the camera. One of the cohosts—either Kathi Goertzen or Dan Lewis—would say something like: "Well, what do you make of what happened in the trial this week, Anne?" As I tried to explain in simple English what I thought was interesting or significant about what happened in the trial that week, the cohosts coaxed me along with encouraging looks and smiles. I'd give it my best shot: "Well, what they tried to do was . . . " inevitably ending with a smile and "Stay tuned." It was awful. I bombed. But they kept asking me back. They kept being encouraging.

It's hard to remember a time before O. J. when the entire nation was talking about how a piece of evidence was handled by the police or how a prosecutor was treating a witness. It was good for democracy that people around the country were wondering why Marcia Clark didn't introduce the "suicide note" or the police chase into evidence. The trial turned into an international education about the justice system in the United States.

This was only made possible by television. What's reported in the newspapers will never have the public impact of watching the drama of the courtroom unfold on television.

We've seen the power of television and the way documentaries have given cold cases a new look. Trials are currently covered by lawyers such as myself who work as analysts and are granted seats at the trial in order to provide that coverage. We come out of the courtroom during breaks to explain to the cameras—and the world that wasn't allowed inside—what happened and what it meant. What I think is interesting, important, and significant might be different from the person standing next to me. The more people who have access to the entire trial, the better.

So why not just put it on television so everyone can see it? There are pros and cons.

We can all agree that it's a good thing for people to be educated, whether it's about their health, or their rights in a court of law. We shouldn't just accept whatever a doctor tells us about our health, or what a lawyer tells us about our legal options. We should educate ourselves and take an active role. Televising court cases educates the public about our legal system and the processes of the law. That's a good thing, for everybody.

Televising court cases can also have its drawbacks. It pours more information out there for public consumption, giving an opportunity for trolls and malicious forum posters to take that information and distort and misrepresent it. Hours of uncut footage are used to create harmful memes, photo shopped pictures and videos, and unflattering sound bites on Instagram and TikTok, as we've seen more recently with the Johnny Depp-Amber Heard case. It is the fundamental dilemma of social media in modern times.

And there are other challenges that arise when trials are televised.

We saw them in full bloom during the O. J. trial.

Firstly, it can take way too long. Everyone involved is "playing" for the cameras, and they often do things completely differently than they would during an untelevised trial, when their only audience is the jury and courtroom spectators. When you're not televised, it's to your benefit to get witnesses and evidence in and out, to be efficient. When you're playing for cameras, everyone's trying to make themselves look better.

There's a great quote from Judge Lance Ito: "The sirens of mythology pale in comparison to the allure of seeing yourself on CNN."[2] That sums it up. Everyone knows that everyone's watching. They know it's what everyone around them is talking about. That it's on all the daytime shows. All the late-night shows. That a late-night host might make hay out of something they get wrong. That the next time they're in a bar they're going to be recognized as the guy who played a part in the O. J. trial. Any time anyone is allowed to speak during a televised trial, they're performing for the world. They know their mom is watching, celebrities and dignitaries are watching, and they'll probably never be in a position like that ever again. So they jockey for more time in front of the camera. Defense attorneys and prosecutors go on and on. Marcia Clark had a number of assistants, and when it was their time to speak, they went on for days. Weeks. There were months when Marcia hardly played a speaking role.

And then there are the witnesses. These men and women who often work arcane jobs, who have never been able to explain to friends and family members what they do or how they do it, get to make their pitch on national television. The medical examiner was on the stand for days in a case in which it was very clear how they died. Their throats were slit. They were stabbed to death! Let's move it along.

But television is intoxicating. And testimony can turn into the courtroom equivalent of some overzealous fan at a ballgame sitting behind the catcher, waving to his buddies back home who are watching on ESPN. It's human nature for people to try to stretch their fifteen minutes of fame into a couple of days, and that can interfere with the accused's right to a swift and fair trial.

This is a problem that judges can mitigate. They can move things along. They can tell prosecutors and counselors they've been over this material before. Judge Ito did the exact opposite. He made the trial a circus. He was a reed-in-the-wind kind of guy who didn't take control of the case. In many ways, he embarrassed the system. He was the wrong judge for the job because he tried to make himself the center of attention.

Every day when O. J. and his team came into court, he'd say good morning to every single one of them. It wasn't just lead attorneys Robert Shapiro and Johnnie Cochran. There were, like, twelve of them. And he said good morning to them all!

That was another part of the problem. He also allowed O. J. to have close to a dozen lawyers, each with a specific role to play, each with a family and group of buddies to wave to when it was their time to question a witness. The prosecution played the same game. Clark had someone specialize in the DNA evidence. She had somebody else question the medical examiner. She had somebody else work on the crime scene. And she had someone else deal with Mark Fuhrman, the LA cop she didn't want to have anything to do with. A little discretion from the judge at the beginning of the trial would have made all the difference.

So, yes, there are problems that come with televised trials, just like there are problems—and expenses—that come with body cameras and the Freedom of Information Act. But the benefits of maximum transparency outweigh the costs.

Just because it's not perfect doesn't mean it's not the right thing to do. Our system isn't perfect. More transparency and more televised trials will come with consequences, even negative ones. But that's still better than the alternative. The more people who know not just the framework of our criminal justice system but also how justice is served, the better.

It was a remarkable thing that the entire world got to see a case from beginning to end, basically everything but the stabbing. They saw the way a celebrity was treated better than anyone else ever would have been. This is the way our system worked for O. J. It showed the imperfections and the frustrations. And it showed the way the rich could bend the system in their favor. It's important that the public is not just told how that can happen, but that they see it for themselves.

Having cameras in the courtroom also allowed the entire world to see why our system works. In a dysfunctional criminal justice system, innocent people go to jail. In a functional criminal justice system, guilty people go free. It is impossible to get it 100 percent right.

Seeing the O. J. Simpson trial allowed the nation—the world—to see that in the United States, you are innocent until you are proven guilty, and if your peers are not 100 percent certain, beyond a reasonable doubt, that you did what the prosecutors say you did, you go free, even if you most likely did it.

After the O. J. trial, Kathi and Dan asked me to come back to talk about some other cases, like the trial of Susan Smith, a mother who was convicted of drowning her children. Smith had taken her two boys, three-year-old Michael and fourteen-month-old Anthony, to the John D. Long Lake in South Carolina, where she claimed a man had stolen her car with the boys inside.[3] She went on the national news pleading with the public to help her retrieve her children for several days before she admitted she had driven the car into the lake, drowning the boys. She had a history of depression and suicide attempts, was molested by her stepmother, and was having an affair with a local wealthy man who had called it off, saying he didn't want children. She was sentenced to thirty years in prison and will be eligible for parole in 2024.[4]

I was still struggling to reach a point where I was comfortable on camera. But every time I went on, I started getting a little better.

Years later, when I started doing national TV regularly, Kathi and Dan would always brag: "We trained her." They did. They also gave me the TV bug at just the right time in my career and just when law started to evolve into entertainment. I could see that the O. J. Simpson trial was the first of something. It wasn't going to be the last time the world was riveted by a murder trial. And I could tell it was going to change the way all of us did our jobs. In the same way that lawyers put on a theatrical performance for judge and jury, those of us who worked on high-profile cases were going to have to do the same for a much bigger jury pool that was not in the courtroom, but who would unmistakably help swing the outcome of the trial.

Kathi and Dan gave me a good introduction, but I knew I had to get better. So I hired someone who used to work at the station to tutor me on the basics: how to talk on camera, how to keep sentences brief, where to look, what to talk about, and how to get rid of the "ums" and the "whatevers."

Later, I hired another teacher who went so far as to put the faces of jurors on conference room chairs for me to practice talking to them. And she helped me get away from speaking in monotone to having inflections in my speech without resorting to "upspeak," which is the tendency of some women to inflect their voice upward at the end of a sentence, as if they are asking a question. It's an unconscious habit that comes from an impulse to not appear too aggressive, but it has the effect of projecting insecurity.

I learned more from the O. J. trial than just how to go on television or try a high-profile case. Watching the case every day—discussing every witness, prosecutor, and defense attorney—at length with friends for two years—was more valuable training for defending clients and prosecuting cases than anything any of us learned in law school.

First of all, every attorney in the trial was among the best in the business.

To watch the defense was to watch perfection. I don't care what your business is—football, insurance, manufacturing—if you can conceptualize, coordinate, and execute a plan as well as O. J.'s defense, you're going to be successful.

The defense used simple themes: simple language, indignation, ideas, and emotions every juror could understand. They took a case that appeared unwinnable, but by owning every piece of the story they wanted to tell and deploying the right experts, the right pieces of evidence, and the right attorney to present it all, they presented a flawless case, perfectly choreographed.

My only quibble was that it wasn't all true. The defense was able to convince the world, the nation, and members of the jury that O. J. Simpson—powerful, privileged, rich enough to hire attorneys good enough to outmaneuver prosecutors like he could outrun defensive ends—was the victim of systemic racism in the nation, the Los Angeles Police Department, and the police officer who found the smoking gun—a bloody glove—at his home the night his wife and her friend were murdered. O. J.'s defense was a case study in the importance of attorneys on the losing side of a case changing the narrative. And doing it in the press.

Disciplined defense attorneys who present flawless cases do not take many wrong steps. Their every move outside the courtroom is as coordinated as the words they choose to speak in front of a jury. Which is why, when unnamed members of O. J.'s defense team decided to talk to the *New Yorker*'s Jeffrey Toobin in the summer of 1994, they weren't doing it off the cuff.

When they highlighted for Toobin the way they were about to change the narrative of the night of Nicole Brown Simpson's murder, it's like they were speaking directly to the jury.

In the July 25, 1994 issue of the *New Yorker*, in a story titled "An Incendiary Defense,"[5] the attorneys opened up a new front in the nation's heated conversation around race and began to change the way the nation thought about O. J. Simpson:

According to news leaks last week, the results of sophisticated DNA tests suggest that the blood of both victims was on the glove found at Simpson's house. If Simpson did not bring the glove from the murder scene to his home, who did? At the preliminary hearing, Robert Shapiro had no answer. He does now— Mark Fuhrman.[6]

That's right, Fuhrman. The police officer who found the glove at Simpson's house. In their telling, he was no longer a cop doing his job. He was the cop who thought he was going to be running point on the biggest case of his career. But he was later told he was going to be a back-bencher. And as O. J.'s defense attorneys told Toobin, he found a way to get back into the action.

> *"Just picture it," one of the attorneys told me. "Here's a guy who's one of the cops coming on the scene early in the morning. They have the biggest case of their lives. But an hour later you're told you're not in charge of the case. How's that going to make that guy feel? So now he's one of four detectives heading over to O. J.'s house. Suppose he's actually found two gloves at the murder scene. He transports one of them over to the house and then 'finds' it back in that little alleyway where no one can see him." That would make him "the hero of the case," the attorney said.[7]*

But the defense wasn't going to stop there. Fuhrman, they decided, couldn't just be a bitter cop or a bad cop. He had to be a racist cop, whose racism inspired him to find a way to put O. J. away for the murder of his white wife.

> *The defense will assert that Mark Fuhrman's motivation for framing O. J. Simpson is racism. "This is a bad cop," one defense lawyer told me. "This is a racist cop." That would be an explosive allegation in any community, but it has a special resonance in Los Angeles. It was, of course, several officers in the Los Angeles Police Department who administered the notorious videotaped beating of Rodney King, in 1991—and it was the acquittal of those cops of state charges, in 1992, that prompted rioting in the city.[8]*

O. J. wasn't just "not guilty." He was the victim. And they knew just the right person to make the case.

> *The projected attack on Fuhrman is just part of a concerted defense strategy to portray Simpson as a victim—of official misconduct and, in a larger sense, of his race. For one thing, the Simpson defense team is considering diversifying its own ranks. One Simpson lawyer told me that the team was negotiating with Johnnie L. Cochran, a prominent black litigator in Los Angeles, to join Shapiro on the trial team.[9]*

This incendiary defense could only work if it was executed perfectly by a team that could take advantage of the prosecution's missteps. And they did.

Los Angeles screenwriter Laura Hart McKinny was doing research for a screenplay about harassment of women in the Los Angeles Police Department. Fuhrman was identified as a member of a group in the LAPD that was opposed to having women in the police force. In a series of recorded interviews she conducted for background material for her screenplay, Fuhrman made a series of racist and misogynistic remarks.

One of O. J.'s lawyers, F. Lee Bailey, asked Fuhrman while he was on the stand if he'd ever used the n-word in the past ten years. He denied it. When the tapes were played back in court, showing he had lied, it turned the courtroom upside down.[10]

For all her immense skills, Marcia Clark and her team should have vetted Fuhrman better. They should have known that he'd used the n-word. They should have addressed this with him on the stand—made a case for the fact that a deeply flawed man like Fuhrman wasn't motivated to put O. J. away out of racism or spite.

But they didn't. And the surprises the jury heard in the courtroom felt like confirmation of what they'd heard about Fuhrman. And it planted the seed of reasonable doubt.

The media played a role in the outcome of the O. J. Simpson case, as well. The O. J. dream team was very effective in exploiting media coverage. You can argue whether or not it was fair, but you can't argue that the media didn't play a role in the outcome, or that we shouldn't take a hard look at the effects of the media and social media on high-profile criminal cases.

I've argued that televising court cases is a good thing. Knowledge is good, right? We don't want to take legal outcomes at face value without educating ourselves and doing our own research. But I've also argued about the potential harm involved in "doing our own research," especially on the internet or on forums filled with false information. And another downside of televising cases is that the media can portray cases in a way that inflames emotion, especially hot button issues like race.

The bottom line is that having criminal cases out there in the media and the popular press, whether it's televised courtrooms or Facebook or chat forums dedicated to specific cases, is here to stay, and we have to find the best way forward in the situation.

One thing is clear. At this point in time we don't try cases only in the courtroom. We can try them in the press. The court of public opinion convenes outside the courtroom. And the party with the best presence in public is likely to be the one who wins.

Being on the losing side of this reality landed Amanda Knox in an Italian jail for four years. Being on the other side set her free.

We are all members of the jury in the court of public opinion, ready to hear all the facts and readily provide our own opinions on them. The news media serves as the prosecutor, feeding us a steady flow of "facts," yet these "facts" are usually one-sided, pointing toward the accused's guilt.

Social media also plays a huge role in the court of public opinion. It serves as a space for us to gather and share our thoughts on the case. Through conversations about a controversial trial, we can connect with others who share an interest, argue with those who disagree with us, and find out about even more pieces of evidence that further confirm what we already believe. We follow these high-profile trials because we find them extremely interesting, and for some people, it almost turns into an obsession to try to find out every piece of information possible. Kind of like a game.

While it may be entertaining, the truth is that the media's information isn't always true, viewers usually only see one side of the story, and the public's entertainment comes at the expense of the defendant's potential loss of liberties.

So who stands up for the defendant? Who tells the media when the sensationalized "facts" don't add up? Who ensures that the defendant receives a fair trial by media?

Remember the article I quoted earlier about Frances Farmer being sent to the hospital to undergo a hearing regarding her sanity? It quotes the doctors and lawyers giving opinions and rulings that would determine her future, which happened to be detrimental to her. But later in the article it quotes Frances herself:

> Miss Farmer spent a quiet night in her cell, drank a cup of coffee which she eyed with distinct disdain, and said:
>
> "Well, where are the instruments? When are you going to start the torture? I thought you would brand me with a hot iron."[11]

Prescient words. It wasn't enough for Frances Farmer to be a famous actress and celebrity beauty. She got steamrolled by the doctors and lawyers who were supposed to be looking out for her and blasted as a crazy loon in the press. I was able to stand up for Amanda Knox, but I was too late for Frances.

The O. J. case was about excesses of passion and the criminal extremes that can result from those passions. In his case, it was the passion of jealousy, and the crime was murder. But passion can lead you to other crimes. In the case of Mary Kay Letourneau, it was love, and her crimes were of a different sort.

THE CRIMINAL PASSIONS
OF MARY KAY LETOURNEAU

LETOURNEAU FOUND IN CAR WITH FORMER STUDENT
February 4, 1998 (The Associated Press): Twelve weeks ago, former teacher Mary Kay LeTourneau [sic] tearfully told a judge she was wrong to have had sex with a sixth-grade boy and to bear his child. "I give you my word it will not happen again," the 35-year-old woman pledged. On Tuesday, a month after her release from jail, prosecutors say LeTourneau was arrested after being found in a parked car at 3 a.m. with the 14-year-old boy she had admitted raping. Her arrest will likely send her back to prison and has prosecutors and some child advocates saying, "I told you so."[1]

It was the strangest of love stories. The teacher and her student. Compelling and revolting at the same time. Mary Kay Letourneau was thirty-four. He was twelve. After pleading guilty in 1997 to having sex with a minor, she gave birth to his child while awaiting sentencing. She made a plea deal and was released after three months in jail. Part of her parole was a ban on her contacting him again.

Shortly afterward, the police found them together in a van. Her plea deal was revoked, and she went back to prison, where she gave birth to his second child. When she got out, they got married.

Nothing could keep them apart.

Mary Kay Letourneau was a thirty-four-year-old married mother of four and a sixth-grade teacher at Shorewood Elementary School in Burien, Washington. One of her students was twelve-year-old Vili Fualaau. The pair developed a friendship that turned into a sexual affair. On June 18, 1996, police found the two in a parked car in a compromising position. They both gave false names, and Vili lied about his age, saying he was eighteen. When the police called Vili's mother, she said to release him with Mary Kay because she was a trusted teacher. Later, a relative of Mary Kay's husband contacted the police about the inappropriate and illegal relationship, which led to her arrest on March 4, 1997. She pleaded guilty to two counts of second-degree child rape. On May 29, 1997, while awaiting sentencing, she gave birth to Vili's child, a daughter. She spent three months in jail, was required to undergo sex offender treatment, and was forbidden to have further contact with Vili. Her husband divorced her.

Mary Kay and Vili wrote a book together, which was published in France, entitled *Only One Crime, Love*. She was released from prison in 2004 and they were married in 2005.

Nobody could keep them apart.

America had never seen anything like the Mary Kay Letourneau case before, and I don't think we'll see anything like it again.

This was a grown woman who behaved horribly, immorally, not to mention illegally, and abusively with a child. One she loved. One who loved her. And one to whom she was later married for fifteen years.

I first heard about the Mary Kay Letourneau case one morning while I was getting ready for work. It was in the spring of 1997, and I heard a news reporter on television explaining that a local teacher had been arrested. She'd apparently been having a relationship—and a sexual one at that—with a twelve-year-old student. That was young enough to stop me in my tracks.

Like the rest of the nation, I couldn't turn away from the story. It was a perversion of the cliché story of the little kid having a crush on his teacher. Except this time the teacher didn't just cross boundaries. She obliterated them.

Though it does not excuse what she did, Mary Kay had an extremely odd, even tragic, upbringing. She grew up in Corona del Mar, California, in a mansion on

Spyglass Hill with a panoramic view of the Pacific Ocean.[2] Her family members were extremely smart. Three of her brothers went to Stanford and one of them worked in the Trump administration. But there were also some odd things about them.

Mary Kay's father, John G. Schmitz, was a one-time California congressman who was so conservative that most conservative people couldn't stand him. People used to protest outside their house, blaring German marching music. Her mother, Mary Schmitz, opposed the Equal Rights Amendment (ERA) and debated Gloria Allred. In the summer of 1973, just before the start of sixth grade, Mary Kay was left alone, as she often was, to care for her three-year-old brother, Phillip.[3] Her father was away on business, and her mother was off doing church or anti-ERA activities. Mary Kay was playing in the pool with her older brother, Jerry, and didn't notice that Phillip had slipped off his life jacket and entered the deep end of the pool. No one noticed he was missing until her mother came home and went looking for him, and found his lifeless body in the bottom of the pool.[4]

Expecting a sixth grader to watch a three-year-old is too much responsibility, but the family held her responsible nevertheless. I think that event had a long-lasting impact on her.

Over the years, she'd been diagnosed with different things like bipolar disorder, narcissistic personality disorder, and histrionic personality disorder. She didn't believe any of them and never stuck with treatment. On the one hand, she was super fun—the favorite teacher—conducting her class like a symphony. On the other, she was having sex with her student, sometimes even at school.

Mary Kay Letourneau died of cancer in 2020. I don't think she ever really grew up. I think that's one reason she got so close to some of her students. She fit in well with the girls she taught. She would have long, late-night girl-talks with some of them on the phone. She was very childlike.

She always had a naïve innocence about her. When I would see her in prison, she would come running across the lawn to see me, like a golden retriever. Just happy to see me, without a care in the world.

If you had met Mary Kay, you'd think she was just another mom. She had six kids. One went to Georgetown. At the time I visited her in prison, one of them was the same age as Vili when they first met. Any time we were together, she was constantly texting with her kids: "Just got the dog," "What time is practice?" She was the ultimate soccer mom.

After years of cashing in on the idea that their relationship was a love story, Vili's family decided to try cashing in on the idea that it was not. They sued the Shoreline school district where Vili was a student and the Des Moines police department that found them together and didn't do anything about it. I was hired to defend the Des Moines police department against the family's civil suit. That trial laid bare for the first time the details of the relationship. And it turned out that my best arguments for the Des Moines police department were essentially arguing from the point of view of Mary Kay Letourneau. You may not like it, but that's my job. Everyone has the right to have a day in court, and to have the best argument put forward in their defense. That's the way our legal system is constructed. And it's the best way.

The allegations against the school were simple: she became involved with him at school while she was his teacher, and there were red flags everywhere. Some of their favorite places to have sex were her car or the teacher's bathroom, where they'd say they were going to wash out paint brushes. They said "I love you" to each other in the hallways. It was obvious what was going on, but nobody wanted to think it. Or believe it.

And then there were the cops. My clients.

Several officers caught them together late at night in a van outside an Anthony's restaurant in Des Moines, just outside Seattle. There was a sleeping bag in the back. She was wearing little more than a T-shirt. She lied about his age and told the cops he was eighteen. He was twelve. She said she was supposed to be with him.

It was all very suspicious. The officers put Mary on the phone with Vili's mom. His mom was, like, "oh, he's with Mary? That's fine." The mom was as clueless about what was going on as the school was. The police were concerned, so they referred the case to a detective, but nothing really happened. This was 1996, before law enforcement and teachers were required to report suspected child abuse.

They should have interviewed Vili, but they didn't. They never should have put Mary on the phone with his mom. There are a lot of things they should and should not have done. The relationship went on for another year before Mary Kay was arrested. And she'd become pregnant.

What's always intrigued me about the Mary Kay story was not the sex—we have plenty of those cases—but it was the relationship between the two. I'm not condoning it. It's immoral and unethical, not to mention illegal. But I've been interested in human behavior since I was a child and I sat in for my dad's secretary and accompanied him to the psychiatric hospital.

It had so few of the hallmarks of a predator/victim relationship. Mary Kay's dad was going through cancer treatment, and she was having a hard time. She felt that Vili was there for her and understood her. She knew that she was wrong to have sex with him when he was a child. But she also felt like her love for him was bigger than the ocean, that they were soulmates. She was committed to, even obsessed with, him, when she was in prison and out.

She put notes to him in with the breast milk for their babies. She said violent, threatening things to him in the notes, like if he slept with someone else, she'd cut off parts of his penis. She drew pictures of it. She wasn't well. When I would visit her during the trial, she used to tell me, "You won't be able to resist him." I was like, "Um, he's a kid. I'm sure I can."

The case got blown up in the media. The two trials of Mary Kay Letourneau, in 1997 and 1998, for child rape and violating the terms of her parole by not staying away from Vili Fualaau were covered by all the major media. Court TV covered them gavel to gavel, just as they had with O. J.

When I defended the Des Moines Police Department in the separate civil trial, I found that the Venn diagram of Mary Kay's arguments from four years prior and mine often overlapped. I argued that the cops in Des Moines, while they made mistakes, were justified not to press the matter.

It's hard to remember what the time was like then, but in a pre-Mary Kay Letourneau world, people didn't see a thirty-something teacher together with their student—even in a compromising situation—and immediately think sex. They thought it had to be something else.

"Nobody thought they were together," I argued. "Look at her and look at the way he looked in sixth grade. Look at her, I mean, do you think a cop would think they were together?"

The truth was nothing could keep them apart. She was arrested and went to jail. It didn't keep them apart. She went to prison. His family sued her. It didn't keep them apart.

I did my job. I defended the police. The jury agreed. The family got nothing. Except a daughter-in-law. Three years after the end of the trial, Vili and Mary tied the knot and were married for fifteen years.

I got to know Mary during the trial. She didn't testify, but she wanted to tell me everything. She wanted it to be a love story. One in which the two of them won. After the trial we stayed in touch, and over the following years became friends.

I think Mary Kay's story was all about that fateful day in California when her little brother, Phillip, slipped out of his life jacket and fell to the bottom of the family's pool and to his death. Mary Kay was just shy of twelve years old, the same age as Vili when she met and fell in love with him. I think Mary Kay never grew up. Her psychological growth stopped that tragic day at the pool when her brother died.

I'll never stop thinking about the case of Mary Kay Letourneau. About human nature. About consent. About love. And about these two people who were, by all accounts, very much in love. I can't defend what she did, but I could tell the world that the cops weren't able to keep them apart. Nothing could.

There's another case I don't think any of us will ever forget. Maybe because he looked like a movie actor. Scott Peterson.

10

SCOTT PETERSON: IF LOOKS COULD KILL

I've got one for you. There's a nice couple who live in a nice neighborhood. The wife is pretty and wears a smile well. She's also pregnant. First time. Can't keep that smile off her face.

The husband is handsome. You might not see him up on the big screen, but he's plenty good looking enough to play the manly type in a movie. He's got a good job, too. Likes to fish.

Together, they light up the neighborhood. They're the kind of couple you hope will buy the house next door. You're happy to watch the house when they're gone. You're looking forward to checking in on the baby. You've got a casserole ready to go in the freezer.

The day before Christmas, she disappears.

Parts of the fetus turn up on the beach.

Then her torso.

MODESTO POLICE SEEK TO IDENTIFY BODIES ON SHORE
April 16, 2003: The Modesto police were seeking help from DNA experts today as they studied the possibility that the bodies of a woman and an infant boy found washed up on the shore near Berkeley were those of a pregnant Modesto housewife and her baby. Laci Peterson, a 27-year-old substitute teacher, was almost eight months pregnant when she vanished on Christmas Eve. The infant found on Sunday had

his umbilical cord still attached. Autopsies were being conducted to determine their identities, but the advanced state of decomposition prevented immediate conclusions.[1]

People like to follow along with manhunts, missing persons, and trials because everyone wants to be an armchair sleuth. It's like watching *Law & Order* if *Law & Order* were a reality show. And was participatory. In the age of Facebook and Twitter, people feel like they can affect the outcome of the trial, and they're not wrong.

Not every case becomes an international sensation. One of the main reasons Amanda Knox's story became a global tabloid affair is that she was the girl next door. Everyone wanted to know: Would I know a killer if they lived next door? Would you have the victim for dinner? Would you marry the killer?

This is the same reason the nation was captivated by the trial of Scott Peterson, the pretty-good-looking husband and father-to-be who killed his pregnant wife and unborn son.

People like to compare Amanda's case with Peterson's. And although the cases are very different, they shared many similarities, starting with the fact that they drew sensational worldwide coverage. Beyond that, both cases were a bit odd, as there was precious little direct evidence tying either accused to the murders, and there was a presumption of guilt more or less from the start.

But when people compare Amanda Knox to Scott Peterson, they're talking more about themselves than they are the cases. The stories captivated the world in ways others don't, because so many people could see themselves in the cases. The Petersons were the couple on top of the wedding cake. Everyman married to Everywoman living in Small Town, USA.

Like Amanda, Laci Peterson was the girl next door, someone everybody could relate to. It made women everywhere wonder: Would I know a murderer if I married him? She married him, right? How could she not have seen it? We all think we would have seen it. But do we ever?

One of the most unfortunate similarities between the two cases is that they both looked guilty. There's a reason why people point fingers at suspects who look guilty. Oftentimes, they are. Scott Peterson had guilty written all over him.

The Scott Peterson case didn't start as a murder investigation. It was a missing person case first. Search parties were out looking for Laci in what appeared to be a Christmas Eve abduction.

One thing that stood out is that Scott didn't seem to show any emotion. It was supposedly the most horrifying thing that could ever happen to a person: your wife, eight and a half months pregnant with your son, has vanished. And yet you don't seem the least bit shaken up about it.

"I saw more reaction out of [Scott] when he burned the God-darned chicken," Harvey Kemple, Laci's second cousin, later testified.[2]

When she disappeared, he behaved like she wasn't coming back. He ordered two porn channels on cable. He looked into selling his house—quickly, even furnished.

This is not the way innocent people behave.

Then more of the pieces started falling into place. It turned out Scott had been seeing someone—a masseuse named Amber Frey. He'd even skipped a Christmas party with Laci to be with her.

He went on TV, but it only made him look more guilty—more removed, more convinced that his wife was dead, never coming home—and like he didn't care. In an interview on ABC, Diane Sawyer asked him if he'd killed his wife, and he coldly responded that he hadn't, explaining: "Violence towards women is unapproachable. It is the most disgusting act to me."[3]

Then he told Sawyer that he'd told Laci about the affair, and that they were dealing with it. But it didn't cause a rupture in their relationship: "It wasn't anything that would break us apart."

Sawyer spoke for the world when she asked: "Do you really expect people to believe that an eight-and-a-half-month pregnant woman learns her husband has had an affair and is saintly and casual about it? Accommodating? Makes a peace with it?"

"Well, yeah," Scott said. "No one knows our relationship but us."

Later in the interview, he told Sawyer: "She was amazing," before catching himself: "Is amazing."

All the while, Scott had become the primary suspect in Laci's disappearance, and police put a tracker on his car. They noticed that he'd been returning to the bay where his wife and child's partial remains would eventually wash ashore. And they got his girlfriend, Amber, to play ball. They recorded her conversations with Scott.

"Our relationship will grow," he told her. "I have confidence in that."

Police arrested him on April 18, 2003, at a golf course in La Jolla, just north of San Diego—his dark hair dyed blonde—carrying his brother's ID and a box of Viagra. He said he was planning to go golfing with his brother. His Mercedes Benz was stuffed with clothes, camping and survival gear, four cell phones, and $15,000 cash.[4]

It's almost as if he didn't want to look innocent.

I've never seen anyone else who appeared as guilty as Scott Peterson.

The first day I covered the trial for Court TV, I walked in with Gloria Allred and Nancy Grace, and the three of us sat together in the crowded little courtroom. I looked over at the jury and thought: *Oh, wow, these people hate him.* You could see it in the looks on their faces. I thought to myself: *He is so going down, it's not even funny.*

But he seemed to think it was. He was smirking constantly. Like the whole thing was a game. A chance for the attention of the world to finally land where it belonged: on him.

At one point, they showed pictures of him fishing as a kid, and he looked at them and smiled, like: *Oh, look how cute I was! Finally, my story is being told!*

He was bizarre and inappropriate with his attorney, Mark Geragos. He kept acting like they were buddies, just a couple of colleagues yucking it up.

Like we'd seen before the trial, he didn't act the way you'd expect. He never broke down: "Oh my baby. My wife." There was none of that. You expect people to be sad, even devastated. He seemed thrilled. It was all about him.

Even Scott's mom looked guilty. She was very strange. She showed up in court every day with a walker. But when I saw her at Saks Fifth Avenue at the Stanford mall, she was fine, up and around, shopping for shoes. The whole thing was completely bizarre.

From the moment I walked into the courtroom, it looked like the jurors were trying to restrain themselves from walking up to Scott and wiping that smirk off his face. They hated him. It's not just that he was acting inappropriately—being accused of murder does not bring out the best in people—but that he was acting disrespectfully to a beautiful young woman and baby. You could see it in their eyes: Whether he killed them or not, loved them or not, he owed them some respect. He gave them none in the courtroom.

During the day, people would line up in front of the Court TV truck, wanting to talk to Nancy Grace and get on the air. Professional and otherwise, they lined up offering their opinions, angling for their chance to comment on the case the world was watching that week.

Nancy and I covered the trial together a lot, and we became close friends. Every night, we'd get together back at the hotel's hospitality suite to wind down and talk about the trial—how the lawyers were handling things and what we'd do differently. Standard shop talk.

With Nancy, the talk always turned back to Laci and her son. She's always been about the victims. But we also couldn't help but shake our heads at Scott Peterson's attorney, Mark Geragos, who we both saw as something of a lazy showboater, unprepared for the trial. His case rested on the fact that there was slim to no direct evidence.

"You want to say his behavior is boorish; we are not going to dispute that," he told the jury during his opening statement. "But the fact is that this is a murder case and there has to be evidence in a murder case."[5]

That much was true.

There seemed to have been an extremely clean crime scene. The theory was that Scott killed Laci in the house, then moved her body—or parts of it—into a van, concealing them in large umbrellas. And, in fact, a neighbor claims to have seen him move the big umbrellas into his van.

But the house was clean. There was nothing amiss in the bedroom. And the kitchen was spotless. There was even a mop and bucket in the kitchen, not long after the housekeeper had been there, something Diane Sawyer asked him about and, of course, he had an answer for: "Dog, two cats, muddy backyard. She mopped those floors every day. And I emptied the bucket when I returned that afternoon."

There was no DNA or fingerprints that suggested foul play. No sign of a struggle. Just a bit of Laci's hair on a pair of pliers on his boat.

This all assumes that Laci died in the house. We really don't know for sure. But either way, a lack of direct evidence does not mean a crime wasn't committed. Circumstantial evidence, despite its unfortunate name, is just as valid as direct evidence. I even find it more convincing.

Direct evidence is, for instance, someone's testimony: "I saw him walk into the house, and then I saw her stumble out the back with a bullet wound in her side," or something like that. Circumstantial evidence is something you can deduce from evidence presented in the case.

Think of circumstantial evidence like footprints in the snow: you go to bed at night, it starts snowing, and your yard, porch, and front steps are covered in snow. When you wake up in the morning, there's a newspaper on your porch and there are footprints leading to the newspaper. You didn't see the paper carrier deliver the newspaper. All your neighbors were asleep when she dropped the paper off. So, on the surface, you have no direct evidence that your paper carrier delivered the paper. But you do have circumstantial evidence. It's simple and convincing.

You know people say, "Oh, well, it's just circumstantial." That's a misnomer. Circumstantial evidence and direct evidence are equal in the eyes of the law. They're both compelling. Circumstantial evidence doesn't lie. It speaks for itself, and its story stays consistent. Direct evidence can be unreliable. Witnesses can lie, remember things incorrectly, or their memories can become blurred by the passage of time. Circumstantial evidence doesn't change.

I think jurors like circumstantial evidence, too. It makes them feel like they're figuring things out for themselves, not being told to force pieces of the puzzle where they don't belong.

And Scott was dead to rights on circumstantial evidence.

He was fishing on Christmas Eve. He was seen moving something big out of his house. He'd cleaned tarps that had been on his fishing boat with gasoline and fertilizer. He was moving on with his life—stocking up on porn, getting rid of the house—behaving as if Laci was never coming home.

And he was obsessed with visiting the bay where the bodies eventually washed up. He kept visiting there. As if he was waiting for something. An expert on tide patterns said the body would have been ditched in the area of San Francisco Bay where Scott said he had been fishing. Heck, fisherman said he didn't have the right gear to catch the fish he claimed to have been fishing for!

There was a huge crowd outside the courthouse the day the jury returned the verdict. And when the judge read that they'd found Scott Peterson guilty, the crowd erupted into huge cheers. It was like nothing I'd ever seen. It was a visceral reaction. All these people turned out, just furious, wanting justice for what a man had done to his wife and son.

As Nancy said, "Laci didn't even have the arms to hold her baby." (Meaning in heaven.)

Scott Peterson's case was similar to Amanda Knox in that judgments were made early on in both cases that they looked guilty. Scott grinned and joked with his lawyers in the courtroom. Amanda hugged her boyfriend and did cartwheels. Scott bought porn and got ready to put his house on the market. Amanda bought lingerie and ate pizza. In both cases people said they didn't seem to show remorse for the victims. People said Amanda didn't act "correctly" for a person whose friend had just died.

From an outside perspective there was nothing to separate Scott Peterson from Amanda Knox. Externally, from the perspective of the media, they were identical. Young, beautiful people acting callous after the murder of someone close to them, which demonstrated their guilt.

To the media, that was all that mattered. In the court of public opinion, the first impression, as I've said before, is the most important. And that opinion, in both cases, was "guilty as charged."

But there were important differences.

Scott Peterson had the torso of his wife and the fetus of his unborn son wash up on the shores of San Francisco Bay where he had recently gone "fishing." He was having an affair and therefore had a motive to get rid of his growing family so he could be with the other woman. And there were no other possible suspects for their murders.

Amanda Knox faced accusations of belonging to a cult that indulged in a sex orgy where none of her blood or DNA showed up at the crime scene. She had no conflicts or motives to kill her roommate. The real killer's blood was sprayed all over the room and his semen was in the victim's body.

So what this boils down to is two young and attractive people acting in ways that others say "look guilty," and they are both portrayed in the press as "guilty," and yet the evidence fits for one but not the other.

In summary, Scott Peterson killed his wife and her unborn baby. Amanda Knox did not kill her roommate.

If Scott had been a better actor and faked a show of remorse, he might have gotten away with it. Amanda's behavior resulted in four years in jail which could have become her whole life.

I talk about both these cases because, in addition to being personally involved in some way, either as lawyer or commentator, they show how powerful impressions are. How the media can act like an accelerant for those first reactions in the court of public opinion.

I highlighted in the O. J. case how important it is for the public to be able to follow along with the trial, and the important role that televising the trial had in informing the public. I also pointed out how this publicity can be a good thing. But I also point out in this book how the public can form snap opinions and can make up their minds before all the facts are in, and the media can present a biased viewpoint. So it can cut both ways. That's why we have courts with judges and juries and attorneys to represent both sides so everyone can get a fair hearing.

Scott Peterson was put in prison for the rest of his life due to a bounty of circumstantial evidence. In the end, Amanda Knox was exonerated because the evidence, both direct and circumstantial, rightly pointed toward Meredith Kercher's real killer.

MICHAEL JACKSON: WELCOME TO NEVERLAND

What if you were a kid, and someone invited you to a sleep over at a place that had three miniature railroads you could play on, a Ferris wheel, a carousel, a pirate ship, Super Slide, roller coaster, bumper cars, and an amusement arcade! I'd say yes if I were a kid; wouldn't you?

Welcome to Neverland, the magical ranch of pop music star Michael Jackson. Neverland not only had cool rides and stuff, it had a petting zoo! How cool is that? You could meet Bubbles the Chimp, whom Michael dressed like his twin and took with him on tour, not to mention orangutans, snakes, giraffes, flamingos, elephants, tigers, and Rikki the Parrot!

But wait, why would a grown man want to spend all of his time hanging out with . . . kids? Nobody seemed to ask that question back when the King of Pop was strutting his stuff on stage and doing the moonwalk. But what goes up must come down, and Michael eventually did come down.

POLICE RAID JACKSON RANCH
FOLLOWING FRESH ALLEGATIONS FROM BOY, 13

Nov. 18, 2003: Police yesterday carried out an extensive search of Michael Jackson's ranch in the US as part of an "ongoing criminal investigation". The raid on the singer's Californian home Neverland, a 2,600-acre estate in Santa Barbara county, about a two-hour drive from Los Angeles, was carried out in the morning by the local county sheriff's department accompanied by members of the district attorney's office. More than 40 police vehicles were present at the raid which continued for several hours and was backed by a search warrant. The estate contains a children's zoo . . . [1]

By the end of 2004, I was in desperate need of some new scenery. It was my midlife crisis. By every measure, I'd been a successful attorney for twenty years. I had represented high-profile clients, had an entire case followed on national television, and made enough money that I could afford to take a flyer on the restlessness that was nudging me out the door.

I decided I had two options: I could go to work as a district attorney in Manhattan for a couple of years or I could spend the next six months with Michael Jackson. I packed my bags, told my partners I'd be in the Marion Davies Room at the Santa Maria Inn, and caught a plane for Neverland.

My plan was to cover the Jackson trial from inside the courtroom. I liked TV and wanted to do more of it. I knew the trial would take up the better part of a year, and if I spent the whole time going on TV every day, maybe I'd get better at representing my clients on TV. At a minimum, I knew I could only become a better lawyer by watching defense attorney Tom Mesereau try to convince a jury that a man who had sleepovers with children was not a pedophile.

One minor hitch was that I didn't have a press pass or the backing of a network, and I knew hundreds of credentialed journalists would be angling for space in a courtroom that's barely bigger than your living room. But I knew I had to be there. I was ready for a change. And I'd been obsessed with Jackson since I was a little girl. It started with my Panasonic radio. So yellow . . . canary yellow! It was perpetually tuned to Seattle's KJR 95.7. It was all any of us in the seventies who lived in *Brady Bunch* houses with car ports, rec rooms, and breakfast nooks wanted to listen to. My friends and I had Michael Jackson trading cards and pored over every LP and 45 we could get our hands on.

In the summers, we spent our days around the pool. The teenagers all had their transistor radios tuned to KJR. At night, when I was supposed to be asleep, I'd lie in bed listening to Roberta Flack, the Bee Gees, and the Jackson 5.

Michael was always my favorite. He and I were the same age—though, technically, I was born a few weeks earlier. It wasn't just that he was brilliant, beautiful, and famous. He was one of us. He was a kid! I wanted to be an actress. Knowing that, like me, Michael Jackson was a kid, made me feel as if my dreams could come true.

The Michael Jackson story didn't stay as bright as my Panasonic radio.

It took me a while to accept the fact that Michael had a disturbing side. I didn't want to believe what I was hearing. But when he paid the family of a child, Jordy Chandler, a $23 million settlement in 1993, my mind was made up. You don't pay that kind of money to a kid's family for a crime you didn't commit. It doesn't work that way. Especially when you're constantly teetering on the brink of bankruptcy like Michael was. After all, grown men don't have sleepovers with thirteen-year-old boys.

This time, Michael was on trial for allegedly molesting (among other felonies) a thirteen-year-old boy named Gavin at his nearby Neverland Ranch. *The People v. Michael Jackson* was to take place at the Santa Barbara County Superior Court, a picturesque Spanish-style building. There was a swimming pool out back, and it was surrounded by ball fields and the scenic town of Santa Maria. The courtroom itself was tiny.

It was to be decided there whether the biggest pop star in the world was going to be the prison system's most popular inmate.

When I got to Santa Maria, I still didn't have a press pass, but I leaned on a few people I'd met covering the Peterson trials for Court TV. They all said the same thing: just go do it. Tell them you're here to cover the trial. So I did.

I stood in line with everyone else trying to get inside and made my case: "Hi, I'm Anne. I've been a lawyer for twenty years and spent the last handful of them explaining the inner workings of high-profile trials on national television. You may have seen my work on Court TV." Critically, I told them I'd sing for my supper: if you let me into the courthouse, I said, I'll explain to the world what's going on inside.

That caught their attention. A lot of people wanted to get in. But few of them knew how to explain what was going on in terms that people would understand. There were no cameras allowed inside. But the court wanted the public to know what was going on. After high-profile embarrassments, like the way Judge Ito handled the O. J. trial, the Santa Barbara County Superior Court wanted to reassure the public that they could handle a trial. They went for it and gave me credentials.

Meanwhile, CNN asked if I'd be their "eyes and ears" in the courtroom. I was in. Finally, I had my press pass, a media outlet to work with, a beautiful hotel room with a Juliet balcony, and a permanent place in the massive media tent city. And it *was* a city, or at least a summer camp. Every news organization with a video camera and satellite truck was there. Each of them got just a few feet of space: NBC, CBS, ABC, and all the cable news types like CNN, MSNBC, Fox News, etc. There were loads of foreign press, too.

To get better access, networks bought the rights to all the nearby rooftops and built temporary structures two stories high with a full production room and space for interviews and live coverage. It was a little media village. The press filled all the hotels—to say nothing of the bars and restaurants. The local chamber of commerce was so thrilled with the business that they threw us a huge Santa Fe barbecue. Locals were having visitors into their homes for dinner. The town could not have been more hospitable.

Our days started early. I was on camera most mornings starting at 4:00 a.m. to brief CNN's East Coast viewers about what was going on in the trial and what to expect during the coming day. J. Randy Taraborrelli, Michael's biographer and sometimes confidant, was out there with me every morning in the next stall. We became close friends.

It wasn't always comfortable. It was cold out there at four in the morning. We wrapped ourselves in blankets and tried to keep bugs from flying into our mouths. As soon as the camera shut off, I'd go to a 7-Eleven across the street for coffee and a newspaper.

Because I actually showed up every morning, I started getting asked to appear on more networks desperate for some analysis of the proceedings for their morning shows. The CBS network kept booking flaky guests, who wouldn't show up, for their morning hits. I was already awake and in makeup, so I chipped in whenever they needed me. They were so grateful that they kept giving me fruit baskets and other thank-you gifts. I couldn't be happier to do it.

Those gigs weren't paid, but I was there. I didn't need money; I needed experience on camera, and I wanted to be there for the colossal trial of the world's biggest pop star.

Hours after many of us had been up and at the courthouse and had made multiple trips to 7-Eleven, Michael and his entourage of lawyers, bodyguards, and hangers-on would arrive in a motorcade of SUVs from Neverland. Everyone would scramble to get their shot of the King of Pop walking under an umbrella, dressed as dapper as can be in one of his prep school dandy outfits.

The jockeying had to be done while staying on the right side of Michael's fans. Every morning, they'd show up at 4:00 a.m., too, entering a lottery for a chance to be in court for the day. Those who weren't lucky enough to get a spot would stand outside yelling, alternating between "we love you, Michael!" and "Screw you, Fox!" (or whoever they were angry at that morning). They had names for anyone who didn't say nice things about Michael. Nancy Grace—who has spared few figures that have crossed her transom—was "Nancy Disgrace." Diane Dimond was "Diane Demon." They were pretty nice to me, because I didn't take it to Michael the way the other media figures did. And most of the fans were benign, if loud. Though there was one known to throw rocks.

Most members of the press couldn't get into the courtroom, so they watched the trial from a nearby overflow room. I got inside most days because I was a legal analyst and was briefing multiple press outlets.

I'll admit that I was starstruck on the first day, much more than I thought I would be. He came in, there was a huge crowd, he was waving, and I'm staring, thinking: *Oh, my god. It's Michael Jackson.* But that wore off pretty quickly. Partly because Michael Jackson didn't look like Michael Jackson. He was so small. So frail. Fragile, almost like a doll. I used to sit there looking at him and thinking: *I don't know who that person is, but I know he's not Michael Jackson.*

Due to all the security concerns, the trial didn't break for lunch, but got out early. On his way out, Michael was always escorted beneath an umbrella and whisked into a car in his motorcade and driven away. One day he brushed right up next to me on his way out and whispered: "Tell them I love my fans."

Once Michael left, I'd go back on the air with various networks, explaining what had happened during the day. I'd also often brief the international press pool.

Much like the O. J. trial, the entire world was fixated, for a time, on the American criminal justice system—following the trial but, with no cameras in the courthouse, not being able to see it. It was my job to explain not just what had happened, but what it meant in the context of the day's proceedings and our legal system.

This was a pedophile case, and I had a lot of experience working in sexual-assault cases, so I could address things the prosecutors were introducing into evidence and why. For example, in most states you can't introduce pattern evidence to say: look, this person did this bad thing in the past and that means they're *always* bad and they did *this* bad thing. That's not the case in California. The state allows prosecutors to show evidence that suggests a long pattern of bad behavior. In the case of Michael Jackson, prosecutors sought to bring in evidence to suggest a history of pedophilia. And pedophiles, they explained, tend to be repeat offenders.

The prosecutors also introduced a lot of female pornography found at Neverland. I was able to explain to the press that the reason the prosecution was introducing evidence like that—which could be construed to demonstrate that Michael preferred women over young boys—is that the prosecution was trying to argue that he was grooming the boys, showing them some things they might be more comfortable with at first.

While all of this was admissible, I think the prosecution overplayed its hand. I think one of the reasons the prosecution lost was that it spent too much time trying to paint Michael Jackson as a bad person, and not enough time explaining—and narrowing in on—why he was guilty in their specific case.

After I spoke to the international press pool, I made the rounds on US cable shows. In addition to CNN, I was talking to Nancy Grace twice a day—Court TV in the afternoons and *Headline News* at night. I'd also drop in on Keith Olbermann (before he burned his last bridge at MSNBC), Joe Scarborough, and various hosts on Fox. All of them wanted the same thing: tell us what's going on and what it means.

Eventually, all the cameras were turned off and we'd gather to decompress and enjoy each other's company. It was almost like a sorority of sorts.

Yes, we were all working to cover the trial of a man accused of assaulting a boy. Still, we had to have some fun. If we weren't, we wouldn't be any good at our jobs.

There were moments that made us all queasy, but untangling the justice system was what we did. It was our natural element. It was what we loved to do.

Award-winning crime writer Aphrodite Jones and I developed a fast friendship. She was dark and sultry. I was bright and happy. She had an apartment where we'd hang out and talk about the case.

TV can be cutthroat, but the reporters, hosts, and analysts couldn't have been nicer to me. They knew I was trying to get better, and they gave me tips. Aphy taught me how to wear concealer under my eyes. Nancy and I would often talk about how to improve.

At night, Randy Taraborrelli, who I considered my work husband because of all the time we were spending next to each other, used to drive me around in his convertible listening to old Michael Jackson bootlegs. He'd known the family since he was a kid. He always thought Michael was a case of arrested development; that he could act inappropriately with kids, but that he wasn't a pedophile. Driving around at night, he'd listen to the bootlegs and say: "Little Michael, this shouldn't be happening to you."

I didn't want Michael to be guilty, either. But I felt like we all knew he was a pedophile. How many times do I have to say it: grown men don't have sleepovers with thirteen-year-old boys.

To me, the case was generally fascinating for two reasons. First, there was an F. Scott Fitzgerald, "show me a hero and I'll write you a tragedy" element to it. How could somebody who was so loved and successful have such a fall from grace? How was that going to play out in the courtroom? Second, I didn't think Tom Sneddon had a case.

Sneddon, Santa Barbara County's district attorney, had been after Jackson for years. He's the prosecutor who got a warrant to photograph Jackson naked in the early nineties as a result of the Jordy Chandler case, the one memorialized in Jackson's song, "D.S.," featuring the lyrics: "Tom Sneddon is a cold man." Worse, he wasn't an effective prosecutor.

Sneddon was obsessed with finding Michael Jackson guilty. He laughed and scoffed and gloated during public statements about Jackson. And he let that obsession cloud his judgment regarding his ability to get a guilty verdict. Sneddon fell into the trap prosecutors fall into when they are more confident in the guilt of their subject than the strength of their case: they try the person for their character, not for a crime. They want the jury to be confident the accused is a bad person, not that they're guilty of a crime. They're so convinced of the person's broader guilt that they don't see that they're looking at a bad case or that there is a lack of evidence tying them to the crime they're on trial for.

Mignini did this when he prosecuted Amanda Knox. The rest of us do it all the time. We're all Tom Sneddons. When we find something we want to be true, we block out conflicting information. We search for ways to reinforce our belief, which is called confirmation bias, which we learned about earlier in the book. It's a universal behavioral characteristic, and it's been well-researched and character-ized by psychologists.[2] It's a search for what we *want to be* fact, rather than the actual facts. It's one thing for this to play out among armchair legal analysts on Twitter. It's quite another when it happens in the prosecutor's office—in Santa Barbara or Perugia, Italy.

Sneddon's opening statement was disorganized and weak. It opted for personal attacks over substance. CNN's Jeffrey Toobin opined that the prosecutor's opening statement was the worst he had ever heard, and I couldn't agree more. During the course of the trial, Sneddon displayed several hundred images of legal pornogra-phy found in Jackson's home (depicting women) that had no bearing on the pedo-philia charges. This showed that Michael Jackson liked pornography—as do many Americans—not that he molested a child.

The witnesses the prosecution called were a motley crew of people who had sued Michael Jackson, owed him money, had stolen from him, sold stories to tabloids, or been fired by him. One was a travel agent who was accused in a federal investi-gation of unlawful surveillance and profiting off Jackson. One robbed a Jack-in-the-Box while the trial was going on and ended up in custody in Las Vegas. We watched as Debbie Rowe, Michael's ex-wife, mother of two of his children, and witness for the prosecution, offered testimony that was the opposite of what the prosecutors expected. They thought she would say that a video she made in sup-port of him was coerced; instead she said she was eager to make the video in order to support him. She said he was surrounded by "opportunistic vultures" who exploited his fame and stole his money.[3]

The prosecution did not present a systematic case or even consistent themes to the jury. They basically decided to toss it all in there. They were so sure Michael Jackson was guilty and that a jury would find it hard to believe that a man who has sleepovers with children was innocent, that they would easily get a conviction.

The defense, on the other hand, successfully argued that if you cannot believe the family of the boy beyond a reasonable doubt, you must acquit. The family was the case, which is the way the case fell apart. After all, the boy's mom, Janet Arvizo, had to plead the Fifth Amendment regarding perjury and welfare fraud. Once, when she didn't think the jury was paying enough attention to her, she snapped her fingers at them. But that was just her courtroom misbehavior.

This is a woman who traveled with Michael Jackson, accepted his gifts, and used his credit cards. She saw no evidence whatsoever that her son was being molested by Michael Jackson. This is a woman who filed a claim against J.C. Penney, alleging that she had been sexually assaulted by employees and beaten—and made off with a $165,000 settlement. She failed to report this money to the welfare authorities while she was receiving full welfare.

Janet Arvizo, the mother of the boy Michael Jackson was accused of molesting, lied and caused her children to lie.[4] She lied on welfare forms. She lied under oath during the course of the J.C. Penney case, saying that her husband never beat her,[5] and then during the course of her dissolution, she alleged under oath that her husband had beaten her.[6] She had at least one of her children lie and say they were molested by their father. She told a paralegal in the firm assisting her that she had lied and forced her children to lie but if the paralegal were to repeat that to anyone, she "would be killed by the Mexican mafia."[7] She said she wanted her children to be actors and actresses and that she needed to help get them money through Michael Jackson. She also made newspaper appeals for money for her son's cancer treatment, when in fact that treatment was covered by insurance. The editor from the newspaper testified that she believed the mother was a con artist.

She got money from celebrities like George Lopez, purportedly for cancer treatment, and spent it on herself.[8] She took money from charitable sources meant to benefit her cancer-stricken son and spent it on herself.[9]

Arguably, Michael Jackson was just the next extortion target for a woman who "had always relied upon the kindness of strangers."

This is the bottom line: Even if this mom didn't believe Michael Jackson was a pedophile, he was *objectively creepy*. He admitted in a *national television interview* that he slept in bed with children. What kind of a mother is going to let her child stay at Michael Jackson's house after that? And what kind of a jury is going to think she's anything other than opportunistic?

The whole time she testified, Tom Sneddon sat in the front row of the courtroom holding his head in his hands.

Part of the job of a prosecutor is picking cases to prosecute. When you pick a case, you're not picking the ones in which you think the accused is guilty. You're choosing to prosecute cases in which you both believe the accused is guilty and believe you can convince a jury beyond a reasonable doubt that the accused is guilty.

When I was working in the prosecutor's office in Seattle—and in the office's special sexual assault unit—we had a standard that a case had to clear in order for us to pursue it. That is the case with most, if not all, prosecutors' offices.

Our standard was: Would a reasonable jury be justified in convicting—on a "beyond a reasonable doubt" standard—when considering the available defenses and the admissible evidence in the case?

That meant we asked ourselves: What evidence can we present to the jury? What would our argument be? What would the defense's arguments be? And, do we think that, stacked up next to each other, our case would be so much more compelling than the defense's case, that a reasonable jury would agree, unanimously, that the accused was guilty beyond a reasonable doubt?

A lot of cases don't meet that standard. A lot of cases in which I thought the accused was guilty didn't meet that standard. There can be a lack of evidence, a lack of corroboration, or credibility issues. Sometimes people have a motivation to lie about the situation. They might be suing in civil court for a bunch of money and think that a guilty verdict in a criminal court will help them get a bigger payday. There are plenty of things. But I've had to turn down prosecuting cases involving people I believed. People have looked me in the eye, told me their story through tears, and I've believed every word—and then had to tell that person that, although I thought the jury might believe her, I didn't think all twelve of them would believe beyond a reasonable doubt, because the evidence wasn't strong enough.

You don't want to ask a jury to take a leap of faith. You've got to have the evidence. If there's no evidence, you can't go forward. If there's no corroboration, if there isn't anything to support the claim, you can't proceed.

But, frankly, most of the cases that I wouldn't move forward with as a prosecutor—and that most people wouldn't bring charges on—were ones in which there were real credibility issues with the complaining victim. Perhaps someone had made a false claim of rape in the past or somebody's story didn't match up with the evidence. I'm not saying anybody was lying. I'm not saying they weren't abused. I'm saying if I can't prove it—then it's not a case I'm going to bring forward.

As a society, that's how we want prosecutors to behave. We don't want them going into cases thinking: *Well, if we get a sympathetic jury, we might be able to paper over the fact that we really don't have any evidence.* We want a high bar. We already put more of our citizens behind bars than any other nation. It's something we're outraged over until we're outraged over the fact that we're not putting more people behind bars.

As much as I may have wanted to, I couldn't wing it. I couldn't say: "OK, fine, it's possible that a reasonable jury would find this guy guilty. And I think that if I get the *right* jury, I just might be able to pull this off." Nope. You don't do it. Because it's not fair to the accused or to the victim.

It's not fair to the accused because—as shocking as this might sound—sometimes we're wrong. Sometimes we think people are guilty, but they are not. The high bar we need to clear keeps innocent people from going to prison, and it should also keep innocent people from having to endure the shame and pain of a trial. It's *difficult* to find people guilty *on purpose*. That's the point.

And it's not fair to the victim, because going through a trial is traumatizing enough for a person who has already been traumatized. Putting someone through the trial of a person they believe is guilty, only to have them watch that person go free in the end, is a crushing blow, which can be deeply damaging.

And particularly in sexual assault cases, which makes it harder for other women to come forward.

The day the Jackson trial verdict came in was complete craziness. I was scheduled to be on just about every network I'd ever covered the trial for, but I lost my Blackberry and had no idea where I was supposed to be or when. A producer ended up just grabbing me and plopping me down in front of cameras. While I was explaining the verdict to the world, I was also coming to terms with it myself.

Off camera, there were fights erupting over jurors. Every network wanted as many jurors as they could get: they wanted to know why they found Michael Jackson "not guilty." I saw producers literally fighting over jurors for interviews:

"You can't have her, you're trespassing!"

"No, no, no. It's our juror, we had him first!"

Seriously. The big prize was getting some of them in the studio on the East Coast for the next day's morning show—a round I believe *Good Morning America* won by putting a bunch of them on a private plane. That night, I was having dinner with a couple of producers who were feeling dejected because they didn't land a juror. At one point, one said to the other one: "Maybe we can go out there and try, like right now, to get one?" I was like: "Guys, it's over. They're on a plane. The trial is over."

The next morning, they tore down Camp Jackson, and we said our goodbyes. I know it sounds cheesy, but some of us had different lives for six months, and we were returning to reality, like kids going home from camp at the end of August. It feels weird to say, but I loved that trial. I needed to learn how to do TV, and covering the trial gave me all the daily experience I had hoped for. I needed to be around people who did it all the time. Everyone down there helped me: both the broadcasters who told me how to apply makeup and look at a camera and the attorneys in the courtroom who taught me what not to do (Sneddon) and how to be a professional under the most high-pressure circumstances. That's something I learned from Jackson's attorney, Tom Mesereau.

I was constantly impressed with Michael's stoic, silver-haired chief counsel. He was a professional of the old school: always immaculately dressed, completely organized, and ever prepared. He was formal, never talking to his client in court. Every time there was a new witness, he'd stand up and say: "Good morning. I'm Thomas Mesereau, representing Mr. Michael Jackson." He was 100 percent professional. And his case was brilliant. He didn't try to convince the jury that Jackson was not a pedophile. He convinced them that he was not guilty of the crime for which he'd been charged.

People who are legitimately creepy—or, even awful, despicable—are not necessarily guilty of the crime they're staring in the face. As I said previously, when prosecutors fall for this, they can fail spectacularly. Mesereau knew his job wasn't to convince the jury that Michael Jackson was a saint. It was to convince them there was reasonable doubt that he had molested the child of a pair of grifters who left their child at the home of a man who had sleepovers with young boys, and paid millions of dollars to the family of one of them. He nailed it.

He didn't let himself get distracted by the tabloid nature of the case. He was practical, eloquent, and unflappable. He has the gift—the practiced talent—of oratory, and he mesmerized the jury with his mastery of the material and his way with words.

During his closing argument, his equipment broke down and he couldn't show his visuals. A lot of people would have folded, given the room an "uhhh, this has never happened before." But Mesereau just barreled through.

The trial was notable for the lack of celebrity friends who showed up. Michael's family was there, sure—even his sister La Toya Jackson, who had feuded with her brother and the rest of the family—but there was no Elizabeth Taylor, Stevie Wonder, or Diana Ross. None of the celebrities well known as Michael's friends. In a sense, it's not surprising. Few people want to be there for someone—even a close friend—while a witness is detailing the ways in which they were molested by that person.

But what's interesting is that four years later, when Jackson died, all of pop's royalty turned out for his memorial at the Staples Center in Los Angeles. Kobe Bryant and Magic Johnson spoke. Stevie Wonder, Lionel Richie, Mariah Carey, and John Mayer performed. Maya Angelou wrote a poem that was read by Queen Latifah. OK, sure, at the time, it didn't seem so strange, either: Jackson had been found not guilty at trial, and his friends and fans turned out to say goodbye.

But then, a funny thing happened. In 2019, ten years after Michael Jackson's death, HBO aired a four-hour documentary called *Leaving Neverland,* in which two men—Wade Robson and James Safechuck—detailed the way they were abused by Michael Jackson as children. It was a reversal of their testimony in the trial, which had helped Jackson win acquittal. Once again, the pop culture establishment abandoned Jackson.

Radio stations stopped playing his songs. The producers of *The Simpsons* said they were going to pull the episode he's featured in from rotation, essentially trying to erase the fact that he'd ever crossed paths with the show. Quincy Jones, the producer of Jackson's most iconic records, even started putting some distance between himself and his most famous collaborator, changing the marketing of a concert in London. Instead of advertising that *Off the Wall, Thriller,* and *Bad* were going to be performed by a symphony, the show was advertised as "Quincy Jones: Presents Soundtrack of the 80s. Defining Albums and Iconic Songs."

This shows both the shallowness and the fickleness of the mob, but also the power of television and the importance of transparency in the criminal justice system. Michael Jackson had been accused of sexual assault multiple times in the past—and paid millions to settle lawsuits. And a young boy had stood up in front of a jury and testified that Michael Jackson had abused him—at the same trial that Robson and Safechuck said Jackson had never molested them. But it wasn't until the world saw Michael Jackson's accusers talk into a camera that they believed them.

I haven't talked to a single person who's seen the documentary and still believes Michael Jackson is innocent. It's extremely convincing. And even though I agree with them, I also find the situation unfair. There was nobody there to make his case. Unfortunately, that is the direction the public is heading: they want to hear that someone is guilty, but they're offended by the idea that anyone would defend them.

I saw Brett Barnes testify at the trial. He said it didn't happen, and I believed him then, too. Macaulay Culkin testified and said nothing happened. I believed him. Jimmy Safechuck denied it for a long time. And I believed him then. When we were at the trial, a lot of these guys testified that they were not molested, but then in the documentary they changed their stories. In trial, when you hear both sides, it's fairer, closer to the truth—and far more difficult to determine innocence and guilt.

By the end of the trial, I was more convinced than ever that it should have been televised, that every courtroom should allow cameras inside.

The whole world wanted to watch. That was a chance for the world to experience the primacy of our justice system.

There is a crisis in civic engagement in this country. Most Americans don't know who their senators are, much less the ins and outs of our justice system. When people are interested in witnessing our criminal justice system—whether they're in the United States or anywhere else in the world—we should accommodate them.

Yes, there are problems that come from allowing cameras into the courthouse. We saw this in the O. J. Simpson case. More transparency, however—not less—will always be better.

Even though the trial was not on TV, it taught me a lot about how important it is, when representing high-profile clients like Amanda Knox, to make a case in the media.

The testimony of Jay Leno, host of a popular nighttime TV show, in the Jackson trial provided a good lesson in this.

First of all, he was brilliant. He had everyone in the courtroom laughing, and he spoke directly to the jury. In the next episode of *The Tonight Show*, he made a big to-do about his testimony. At the end, he held up a gavel and said: "Look what I stole from the judge."

The next morning in court, the judge asked: "Has anybody seen my gavel?" The entire courtroom laughed—even the jurors, who although they were not sequestered, had been instructed to abstain from viewing any media coverage of the case.

That's everything you need to know about how what happens in the press affects what jurors hear and what goes on in a courtroom. While the accused is being tried in a court of law, they're also being tried in the court of public opinion. In a court of law, it was found that there were reasonable doubts about Jackson's guilt, and therefore he was found not guilty, even though the court of public opinion later found him guilty.

In the end, I'm happy with the outcome of the Michael Jackson case. We stood by the high bar of not sending someone to jail for twenty years if we aren't completely sure. But after his death a documentary painted a different picture. Largely because some of his victims who said he was innocent at trial sang a different tune on camera for whatever reason. But we never had the chance to cross-examine that court's witnesses. So we'll never really know for sure. But still, I think justice did its job.

The courts didn't have enough evidence at the time of the Michael Jackson trial to find him guilty beyond a reasonable doubt. So they set him free. And that is the way it should be. When it doesn't play out the way it's supposed to, you can have a disaster, as we saw in another high-profile case where the prosecutor went straight to the media.

That prosecutor's name was Michael Nifong.

12

THE DUKE LACROSSE DEBACLE

On March 13, 2006, two women named Crystal Mangum and Kim Roberts showed up at a party for players on the Duke University lacrosse team. It was at the off-campus home of a few team captains in Durham, North Carolina. The women were hired to strip for $800.[1] The men had requested a white girl and a Hispanic girl but got a black woman (Crystal) and a mixed race black/Asian woman (Kim) instead. Kim arrived in her own car, and Crystal was dropped off by a male, and was, by her own admission, under the influence of alcohol and Flexaril (a muscle relaxant).

As the women began their performance, one of the players asked if the strippers had any sex toys, and Roberts asked if his penis was too small (probably not using that exact language). The player then brandished a broomstick and suggested she could use it as a sex toy. The women then stopped their performance and locked themselves in the bathroom. After being coaxed to come out, Mangum wandered around in the yard, half naked and shouting. Mangum claims she was then locked in a bathroom, where she was raped, beaten, and choked for half an hour.

Eventually the women resumed their performance but were then spooked by the original player who had made the broomstick comment, and they stopped again. Roberts drove Mangum away from the party. Mangum claimed one of the players shouted a racial slur at her as they were leaving. The two women got into an argument, and Roberts drove to a Kroger store. Roberts asked Mangum to leave, but she refused to get out of the car. Roberts alerted Kroger security, who called the police. Mangum was observed to be impaired, under the influence of drugs and/or alcohol and unable to walk. She was taken to a psychiatric facility, where she claimed she had been raped. From there she was transported to the emergency room of Duke University Medical Center, where she underwent physical examination. She had a swollen vagina, which was attributed to using a vibrator for the entertainment of a couple at a hotel prior to the Duke lacrosse party, or to a yeast infection, but she didn't have signs of trauma related to rape. She had a few cuts on her leg, which were seen on a video from before she went to the party.

At 2:00 a.m., after the party, one of the players, Ryan McFadyen, sent an email to team members:

To whom it may concern, tomorrow night, after tonights show, ive decided to have some strippers over to edens 2c. all are welcome.. however there will be no nudity. I plan on killing the bitches as soon as the[y] walk in and proceding [sic] to cut their skin off while cumming in my duke issue spandex . . all in besides arch and tack [two of his teammates] please respond.[2]

He meant the email to be an ironic parody of a scene from the film *American Psycho*. Some of the team members responded with other content from the film, showing they got the reference.

Based on Mangum's accusations, three of the Duke lacrosse players—Reade Seligmann, Collin Finnerty, and David Evans—were accused of sexually assaulting her. The Durham Police Department somehow got wind of the McFadyen email, searched his room and computer, and lodged charges against him of "conspiracy to commit murder" based on the email. The judge in the case inexplicably unsealed the email from the indictment against McFadyen, and it was published by the *Durham Herald*, taken out of context, by implying premeditated intent to do violence to the women. After that, all hell broke loose.

I always call Amanda Knox's case "Duke Lacrosse Italian Style," because, like Amanda, the Duke lacrosse team found itself up against someone who was less a prosecutor and more of an unguided missile: Michael Nifong.

Nifong was the fifty-six-year-old acting district attorney for Durham County in North Carolina, home of Duke. He'd started out in the district attorney's office as a per diem lawyer and worked his way up the ladder to chief assistant. He'd recently gotten an opportunity when the former district attorney (an elected position) was appointed to the Supreme Court of North Carolina, and the governor appointed

Nifong to serve out the rest of his term. Nifong's ambition was to run for the office in the following year, and in the Duke lacrosse case he found an excellent opportunity to get his name in the papers and make a good impression on the voting public.[3]

Duke had an excellent academic reputation. It was known as being one of the premier universities of the South. But it was also known as being preppy, and a place where rich white kids from powerful and influential families in other parts of the country went to school. In contrast, the local residents of Durham were not typically wealthy and were more likely to be black. This created an uncomfortable town and gown dynamic that Nifong was able to exploit.

The Durham police posted a message on an internet message board saying they were interested in information on Seligmann, Finnerty, and Evans related to the rape charges. They did a photo lineup for Mangum where they only showed photographs of Duke lacrosse players with no "fillers," ensuring that at least some of the players would be identified as guilty. Nifong immediately held a news conference where he invoked white privilege and racism in accusing the three boys. During the next three weeks, Nifong held fifty press conferences and interviews. Neither he nor any of his assistants interviewed the accuser, Crystal Mangum, at any point during the entire disaster.[4] She changed her story about what happened twelve times, sometimes implicating one or more of the three players, other times not. The three players offered to take lie detector tests, but the Durham police demurred. Later the police accused them of not cooperating.[5]

Nifong subsequently ran for the position of district attorney of Durham County. He won the Democratic primary, and then the general election by 833 votes.

The charges rocked Duke: three students charged with first-degree rape, first-degree kidnapping, first-degree sexual offense, common-law robbery, and felonious strangulation. The author of the email also faced the charge of conspiracy to commit murder. The email itself was brought forth as evidence of how "sick" and "twisted" the accused were.[6] A "Take Back the Night" protest against sexual violence, in which five hundred people walked from the Duke East campus to the main campus, saw the players' names and photos distributed. Ironically, McFadyen attended and voiced his support. Others at the march defaced the photos. The coach was forced to resign. Professors spoke out openly against the players. The rest of the lacrosse season was canceled, ruining prospects for six members of the team who were All-Americans.

Media outlets across the country covered the story extensively. Selena Roberts, famous for getting the scoop while at *Sports Illustrated* that baseball star Alex Rodriguez used performance enhancing drugs (she later wrote a bestselling book called *A-Rod*),[7] published a commentary about the Duke players on March 31, 2006, in the *New York Times*. She described the players as "a group of privileged players of fine pedigree entangled in a night that threatens to belie their social standing as human beings" and falsely claimed they had observed a "code of silence," saying they were like "drug dealers and gang members engaged in an anti-snitch campaign."[8] It implied that the victim may have been given a date rape drug and that no semen was found because she used condoms (false and false).

She said Mangum was "reportedly treated at a hospital for vaginal and anal injuries consistent with sexual assault and rape." That was also totally false and was presumably derived from a fake "memo" written "from memory" months after the fact by Sergeant Mark Gottlieb of the Durham Police Department. Roberts's column went on to imply that the defense lawyers had deceived the public, when in fact it was the prosecutor, Nifong, who practiced the fine art of deception. She referred to students "daily banging pots and pans" and demanding that the president of Duke do something about the situation. She quoted research professors about the team's code of silence and suggested maybe the president was also afraid of being a "snitch."[9] That also couldn't be farther from the truth, since the players had gone out of their way to cooperate with the investigation from the beginning.

Ultimately, the only person to be sentenced to any time over this case was Nifong himself. He was charged with lying to a judge and sentenced to a day of jail.[10] Nifong was found to have conspired to withhold DNA evidence that would have exonerated the players. He claimed he "had a bad memory."[11] Additionally, he was disbarred by the North Carolina Bar Association, resigned from his position as Durham County district attorney, and, in the face of $180 million in lawsuits filed by Duke players, also declared bankruptcy.[12] The case against the players was dismissed and declared to be the result of "a tragic rush to accuse."[13] The three accused players each won $20 million in civil suits against Duke University. McFadyen didn't do so well. His ambition was to become a trader on Wall Street, but every time he did an interview, they would Google his name and it killed his prospects. Eventually he legally changed his first name to "John" to escape the Google death sentence, and now he works for a business managing residential complexes in Connecticut.[14]

Selena Roberts never apologized for her malicious and vindictive column about the Duke case. The *Times* followed up with a series of supposedly self-examining editorials that progressively diminished their own role in the creation of the Duke media circus. Selena faded away from writing about sports for big media outlets like the *New York Times* and *Sports Illustrated*. Why did she leave? "Eventually you get tired of your own voice," she said. She also supposedly found a million dollars in her deceased mother's house.[15] Life is sometimes stranger than fiction.

The Duke lacrosse case is the study of a prosecutor whose personal ambition caused him to make errors of judgment that ruined his life and the lives of others affected by him, and of the media that aided and abetted him. Michael Nifong is a classic case of what the ancient Greeks called *hubris*, or the arrogant belief in your own qualities or course of action, which causes you and others harm. In that sense, he is a tragic figure if you want to look at it that way. It's also a story of the tragic consequences of a rush to judgment based on preconceived ideas and biases and how that can ruin people's lives.

But just so you don't think that only America produces out-of-control prosecutors who, blinded by personal ambition, ruin people's lives, and journalists who will do anything for a scoop, there is another prosecutor named Giuliano Mignini with his own merry band of scribblers.

13

AMANDA KNOX IN THE COURT
OF PUBLIC OPINION

FOXY KNOXY SINGING AND SMILING AT MURDER TRIAL
*MURDER suspect Amanda Knox smiled and sang during her
court appearance over the killing of Meredith Kercher,
it emerged yesterday. Knox, 21, or Foxy Knoxy as she
styled herself on her social networking website, is known
to sing in jail to pass the time. Yesterday it was
claimed that during breaks in the pre-trial hearing she
sang hits by the Canadian singer Feist. Suspect Rudy
Guede, 21, also appeared but Knox's Italian ex-boyfriend
Raffaele Sollecito, 24, was not present. A source at the
court in Perugia, Italy, where British student Meredith
died, claimed Knox "never said a word" during the hearing. "But outside, when there were breaks for water and
coffee, she was smiling and singing"* . . .* [1]*

Amanda Knox didn't have a chance. Before she had set foot in a courtroom, the
Perugian prosecutor Giuliano Mignini had put her and Raffaele Sollecito's pictures
up on his wall next to the Mafia Dons he had bagged.[2] He declared "caso chiuso!"
or *case closed* for Amanda Ka-nox, as he would declare in his butchering of her
name. Before the first piece of evidence was presented in a court of law, the British
tabloid hacks had scoured the internet and found her referring to herself as "Foxy

Knoxy." It didn't matter that she was referring to her moves on the soccer field many years before. The name stuck, and they were off to the races.[3]

> "THE WILD, RAUNCHY PAST OF FOXY KNOXY"
> Dec. 3, 2007: Amanda Knox—accused of killing Meredith Kercher—has been portrayed as a blameless girl led astray when she moved to Italy. But as this investigation reveals, she already had a dangerous appetite for drink, drugs and sex . . . [4]

Amanda Knox was to be tried in the court of Facebook and Twitter, blogs and social media, English tabloids and the court of "guilty at first glance," not in the court of law. She fit into the European stereotype of the *femme fatale*. She reminded the British and the tabloid hacks pandering to them of everything they hated about Americans. The story became an opportunity to express long-suppressed misogyny and xenophobia. It became a cesspool and a magnet for sociopaths and sadists.

Typical was a book rushed to press by an Italian "true crime" writer named Fiorenza Sarzanini. In her book *Amanda and the Others*, as well as in interviews, she stated:

> *Amanda Knox's secret diary revealed that Foxy Knoxy was always thinking about sex. On top of her list of things to do before leaving for Italy, Amanda Knox wrote in her diary that she needed to visit a sex shop to buy condoms. . . Knox isn't obsessed with sex but she sees it as one of the predominant aspects of her life. . . This has influenced her life in the sense that it influences her relationships with both men and women. . . . It's as if you (Knox) were always hunting men. You list your conquests as if you were displaying them like trophies.*[5]

There's an iconic piece of video footage in this case, just a few seconds long, of Amanda kissing Raffaele out in front of the house where her roommate had been slaughtered just a few hours before. The short clip spread like wildfire across TV news, was picked up by the tabloids, and commanded the attention of a newly emerging social media website: Twitter.

From that moment forward, everyone *wanted* Amanda to be the killer. The prosecution insisted on it. The tabloids salivated over it. Readers and Tweeters were instantly convinced. Every other bread crumb that came out later was used to support this narrative. And the press and everyday busybodies went looking for anything they could find. As we've come to expect, digging through the social media life of a teenager yielded plenty of ammunition.

You know how they say to be careful what you put on social media? Well, they rarely say it could land you in an Italian prison for four years, but that's what happened.

There were the obligatory drunk pics. But there were also pictures of her or Raffaele hamming around with a machine gun. A machete. Knives. Party pictures. When it came out that she'd slept with a man she had just met on a train, the trifecta was complete; this immoral, sex-crazed American whore who was sleeping her way across the continent graduated to murder. And it stuck. One of the guys in my group advocating for Amanda was convinced she was going to become an old woman in prison, bent over working in the fields of Italy.

"She's never coming home."

He said it over and over and over. It's what the world wanted.

Amanda Knox was to social media what O. J. was to cable TV. The world followed along with the O. J. trial in real time in the first true cable TV trial. The internet existed when Michael Jackson was on trial, but the medium wasn't a driving factor. They followed along in reenactments and talking heads. But by the time Amanda was arrested in Perugia, Twitter had come into its own, and the Facebook news feed was changing the way the world got its information. The world followed along—and participated—in real time, tweet by tweet, link by link, for the first time. Amanda's case hit at exactly the right time, and it was everywhere.

Things got worse when the trial really got going. The prosecution said Amanda was behind the killing and had been assisted by her boyfriend, Raffaele, and by Rudy Guede. They fast-tracked the trial with Rudy and tried Amanda and Raffaele separately.

The evidentiary hearing was closed to the press, so the only things that got out were strategic, salacious leaks. The press was desperate for it. Readers were voracious. And the tabloids ran with whatever they could get their hands on. Did they know what they were running was true? Did they care? In the Netflix documentary, *Amanda Knox*, Nick Pisa, one of the tabloid journalists who covered the trial, said he would stop at nothing to get the story.

"A murder always gets people going," he said in the film. "Bit of intrigue, bit of mystery, a whodunit . . . What more do you want in a story?" About getting the scoop on the Amanda Knox case, he said if he didn't write it, someone else would: "To see your name on the front page with a great story that everyone's talking about . . . it's just like this fantastic buzz. It's like having sex or something."[6] Pisa comes across in the film as . . . less than noble. Let's just leave it at that.

For a while, the gossip was that the murder was sparked by jealousy, theft, and a quarrel between roommates. A lot of it was driven by cultural differences between the roommates' backgrounds as English, Italian, and American. In eco-conscious Seattle, not flushing the toilet after you pee is considered virtuous. It saves water and helps the environment. "If it's yellow, let it mellow; if it's brown, flush it down." But for the English and Italian girls, that meant Amanda wasn't clean! What's more, she left her vibrator out! When looked at through this light, the feces found in the toilet came off as a surefire indictment of Amanda. Never mind the fact that it was actually the real killer, Rudy Guede, who took a crap after killing her roommate and didn't flush.

Pretty soon, the narrative evolved into a ritualistic, satanic sex slaying—with Amanda running the show. They said she forced Raffaele to participate. It was almost too rich: the demonic American girl and the idyllic Italian boy who had to be forced into sexual servitude. She was no longer Amanda Knox. She was *Foxy Knoxy*.

HOW ANGELIC STUDENT ORCHESTRATED 'SATANIC' MURDER
Finding the front door open, a window broken and blood-stains in a bathroom, they forced open the locked door of Miss Kercher's bedroom to find her body in a pool of blood on the floor, mostly hidden under a duvet and naked except for a T-shirt yanked up around her armpits.

The injuries on her body suggested she had been forced to kneel, with her face pushed into the floor, and raped at knifepoint before being killed by a combination of strangulation and three deep stab wounds to her neck. Arturo de Felice, the local police chief, revealed that Miss Kercher had been killed by three people who had been high on drugs and tried to force her to take part in what was later described as a "satanic" group sex session, then held her down and stabbed her in the throat when she refused.[7]

If there was going to be a killer, it had to be Amanda Knox. From the Madonna-whore complex to the fear and loathing of wanton American women, she just fit the part in the play everyone wanted to see.

It didn't help that every time there was a camera, she looked straight into it—consumed it. It's not a long leap from that chilly gaze to the way we remember Charles Manson owning every camera that was thrust in his face.

If there is any question about the sexism of all this, let's not forget that there were three people tried for Meredith Kercher's killing. But it didn't turn into the story of a gang-rape murder. It became the story of a young American woman who was a sex-crazed satanic killer.

Everybody—the tabloids, readers, social media gawkers—wanted this story. It was like a blockbuster movie that had been market tested: two of the main characters were eliminated and only one remained—the woman, of course. If this had to be a movie that involved other characters, they had to be pawns. She had to be at the center of it all. The one in charge. The corrupting influence. The main character.

This is all the more shocking when you consider that the prosecution really didn't have *anything* on Amanda, but they had *everything* on Guede. They had his fingerprints and his blood. His feces were in the toilet. His DNA was inside Meredith, whom he'd raped.

They also had motive: he was a known crook, a wandering burglar, and her money was missing. He was obsessed with Meredith. They had his confession.

Plus, a rape/murder fits the profile. That's a crime that actually happens. A man whom a woman knows follows her back home and . . . that's how these things happen. What usually doesn't happen—except in movies—is what the prosecution and the tabloid press insisted had happened: that a group of two men and one woman gang-raped and killed a woman. I'm not saying it never happens, but when you have everything on one guy and nothing on the others, that idea is more than a reach.

After Mignini had arrested Guede, he couldn't let go of Amanda and Raffaele. He came up with a scenario where the three of them acted together. He claimed that Guede couldn't act alone. That together they staged a break-in. This was in spite of the fact that there are numerous examples of an athletic young man overpowering a woman, and the physical evidence clearly showed that a rock had been thrown through the window from the outside in the course of a break-in.[8]

So why is it that when the world thinks of the poor woman who was killed in her house in Perugia, we think of Amanda Knox and not Rudy Guede? There are several explanations.

Nina Burleigh, author of *The Fatal Gift of Beauty: The Trials of Amanda Knox*, looked back later to say that the case was, in some ways, the birth of the "fake news" phenomenon:

> *The Amanda Knox phenomenon marked the first time a bizarre cult of credulity emerged online, with tens of thousands of people energetically subscribing to the most heinous possible scenario, while refusing to accept more reasonable alternatives. A now-familiar scenario played out: Vicious social media swarms led by trolls using online pseudonyms. Accusations of fake news hurled at reputable outlets, while demonstrably fake news was published regularly. There was doxing. Lawmen attacked as shills. Journalists accused of "being on the payroll." A theory in which everyone is connected by money or in the case of the Magistrate's version of the case, by deviant secret cults with midnight membership lists who meet by the light of the moon.[9]*

Even more basic than this, though, is that the truth just wasn't good enough. Not for readers, not for the writers, and certainly not for prosecutors who worked for them and wanted to give them what they wanted. What they expected. The prosecutor in charge did everything he could to give it to them.

14

DNA, O. J., AND THE WRONG LESSONS LEARNED

O. J. got off, in large part, because the DNA evidence was called into question.

This gave the wrong idea about DNA. The trial made getting off because of DNA evidence seem like it's an excuse to protect the guilty, or at least help the guilty get off, because people make mistakes. It's really about protecting the innocent.

But in the court of public opinion, anything that's not allowed into the courtroom is viewed as a scandal, something that's being covered up, depriving the jury of the tools needed to find someone guilty. In the case of O. J., his attorneys were able to raise doubts about the DNA evidence—that it was contaminated by the police—even though it's really a stretch to think that happened. The contamination was that Detective Fuhrman had transported the glove that was saturated with O. J.'s ex-wife Nicole Brown Simpson's blood from the crime scene and planted it in O. J.'s house. There was a mountain of other DNA evidence, but since they were able to plant that idea in the mind of the jurors, they used that to disqualify in their minds everything else. It's extremely unlikely that Fuhrman transported the glove, and there was no evidence that he did, but the defense attorneys did their job and planted that idea in the minds of the jurors. That idea stuck, and they won their case.

In the case of Amanda, the DNA evidence they had . . . was probably contaminated by the police.[1]

First of all, not all DNA evidence is equally compelling, and not all courts look at DNA evidence the same way. Patrizia Stefanoni, the Perugia, Italy, forensic laboratory technician who analyzed the DNA evidence, used a lower standard than other courts. So what was considered admissible in the first trial would likely not be considered admissible in the United States, and probably most courts in Italy or other countries.

The DNA evidence they supposedly had on Amanda and Raffaele boiled down to a knife that was argued to be the murder weapon and Meredith's bra clasp. The knife was randomly grabbed from a drawer in Raffaele's apartment on the other side of town from the house where the murder occurred, and the bra clasp, collected off the floor over a month after the crime, was the only place in the room where DNA was found after they had supposedly participated in raping and killing Meredith Kercher. The murder was supposed to have been a ritualistic satanic sex killing, yet the only DNA that was left behind by these two killers was a bit on the knife (Amanda) and the victim's bra clasp (Raffaele)? Let's think for a second about what would likely transpire during a ritualistic satanic sex killing. Even just think about the last time you had sex; does it seem possible that all of the DNA from your partner would evaporate? It's not like the prosecution suggested the killers were tidy. They left feces in the toilet, for crying out loud! When Amanda and Raffaele got to the house, the place was trashed. When the police opened the locked door to Meredith's bedroom, where they found the body, they did not find a room that had been sanitized or cleaned. Nothing had been tidied up. It was a wreck.

So, just for starters, it's preposterous to think that after this ritualistic sex slaying that involved two men and a she-devil barking orders, the only DNA for two of the killers would be on a section of a kitchen knife and the victim's bra clasp.

All that said, the experts claimed Amanda's DNA was on the knife. So let's talk about the knife, which was found in Raffaele's kitchen. First, think about the knives in your kitchen right now. Think your DNA is on any of them? If you have a significant other who comes over, could theirs also be on the knives? How about their college roommates? Because that's what the prosecution is alleging here; Meredith and Amanda both had their DNA on a knife from Raffaele's kitchen, which was supposedly used as the murder weapon.

And why did they pick that knife? He could have had twenty in the drawer. Why did they pick that one? Was it covered in blood? The police have never addressed that question. The most likely explanation is they picked the first one they saw, since forensic examination did not find any blood on the knife.

After the arrest in 2007, Amanda Knox and Raffaele Sollecito were imprisoned awaiting trial. Meanwhile, the real killer, Rudy Guede, took a "fast track trial" where he was sentenced to thirty years in prison on October 28, 2008. During the trial for his appeal, on November 18, 2009, Guede made a "spontaneous statement" where he placed Knox and Sollecito at the scene of the murder. As a result, his sentence was reduced to sixteen years.

On January 16, 2009, the first trial of Knox and Sollecito for the murder of Meredith Kercher began in Perugia. On December 4, 2009, they were convicted, with Knox sentenced to serve twenty-five years and Sollecito twenty-six years. They were ordered to pay $7 million to the Kercher family, and Knox was ordered to pay $60,000 to Patrick Lumumba for placing him at the scene of the crime.[2]

Throughout this time, a number of internet sleuths went through the specifics of the case in meticulous detail. Some of them had expertise that was value-added. For instance, the American scientist Dr. Mark Waterbury wrote that there was no evidence of Meredith's blood on the blade or DNA of Amanda on the handle of the knife that had been randomly pulled from the drawer in Raffaele's kitchen.[3] (I mean, let's just wipe the blood off the knife after an evening of murdering, take it home, and put it back in the drawer so it's ready for tomorrow night's steak dinner, right?) He further confirmed that the bra clasp that was kicked around the floor for a month before it was picked up and tested did not contain Raffaele's DNA but was certainly contaminated. Meanwhile, retired engineers used analyses of glass trajectory after breakage to debunk the claim that the broken window in the cottage had been staged by Raffaele and Amanda to fake a crime scene. In fact, the pattern of the glass could only be explained by someone breaking the window from the outside, as Rudy Guede had done when he climbed up to the second-floor window and broke it to enter the cottage.

While Amanda Knox and Raffaele Sollecito rotted away in an Italian jail waiting for their appeals trial, I was to get involved in another case of injustice involving a woman who, like Frances Farmer and Amanda Knox, originally hailed from the Seattle area: Susan Cox Powell.

15

SUSAN COX POWELL: INTO THE WILD

It's good to spend time with your kids, right? So if you're a busy father with a full-time job, you need to carve out some time for your kids, right? So that might mean doing things with them at odd times of the day or night, right? And it's good to spend time outdoors, and to do activities like camping that don't add to the carbon footprint, right? So if you take some time off to go camping with your kids you shouldn't be criticized for that, even if their mother doesn't come along.

On December 6, 2009, Joshua Powell left his home in West Valley City, Utah, with his two sons, Charlie, age four, and Braden, age two, to go camping. In the middle of the night. In the middle of a blizzard. And he was scheduled to go to work at 8:00 a.m. the next day and the kids had daycare. He didn't tell his employer he wouldn't be coming in, but wait, he thought it was Sunday, but in fact it was the early hours of Monday. And Charlie said that mom *had* come along with them. She just didn't come back.

The next morning, when the kids were not dropped off at daycare, their grandma and aunt went to the family home to see what was going on. When nobody answered the door, they called the police, who broke in and found the house empty. They found the wallet, phone, and keys of Josh's wife, Susan Cox Powell, but not Susan. Josh came home with the kids later in the afternoon.[1]

Josh claimed he had no idea where Susan was. He claimed to have last seen her on Sunday night, before he took the boys camping. He spun his tales that pointed to what was most likely a tragic fate for Susan Cox Powell.[2]

BLOOD AND LETTER FROM JOSH POWELL'S WIFE FOUND,
EXPRESSES FEAR ABOUT HER HUSBAND

A safety deposit box used by Susan Powell had a hand-written letter titled "Last will & testament for Susan Powell," according to the documents. She wrote in that letter that she did not trust her husband and that they'd been having marital troubles for four years.

The letter also said that "if Susan Powell dies it may not be an accident, even if it looks like one," according to the documents.[3]

Meanwhile, Josh drained his wife's retirement accounts, canceled her future chiropractic sessions, and withdrew their children from daycare. Subsequently it was revealed that he had talked to coworkers about how to hide a body in an abandoned mineshaft in the Western Utah desert. Charlie drew a picture of his mom in the trunk of the family car.

When I first got interested in working in the media, I knew it was going to help me and my clients in the courtroom and as an advocate for them elsewhere, but I didn't realize how important it would be in the nuts and bolts of working for a client before charges were even filed. In 2009, I stumbled into one of the most important cases of my career. Susan Cox Powell, wife and mother to two small boys, had vanished without a trace. I was hired by her parents to represent the family and to try to help them find their daughter. From the beginning, the most important part of my job was to be on television. Not to prove guilt or innocence, but to look for a mom. At first, we were trying to find her. Eventually, it became about finding out what happened to her.

Just as the media's eagerness to feed the public's fascination with details of the intersection of young women and murder helped put Amanda Knox behind bars for a crime she did not commit, I knew that same rabid fascination could also be redirected to help find out what happened to a mother of two who disappeared.

From the start, we knew two things were true: Susan Cox Powell was most likely dead, and her husband had something to do with it. This wasn't like Amanda Knox doing cartwheels and ordering pizza. Normal people do cartwheels and order pizza. Sane people do not take their diapered children camping at midnight, in Utah, during a snowstorm. Innocent people don't claim to have done so.

Proving it all was another matter.

Like Scott and Laci Peterson, this was another case of what appeared to be a beautiful, happy family. The kind you live next door to and open your home to. So, how did this woman disappear into thin air? The public was fascinated.

The most important thing we could do was keep Susan's face and story on television. This was another example of what I have said repeatedly, that high-profile cases are not tried strictly in the courtroom. They're tried on television. By keeping the case and Susan's face on TV, in the public consciousness, I knew we'd have a better chance of solving the case, too.

A big part of my job at that point was to help Susan's dad, Chuck Cox, get on television and talk about Susan. It was important for him to be really present in the press. Every day there's a new headline. But his daughter was missing, and he wanted to keep her story alive.

I knew if we could keep her face and her story on the mind of the public, evidence, tips, and testimony were bound to come out. *America's Most Wanted* worked because people watched TV and discovered their neighbor was wanted for a decade-old crime. I kept Susan on TV for the same reason.

As things began to unfold, the case kept getting weirder and weirder and, horrifically, more obvious.

Charlie drew pictures of their mom's body in the trunk of a car. The boys said mommy went camping with them but didn't come back. "Mommy's in a mine," they said. Obviously, tragically, they were witnesses to something.

From the beginning, Josh was the primary suspect. Josh had stopped payment to the daycare provider, knowing the kids wouldn't be there on the Monday after that weekend. Susan had a will written out in her safe deposit box, which said that if she disappeared, it probably was not an accident, that Josh had probably killed her. The police found blood in the house and fans drying the couch.[4]

Josh never had any interest in finding his wife. The whole time, he behaved as if she wasn't coming back (just like Scott Peterson did). He wasn't helping with the search efforts. He wasn't waiting at home for Susan to come back. He and the kids moved to Puyallup, Washington, to live with his deranged father, Steven, who was obsessed with Susan (an obsession he chronicled methodically in his journal).

When child welfare authorities issued a search warrant for the home in Puyallup, they found a house of horrors. There were gallows in the house.[5] A picture of a woman with a knife going through her vagina and out through her stomach. Susan's underwear was framed. Police found her hair and fingernail clippings. There were hundreds of images of child pornography in the house. Cartoons of incest porn.[6]

The state ultimately convicted Steven of voyeurism for taking photos of neighbor children through their bathroom window, and later for possession of child pornography. He was sent to prison. Authorities took the kids from Josh, and they went to live with Susan's parents, Chuck and Judy Cox. Still, Josh had visitation rights.

Because Josh was the primary suspect, the police were looking into his past, and it was shocking. He'd been showing psychotic tendencies since he was a kid. He'd molested his sister. He'd killed a family pet. He tried to kill himself. And he'd once pulled a knife on his mother.

The police were adamant: we know this guy killed his wife. We know this guy is a danger to his kids and himself. Don't let him be alone with the kids. He'll kill them.

Despite all this, a few hours a week, while the Coxes were at church, Josh was allowed to have supervised visits with Charlie and Braden. At one point, without alerting my clients or the judge, the state allowed the supervised visits to take place at Josh's house.

Let's stop to think about that for a second: a woman goes missing, a husband's alibi is that he took his sons—one in diapers—camping at midnight, in the mountains while it was freezing, and one of the kids drew a picture of his mother in the trunk. Then he moves his sons to stay with his deranged father—and the state thinks it's a good idea for the kids to be in Josh's house?

The state took the kids out of the home their father shared with their grandfather because they believed it to be unsafe. The state had a duty to these kids. They were responsible to keep them safe. Instead, they let the father see the boys in his home.

Eventually, in the course of the investigation, the police ordered a psychosexual evaluation of Josh that would include a polygraph test. That is what broke him. He knew he couldn't pass a polygraph test about Susan. He freaked out. He knew he was in a corner. But he still had one more in-home visit with his boys before the scheduled test.

On February 5, 2012, a social worker contracted by the state drove Braden and Charlie to their dad's home. When they got out of the car, they ran into his arms. He pulled them into the house and locked the door. The social worker later testified that she'd pounded on the doors and told Josh to open up. Then she heard him speak to the boys.[7]

"I had heard him tell the boys to lay face down, that daddy had a surprise," she testified.[8]

She moved her car. She called her supervisor. Eventually she called the police. It was too late for the boys.

The surprise their dad had for them was a hatchet to the back. Then he poured gasoline into their open wounds and all around the house. He set it on fire.

Josh tortured his sons for ten minutes, but he showed mercy for himself. He put a can of gasoline between his legs and set it on fire. Braden was five. Charlie was seven.

At this point, my job, in representing my clients, Chuck and Judy Cox, became about making sure that the state didn't let this kind of thing happen again. If a husband is going to kill his wife in their home, there are few things that the state can do to stop it. But when small children are charges of the state? That's different. Chuck and Judy, having lost their daughter, and now their grandsons, wanted to do everything they could to keep it from happening again.

Their case would drag on for years. In the meantime, I got involved in the case of another mysterious death, Rebecca Zahau, who supposedly displayed unusual acrobatic abilities in leaping to her death by hanging from the balcony of a multi-million-dollar home where she lived with her boyfriend.

THE MYSTERIOUS CASE OF REBECCA ZAHAU: PROVING POLICE WRONG

What would you say if your daughter's boyfriend called to tell you your daughter had taken off all her clothes, tied her hands behind her back, tied a rope around her feet, stuffed a T-shirt in her mouth, put a rope around her neck, and tied one end to the leg of a bed in a maid's room, closed the door to the room, crossed over to a second story balcony, and then vaulted to her death without disturbing any of the dust on the railing? Oh, and the leap didn't cause the maid's bed to move. And, oh, before she leaped, she painted in black paint on the wall SHE SAVED HIM, CAN YOU SAVE HER. Oh, and by the way, this was a suicide.

Would you believe him? I wouldn't.

This is exactly what happened in the mysterious case of Rebecca Zahau.

On July 13, 2011, Rebecca Zahau was found bound and gagged, hanging from a Juliet balcony at the Spreckles Mansion in toney Coronado, California. John Spreckles had two mansions in Coronado and one in San Francisco, and he settled in Coronado when he started the *San Diego Tribune*. One of the Coronado mansions, built in 1908, was directly across from the famed Hotel del Coronado. It even had a $40,000 room fashioned for the visit of the duke and duchess of Windsor in the 1940s. The mansion, which last went on the market for $17.5 million, was owned by Jonah Shacknai, Rebecca's boyfriend, the billionaire owner of the company Medicis, which made Restylane, a cosmetic face filler.[1]

The pair lived with his five-year-old son, Max (known as "Maxey"). Just two days prior to the discovery of Rebecca's body, Max fell down the grand staircase and was critically injured. He pulled down a chandelier in the fall. A scooter and ball were nearby, as was the family dog, Ocean. Rebecca and her sister, Xena, were home at the time and in opposite ends of the mansion from the central sweeping staircase. Jonah rushed home, and Max was rushed to the hospital. He lived for only two and a half days. The doctor said he had been suffocated. Jonah's brother, Adam Shacknai, flew in from Tennessee for support. He settled into the guest house behind the mansion but never visited Max at the hospital. Rebecca was found dead and hanging before Max succumbed to his injuries.[2] I was asked to represent Rebecca's family.

SHE SAVED HIM, CAN YOU SAVE HER was painted on the door of the balcony room in black paint and large letters. Rebecca's hands were bound behind her back with red rope and perfect nautical knots. Her feet were similarly bound. She had a T-shirt fashioned as a gag in her mouth. The rope from which she was hanging was tied to a bed in the maid's room. The bed had been moved but didn't drag from her weight. Enough rope was used for her to go over the railing but not touch the ground. The soles of her feet were dirty. A neighbor heard a scream around 11:00 p.m. from his den window, which faced the mansion.

Adam claimed to police he "discovered" Rebecca in the early morning, the day after he arrived at the mansion. He later testified in a civil trial he had been in his room in the guest house watching porn on his cell phone that morning and hadn't heard anything. He claimed when he found her, he immediately cut her down and called 911. In his call, he described her as "that girl" and seemed disoriented. His lawyer was one of the first on the scene. He took a polygraph approximately twelve hours after calling 911, in which he admitted to "not having the best bedside manner." He departed for the San Diego International Airport almost immediately, having never been to the hospital.

Later it was discovered that the writing on the door matched his height, and blood from Rebecca's menstrual cycle was found in the master shower and on a knife linked to Adam. We asked famed forensic expert pathologist Cyril Wecht to exhume Rebecca and conduct an independent autopsy. He found four symmetrical injuries to the top of her head. And most importantly, he found that she didn't die from hanging: she died from strangulation and blunt force trauma while on her back. Lividity, which is where the blood settles when you die, was found fixed in her back. Rebecca had not been depressed or suicidal. But the San Diego Police

Department immediately closed the case as a suicide. They left her naked body exposed in the house for seventeen hours. It was filmed by news crews from the air. Interestingly, the French doors to the balcony where she supposedly jumped to her death were noted to have been closed behind Rebecca, as if she reached behind her to close them on her way over the edge. The balcony had no disturbance in the dust on the rail.

The focus in this case landed on Jonah and Adam. But there was also Jonah's ex-wife, Dena, and her twin sister, Nina. The two had supposedly presented themselves at the mansion at 10:10 p.m. the night before Rebecca was found. The motive? Max's fall. Nothing more, nothing less. Adam was another story. There was a plethora of evidence pointing toward him.

Our legal team, including California lawyer Marty Rudoy, presented the case to the authorities. They countered with a "demonstration" of a female police officer untying loosely looped—not knotted—rope from behind her back. There was no evidence proffered to show this to be a suicide. We submitted a twenty-page letter with detailed analysis and took it all the way to then California Attorney General Kamala Harris. She declined to get involved. That was the end of the criminal inquiry.

I was counsel in the criminal probe. It ended there. We later brought in local counsel Keith Greer who, working with Rudoy, brought a civil case in 2018, in which the jury found Adam Shacknai responsible for the death of Rebecca. The burden of proof in a civil case is lower, but there was so much justice in the jury finding civilly that Adam had caused Rebecca's death. As always, our goal was to get out ahead of the game in the media. We had to get out the word that it wasn't a suicide. In the end, the jury agreed with us. We were right. Justice delayed isn't always justice denied. The postscript unfortunately is not as bright: the same San Diego authorities subsequently declined to reopen the criminal case.

We were able to get out ahead of the media game in Rebecca's case. One criminal was able to do this on his own. That was an eighteen-year-old kid named Colton Harris-Moore.

THE BAREFOOT BANDIT: A CRIMINAL GETS AHEAD OF THE MEDIA GAME

Colton Harris-Moore, aka "The Barefoot Bandit," grew up with his mother on Camano Island, one of the largest among the several hundred islands scattered throughout the picturesque Puget Sound north of Seattle. Like many of the islands among the famed San Juan Islands nearby, Camano Island is dotted with vacation homes of rich and influential people, some of whom arrive by boat or private plane on weekends.

But that isn't all there is to the island. There's the "other side" of Camano Island, where people in the service industries live—those who fix the boats and planes or carry groceries for the weekenders at the supermarket. They might live in one of the trailer parks. Alcohol and drug abuse is not uncommon.[1]

That was the side of Camano Island where Colton grew up. But he also wanted to be part of the other side: the private planes and vacation homes.

Colton's biological father was a drug user who was in and out of prison. He walked out of a family barbeque when Colton was two years old and never came back. Colton's stepfather died when he was seven years old. His mother said there was "something off about him." After the death of his stepfather, Colton took to living in the woods off and on, breaking into vacation homes and stealing blankets, food, and water. He had his first conviction for theft when he was twelve.[2]

Colton used to lie on his back and watch private planes take off and land from the Camano Island Airfield. He would fantasize about what it would be like to be rich and able to fly wherever you wanted. When he was seventeen, a neighbor's camcorder was found in his house. He was sentenced to prison, and in April 2008, fled a halfway house to avoid a three-year sentence, going into the wild for good.[3]

Colton broke into vacation houses on Camano Island, soaked in hot tubs, and helped himself to food in the fridge. At first, he just stole what he needed to survive. One time he used someone's computer and credit card to buy a $6,500 pair of night vision goggles. He posted photos of himself in other peoples' houses on Facebook, and pictures of things he would write on the floor of the houses, like "See ya!" as he was exiting a house. Or he would use chalk to trace his feet as he walked out the door and post the pictures on Facebook. Since he never seemed to be wearing shoes in the pictures, he earned the sobriquet "Barefoot Bandit." With his wide grin and natural good looks, he was a hit with the girls, and the Robin Hood-esque storyline captured the popular imagination. A fan Facebook page drew around sixty thousand followers, with many rooting for him to beat the system. Eventually, his thefts increased in magnitude, including cars, boats, bikes, and planes. He taught himself to fly by reading manuals, watching DVDs, and playing flight simulator games on the computer. And he became the focus of widespread media attention.[4]

To understand in part why Colton gained such popularity, it is important to know a little bit about the cultural history of the Pacific Northwest. On November 24, 1971, a man known as "D. B. Cooper" boarded a plane traveling from Portland to Seattle. He handed a note to a stewardess that claimed he had a bomb and asked for $200,000, four parachutes, and the ability to refuel in Seattle. When the stewardess asked to see the bomb, he opened a bag showing some cylinders that appeared to be a bomb.[5]

After arriving in Seattle, he released the passengers, got the money and parachutes, and told the crew to fly to Mexico with the back doors open. Somewhere over southern Washington he jumped with the parachute. Some dollar bills were later recovered in the wilderness, but the mystery of D. B. Cooper was never solved.

After the flight, T-shirts were created with an artist's sketch of his likeness, with these words underneath: "D. B. Cooper, Where Are You?"

People were angry about a lot of stuff back then. The economy sucked, and if anyone could beat the system, they got cheers. The Pacific Northwest also had a kind of counterculture vibe. They liked people who rocked the boat.

Colton was like the current iteration of D. B. Cooper. He stole a plane from the Camano Island Airfield and flew off the island. Ditching it for a car, he drove through southwest Washington, where he saw a veterinary clinic in Raymond. On a whim, he stopped and left a note on the door with $100 cash.

> *Drove by, had some extra cash. Please use this money for the care of animals.*
> —*Colton Harris Moore, (AKA: "The Barefoot Bandit"), Camano Island, WA.*[6]

Colton got out of Washington and, alternating stealing planes and cars, hop-skipped across the country. He stole a Cessna 400 at the Bloomington, Indiana, airport, and flew it to the Bahamas, where he crash-landed it in the water offshore. From there, he stole a power boat. The local police caught up with him off the island of Eleuthera. He attempted to flee, but they shot out the engine of his boat. He threw his laptop in the water and put a gun to his head, but the police talked him out of killing himself.

On July 11, 2010, Colton was captured in Harbour Island in the Bahamas. He said he was trying to flee to Cuba, and then the Turks and Caicos Islands. His mother wanted him to get to a country that didn't have an extradition treaty with the United States. Remanded to the United States and to a trial in Seattle, Colton was represented by notorious Seattle criminal defense attorney (and my ex-husband), John Henry Browne.

But Colton had more going for him than one of the best defense attorneys in the country. Unlike some other criminals who make headlines, he was his own best public relations manager. He portrayed a Robin Hood-esque figure. And giving $100 to take care of the animals . . . Well, who doesn't like pets?

On January 27, 2012, Colton was sentenced to six and half years in prison. He was released to a halfway house in 2016. He tried to raise money online to go to flight school, but that was vetoed by his probation officer, who said that any funds he raised had to go to restitution for his victims. After release, he went to work as a clerk for Browne.

There was another criminal whose case I got involved in who wasn't as appealing on camera or in the courtroom. That person was immortalized by my friend Nancy Grace as Tot Mom.

TOT MOM: DANCING WITH THE DEVIL

911 Operator: *911. What's your emergency?*

Grandmother: *I called a little bit ago, the deputy sheriff. I found out my granddaughter has been taken. She has been missing for a month. Her mother finally admitted that she's been missing.*

911 Operator: *OK, what . . .*

Grandmother: *Get someone here now!*

Mother: *My daughter has been missing for the last thirty-one days.*

Grandmother: *My daughter finally admitted that the babysitter stole her! I need to find her!*

911 Operator: *Your daughter admitted that her baby is where?*

Grandmother: *The babysitter took her a month ago, that my daughter's been looking for her. I told you my daughter was missing for a month. I just found her today, but I can't find my granddaughter. And she just admitted to me that she's been trying to find her herself.*

911 Operator: *And you last saw her a month ago?*

Mother: *Thirty-one days.*

Grandmother: *There's something wrong. I found my daughter's car today, and it smells like there's been a dead body in the damn car!*

911 Operator: Who has her? Do you have a name?
Mother: Her name is Zenaida Fernandez-Gonzalez.
Grandmother: Caylee's missing! Caylee's missing! She took her a month ago! She's been missing for a month!
Mother: I've been looking for her and have gone through other resources to try to find her, which is stupid.[1]

Let me ask you a question: If you were sitting in a jury box and listened to a 911 call in which a grandmother says she just found out her granddaughter has been missing for a month, her daughter kept it a secret the whole time, and her daughter's car smells like a dead body—how much time would you have to think about whether this daughter is a killer?

Just before Amanda and Raffaele went to trial for the first time, the world took a moment to consider the actions of another young, good-looking American woman who was being accused of murder. Her name was Casey Anthony. Or as my friend, Nancy Grace, called her: Tot Mom.

Casey and her two-year-old daughter Caylee lived with her parents in Orlando, Florida. In June 2008, Casey's parents say they had a heated argument with their daughter, and she left the home with Caylee. Despite her parents' efforts to reconcile, Casey refused to come home.

On July 15, 2008—just over a month later—her father learned a car used by Casey had been impounded. He would tell police when he went to retrieve it that he was overwhelmed by a stench. His wife would later tell police, "It smells like there's been a dead body in the damn car."[2]

Cindy Anthony got ahold of her daughter and ultimately reported Caylee had been missing for more than a month in a series of 911 calls chronicled at the start of this chapter.

The story was atrocious from the start. So was Casey, who gave all kinds of stories that fell apart. She claimed that Caylee had been snatched by a nanny—but there was no nanny. She claimed that she worked at Universal Studios—but when police asked her to show them her office, she eventually confessed that she hadn't worked there in years, but had pretended to work there, fooling her family.

INTERNET SEARCHES FOCUS OF THE DAY
IN CASEY ANTHONY TRIAL

June 8, 2011: Internet searches for how to make chloro-form and neck-breaking were done on a computer that a Florida mother accused of killing her 2-year-old daughter had access to, an expert who analyzed the machine testi-fied today at the mother's trial. The queries were done several weeks before Caylee Anthony was last seen, though the expert could not say exactly who performed the searches.[3]

While her daughter was missing, Casey didn't act "right." She didn't act like a mother whose daughter had gone missing. She never showed any concern. She was happy. Upbeat. She got a tattoo that read "Bella Vita"—"a beautiful life."

Instead of spending the month looking for Caylee "through other resources"—whatever that means—she was living it up staying with her boyfriend, shopping, and—here's what made this an international story—competing in a "hot body con-test" at a local nightclub.

In December, months after she'd gone missing—and well after Casey had been arrested—the poor daughter's partially-decomposed remains were found in a gar-bage bag not far from the family's home. There was duct tape in her mouth.

Casey was looking at the death penalty, which seemed to suit most Americans just fine. She quickly became the most hated woman in America thanks, in no small part, to the jailhouse interviews she did, in which she badmouthed her parents and made herself out to be the victim.[4] She was creepy and difficult to watch, even for me, someone who has observed and studied aberrant behavior all my life.

While this was all blowing up, Casey's lawyer, Jose Baez, reached out. He wanted to see if we could work together. I had no idea what he meant. I had no interest in representing Casey. But what he meant was: maybe the teams defending Casey Anthony and Amanda Knox could work together, to jointly fight the sexism and slander in the courtroom and the press.

To Baez, the cases were similar: here were two pretty women who were being wrongly accused in the courts and eviscerated in the press—for something they didn't do. Because they were beautiful. Because they didn't act right. Because the prosecution and the press couldn't resist the story.

I nearly threw up in my mouth.

I was mortified by the comparison. Casey came off as manipulative, as someone who was used to getting what she wanted by whatever means it took. Amanda would have no benefit whatsoever by any kind of comparison.

The whole thing was awful, and I was reluctant to get involved, even as a TV analyst. The case was so disturbing and depressing and, in a way, boring—how anyone could find her innocent, I did not know—that I really wasn't interested in it. But it was taking up so much oxygen, at some point it became unavoidable.

I was convinced Casey was a monster. But I wasn't convinced the evidence existed to put her away. I felt like the case was going to be a test of our system. If the evidence isn't there, if it's not sufficient to convict, then you can't find the person guilty. It doesn't matter how abhorrent that person may be or how horrific it is that a child's death is involved. As a juror, you can't base your decision on passion or prejudice; you have to base it on the evidence. I gradually found myself following it closely and participating in the conversation on TV.

Still, I was loathe to attend the trial, so I did most of my analysis from a studio in Seattle. But when a business trip came up in Jacksonville, I decided to stop by for the end of the trial in Orlando.

Camp Casey, the media circus, was just as sad as I thought it would be. I stayed across the street in a dirty motel. It seemed appropriate, somehow, that my room was so filthy. The whole thing just seemed cursed and bizarre.

The first thing I noticed at the trial was how many young, stroller-pushing mothers turned up every day to try to get inside the courtroom for a peek at the action. The second was what a strong case Jose Baez was mounting.

He argued that Caylee had accidentally drowned in the pool, and her grandfather hid her body. He also alleged that Casey's father, George, who'd been having an affair with a bona fide lunatic, had sexually abused Casey all her life, and was a garden variety degenerate. You could tell this argument had gained traction with the jury.[5]

Amanda Knox escorted by Italian police to a court hearing in Perugia, Italy, on September 26, 2008. She was charged with the murder of her roommate, Meredith Kercher. *(Federico Zerilli/AFP via Getty Images)*

The house in Perugia where Meredith Kercher was murdered in 2007. Amanda Knox was one of her housemates and was accused of the crime. *(Giorgio Benvenuti/Reuters Pictures)*

Giuliano Mignini, prosecutor in the trial of murder of Meredith Kercher, had bizarre conspiracy theories about the involvement of Amanda Knox in a ritual sexual assault and sacrificial murder. *(Antonio Calanni/Associated Press)*

Bathroom sink at the crime scene in Perugia covered with Luminol to detect small amounts of blood, falsely presented in the media as representing a blood spattered scene. *(Perugia Police Department)*

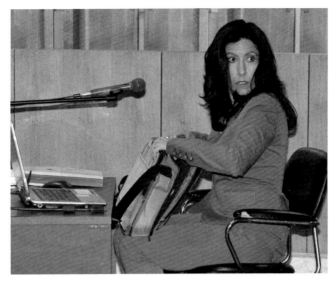

Patrizia Stefanoni, head of the lab that conducted the botched forensic analysis of the crime scene at the house in Perugia. *(Stefano Medici/Associated Press)*

Bremner Family at the top of the Space Needle in 1963 shortly after the Seattle World's Fair. From left, Doug, Anne, Lynn, Steve, Laurnell, and Jim Bremner. *(Family photo)*

Doug and Anne Bremner talk with (on right) their sister Lynn (Bremner) Dickerson at the wedding of their niece, Natalie Bremner, outside of Portland, Oregon, in 2015. *(Steve Bremner)*

Anne Bremner with parents Jim and Linnea Bremner in 2021. Back row, from left, Mike Dickerson, (niece) Madeline Matson, Jim Bremner, Anne Bremner, Linnea Bremner, (sister) Lynn Dickerson. Front: Jacob Moore. *(Family photo)*

Tyrone Briggs with his attorney, Richard Hansen, in a Seattle courtroom in 1987. Accused of robbery, attempted rape, and assault, Briggs was tried three times and eventually acquitted. *(Vic Condiotty/The* Seattle Times)

FRANCES FARMER TO GET HEARING

HOLLYWOOD, Jan. 15. (UP)—
A complaint was filed in superior court today asking a hearing to determine the sanity of Frances Farmer, blond screen actress jailed yesterday after a 24-hour spree.

Dr. Thomas Leonard, a psychiatrist, filed the complaint, and Miss Farmer was ordered removed immediately to general hospital pend-

Left: Frances Farmer in a publicity still for the film *Golden Boy,* 1938. Middle: Headline from the *Spokane Review.* Right: Widely publicized photo of Frances Farmer at her trial. *(Wikipedia)*

Betty and Dan Broderick on their wedding day in 1969. *(Family photo)*

Booking photo of the West Memphis Three, West Memphis, Arkansas, 1993. *(West Memphis, Arkansas, Police Department)*

The West Memphis Three, Jessie Misskelley, left, Damien Echols, center, and Jason Baldwin, after their release from prison, attending a special screening of *Paradise Lost 3: Purgatory* at the New York Film Festival in 2011. *(Evan Agostini/Associated Press)*

O. J. Simpson on trial in Los Angeles, California, for the murder of Nicole Brown Simpson and Ron Goldman, June 21, 1995; when asked to put on gloves found at the murder scene, he whispered within earshot of the jury, "too tight." Defense lawyer Johnny Cochran later said in his closing statement, "if it doesn't fit, you must acquit." Prosecutor Christopher Darden (right) looks on. *(Vince Bucci/AFP via Getty)*

Mary Kay Letourneau and Vili Fualaau in 1997. She was thirty-four and he was twelve when they started their relationship. *(Mark Greenberg Archive/Redux)*

Scott Peterson in a San Mateo County, California, courtroom in 2003, on trial for the murder of his wife Laci Peterson. *(Bart Ah You-Pool/Getty Images)*

Michael Jackson and Bubbles the Chimp meet a teenage fan at the Neverland Ranch in 1986. *(Bride Lane Library/ Popperfoto/Getty)*

Michael Jackson's Neverland Ranch in Santa Barbara, California, 2003. *(John Roca/New York Daily News/Getty images)*

From left, Dave Evans, Collin Finnerty, and Reade Seligmann, Duke lacrosse players accused of the rape of Crystal Mangum, look on during a news conference in Raleigh, North Carolina, in 2007. Prosecutors eventually dropped all charges. *(Chuck Burton/Associated Press)*

Durham County District Attorney Mike Nifong attending a hearing in a courtroom in Durham, North Carolina, April 18, 2006, related to charges of rape against Duke lacrosse players. *(Gerry Broome/Associated Press)*

Susan Cox Powell with her sons, Braden, age two, and Charlie, age four, about 2009, shortly before her death. *(Chuck Cox)*

Susan Cox Powell and Josh Powell in an undated photo. *(Chuck Cox)*

Burning house in Graham, Washington, February 5, 2012, where Josh Powell killed his sons, Charlie and Braden, and then himself by lighting himself on fire. *(Anne Bremner)*

Rebecca Zahau in an undated photograph. *(Wikipedia)*

Left: The staircase in the Spreckles Mansion from which five-year-old Max Shacknai fell to his death in 2011. Later the partner of his father, Rebecca Zahau, allegedly leapt to her death by suicide under a number of improbable circumstances. Right: SHE SAVED HIM, CAN YOU SAVE HER was found written next to the door of this balcony after Rebecca Zahau was found hung. *(San Diego Police Department)*

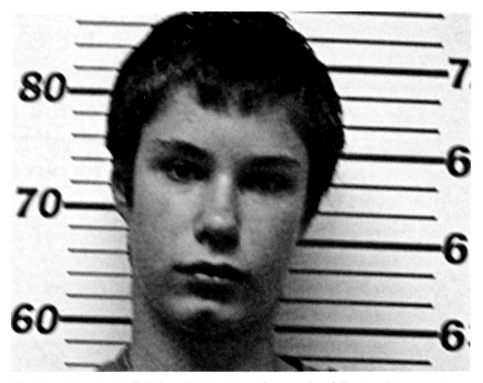

The "Barefoot Bandit," Colton Harris-Moore's mug shot following his arrest in the Bahamas. *(Royal Bahamas Police Force)*

Casey Anthony (Tot Mom) dancing in a hot body contest in an Orlando, Florida, nightclub in 2008. *(Teddy Pieper)*

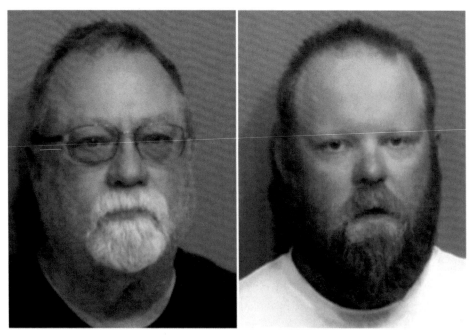

Gregory McMichael's and Travis McMichael's booking photos. *(Glynn County Sheriff's Office)*

9:45
How George Floyd Was Killed in Police Custody

Screenshot of a video of the arrest of George Floyd by Minneapolis police officers that went viral in 2020. *(YouTube)*

Burning Wendy's restaurant in the Peoplestown neighborhood of Atlanta, Georgia, June 14, 2020. Protestors burned the restaurant following the death of Rayshard Brooks at the hands of police after he fell asleep in the restaurant drive-through. *(Elijah Nouvelage/Reuters Pictures)*

Celebrating justice for Susan Cox Powell and her children after the landmark decision against the State of Washington. From left, Rosemary Earp Winquist, investigator, Chuck Cox, father of Susan Cox Powell and grandfather of Charlie and Braden Powell, and Anne Bremner. *(Anne Bremner)*

Kyle Rittenhouse, left, with backwards cap, walks along Sheridan Road in Kenosha, Wisconsin, on August 25, 2020, shortly before killing two protesters and wounding a third during a night of unrest following the police shooting of Jacob Blake. *(Adam Rogan/Associated Press)*

Outside the courtroom, however, it was a forgone conclusion that Casey was guilty. It was a strong case, and every piece of evidence the prosecution produced seemed to point to Casey's guilt. Her daughter had gone missing for a month, and she hadn't even told her own family? Cadaver dogs had alerted their handlers to human remains in her car. Chloroform was found in her trunk. How much more do you need? To many, it felt like a slam dunk. The problem is that the prosecution treated it that way, too.

The prosecutor who delivered the closing arguments, Jeff Ashton, talked about the tattoo, the hot body contest, the boyfriend . . . focusing on stuff to slime her up. But that's not something anyone in America needed help with. Nobody doubted she was a contender for worst mother in America. What was contested is whether the evidence could prove she killed her daughter.

Ashton and his colleagues spent so much time going over what a horrible mother and human being Casey was that I don't think they explained well enough why the evidence pointed toward her guilt.

Specifically circumstantial evidence: how the car, the cadaver dog, the chloroform, and the timing were all damning to Casey.

Baez was able to get up and say there was no evidence about how Caylee died. And if the prosecution can't prove how she died, then how can they prove Casey killed her? This was a brilliant defense, but the questions he raised could have been answered if the prosecution had spent less time trying Casey's character and more time explaining the evidence.

During Baez's closing argument, Ashton started laughing at him. It doesn't get much more arrogant than that, nor does it play well with a jury. Baez already came into this case looking like David against Ashton's Goliath. We all know how that story ends.

I was outside the courtroom with a microphone in my hand when the jury came back with its verdict. When they found her not guilty, my initial reaction—one I kept inside my head—was that this was an outrage. It seemed clear that Casey had killed her daughter and that a killer was getting away with murder. But I sympathized with the jury and understood their decision. They'd heard it all, and the prosecution wasn't able to prove she was guilty beyond a reasonable doubt. As difficult as it is to say, I felt it was a testament to our system—that if the evidence didn't support a conviction, then one wasn't passed down.

It was also a damning indictment of the prosecution. They blew it. Jeff Ashton blew it. He just plain got out-lawyered.

He was so caught up in the salaciousness of the case—just like Prosecutor Mignini was in Amanda's case. All of Ashton's obsession with Casey being a bad mother, a slut, you name it, distracted him from proving the case. It turns out he was terribly wrong.

In 2015, hackers targeted Ashley Madison, a website designed to facilitate infidelity. These hackers, a group known as Impact Team, demanded that the site be taken down or they would release all customer records. The site owners failed to comply, and Impact Team made good on their promise, posting the information for some 32 million users.[6]

When Impact Team's bombshell exploded, Jeff Ashton was caught in the wreckage. It turns out the married father of four had been shopping around for some kink on the side.[7] It was a classic story, like Eliot Spitzer, who prosecuted a prostitution ring as attorney general of New York, only to go down in scandal as the state's governor when it came out that he'd been carousing with a prostitute himself.

The truth is that this was a difficult case. Sane women don't do this. The prosecution's case boiled down to the fact that Casey Anthony didn't want to be a mom. She wanted her daughter out of the picture so she could go about her life and be in all the hot body contests she wanted. But this was a hard, nearly impossible case to make. Because as damning as the evidence, including the 911 call, was against her, who can believe that a sane mother would do this?

I don't think the prosecution really understood what their job was. It wasn't just to make the case that Casey Anthony was guilty of killing her two-year-old daughter. They had to make the case that she was completely sane when she did it. Jeff Ashton failed on both counts. And, honestly, I don't know if I'd be much better arguing the latter.

As it happens, one of the original sins of the prosecution was to ask for the death penalty. Finding someone guilty beyond a reasonable doubt is a high bar to clear. Deciding that a sane mom would kill a two-year-old is even higher. But to ask a jury to be so sure of her guilt that they think she should be put to death for it? Again, it's almost asking for the impossible.

This case showed that proving someone is a bad person isn't good enough. That looking guilty isn't the same as being found guilty. But it also proved that women are capable of being every bit as evil as men. I never thought this was something that would need to be explained, but considering how the culture has shifted in recent years, it turns out that it does.

In his closing argument, Jose Baez made the following point to the jury about the prosecution's case:

> *You see, the strategy behind that is, if you hate her, if you think she is a lying no good slut, then you'll start to look at this evidence in a different light. You'll start to say, "Oh, wait a minute, maybe I'm seeing something that's not there." And start to actually discriminate against her, rather than give her the standard that is afforded to each and every citizen in our country. And that is that the state, that the government, come in here and prove their case beyond and to the exclusion of every reasonable doubt. But you can get away with that if we can get a jury to hate her.*[8]

There's a lot of truth here. And, in this way, the case was very similar to the one going on in Italy. There, a prosecutor obsessed with sex was creating a narrative that this beautiful, depraved young woman who had sex with strangers on trains—sex-crazed to the point of satanic, manipulative, vindictive—could kill the roommate who was supposed to be her friend, but not human enough to show any emotion for it. His play: if they hate her and everything she stands for, the details of the case will just disappear.

Here, a sex-obsessed prosecutor told the story of a mom who didn't want a child, who wanted to sleep around, enter hot body contests, and be a kid herself rather than raise a kid. She was willing to kill to get what she wanted, but unable to conjure the emotions of a loving mother. He believed that if he made the jury hate her enough, it wouldn't matter what details of the case he couldn't connect.

The main difference is that in Amanda's case, the prosecutor was correct; the actual details faded away and he was able to get a conviction via lurid tales of satanic blood orgies and sex-crazed Americans. With Casey, however, the details never quite faded in the face of hot body contests and lies the way Jeff Ashton hoped they would. Two plus two never quite equaled four, and America's most hated mom walked out of the courtroom a free woman.

The same was true for Amanda. It just took a second trial (or more) to get there.

19

TRUMP, AMANDA, AND AMERICA FIRST

FOXY KNOXY, THE GIRL WHO HAD TO COMPETE WITH HER
OWN MOTHER FOR MEN

She is a wholesome-looking young woman who, before her life exploded with the depraved killing of her British flatmate Meredith Kercher, had become adept at presenting two faces to the world.

To many of her teachers and friends in her hometown of Seattle, Amanda Knox was a brilliant scholar, an accomplished sportswoman and the pious, morally upright product of her strict education at a Jesuit-run academy . . .

Then there is the other, secret side of this most enigmatic of accused murderers—the Amanda Knox who, ever since she was an impressionable teenager, has felt driven to aggressively compete with other women, most notably her own mother, for the attention of men.[1]

After the initial trial that found Amanda Knox and Raffaele Sollecito guilty of the murder of Meredith Kercher, the US State Department, the Obama Administration, and Washington State's two US senators were all sympathetic to Amanda's cause, but there wasn't a whole lot they were going to do. In an odd wrinkle in this saga, however, she got a very public lift from a highly unexpected source that came to her defense:

> *Well, I think I'm good at judging people, and I study people, and I became rich because I understand what people are about. I watched the Amanda Knox case unfolding in news reports . . . and after watching it for a little while, I said, "This is not a guilty person."*[2]

Sound familiar? Donald Trump apparently had second thoughts about half the people he had chosen for his cabinet as president, but from the start, he was 100 percent right about Amanda Knox. When she was found guilty, he even called for a boycott of Italy until she was released from prison. My late, wonderful friend, Kathi Goertzen, the Seattle news anchor who gave me my first break on TV, flew to New York to interview Trump—at the time, just a reality TV star with a real estate empire—to get his thoughts on why he was calling for a boycott.

"There's no evidence that links her to this crime, other than she said some unfortunate things after being tormented for hours and hours and hours," Trump told her.[3]

Trump had the Amanda Knox case down cold. He even had the prosecutor's number.

"I know exactly what this guy is all about. He's a maniac . . . it wouldn't matter to him if she was innocent or guilty," Trump said. "He just wanted to bring in the scalp."

Of course, he couldn't resist taking a swipe at Obama.

"I think the president should get involved. This is a miscarriage of justice. I think the president should absolutely get involved, and I think people should boycott Italy. They shouldn't go to Italy. This is not a close call. This isn't somebody that may be guilty. She's not guilty," Trump concluded.[4]

But there wasn't much the president could actually do, short of creating an international incident. So, rather than spend our time lobbying politicians in the United States, we focused our efforts on Amanda's appeal.

The appeal is a *trial de novo* in Italy—literally, a new trial. Unlike how appeals work in the United States, you are basically tried all over again. However, like in the United States, these cases are heard in front of a new judge. One of the first things the judge did was appoint a new panel of forensic experts to evaluate the evidence in the case. For that, they went to La Sapienza in Rome, one of the most prestigious universities in Italy. They got the cream of the crop to weigh in on the DNA and other evidence. This was a far cry from Patrizia Stefanoni, who ran the clown show forensics lab in Perugia. She was basically just a lab manager, far from an expert.

Amanda's family, meanwhile, was spending every penny they had supporting her. Our group was working for free, but her lawyers in Italy were, understandably, getting paid by the hour. It was a big case, and she needed the best lawyers she could get.

Her family was mortgaging houses and maxing out credits cards to help with her defense and to go to Italy to be near her. Her parents, sisters, grandmother, and other assorted relatives took turns staying in a rented home in Italy near the jail where Amanda was kept.

Amanda's parents, Edda and Curt, had been divorced for years, but after Amanda was arrested, both spent huge amounts of time in Italy, comforting their daughter, advocating on her behalf, and sparring with the press. Edda remarried a nice man named Chris Mellas, who is younger than she is. Curt became the de facto spokesman of the family. He has an unflappable way about him, and the role was perfect. Edda, as you'd expect, was extremely emotional all the time. I think she always regretted not telling Amanda to get out of Italy—for Germany, France, anywhere—as soon as things started to point toward her.

Sure, it might have looked a bit guilty, but who cares? She hadn't been detained; she hadn't been questioned at the station. And if she had come home to the United States, there's no way she would have been extradited. The evidence was so weak that the feds never would have gone for it. I always sympathized immensely with Edda.

20

DNA EVIDENCE FALLS APART IN AMANDA'S CASE

On June 27, 2011, the appeals trial of the conviction of Amanda Knox and Raffaele Sollecito for the murder of Meredith Kercher began. The court called on DNA experts Stefano Conti and Carla Vecchiotti, who concluded that Patrizia Stefanoni, who was in charge of the police forensic laboratory analysis, had violated standard scientific protocols in so many ways that the results she had reported and testified to were completely unreliable. In a 149-page report, Conti and Vecchiotti confirmed there was no trace of blood on the so-called murder weapon, and they revealed that proper scientific methods found none of Kercher's DNA.[1] This was the steak knife police had randomly snatched from a drawer in Sollecito's apartment on the other side of town, and that Stefanoni had testified had the DNA of Knox on the handle and the DNA of Kercher on the blade. Furthermore, Conti and Vecchiotti found no evidence of cellular material on the bra clasp retrieved from the murder scene. Let me say that again: There were two pieces of physical evidence that the prosecution had hung its hat on. One of them was that Amanda's and Meredith's DNA were both on a knife supposedly used to kill Meredith, and then it turned out that the supposed murder weapon didn't have Meredith's DNA on it. The other "evidence" was that Raffaele's DNA was found on the murder victim's bra clasp, but the experts found NO evidence of cellular material in the samples taken from it.[2] Unfortunately, that information didn't come out until *after* an Italian court locked up Amanda.

A single sentence on page fifty-five of the Conti-Vecchiotti Report (English translation) captures the essence of their findings: "The hypotheses formulated by the [Police] Technical Consultant about the nature of the material analyzed are wholly arbitrary in that they are not supported by any scientifically objective confirmation."[3]

But let's take a look at how the tabloids reported this. Did Nick Pisa, the tabloid journalist we discussed earlier, take this as an opportunity to tell the world that the knife the prosecution believed killed Meredith Kercher—the knife that had allegedly been used in a ritualistic satanic sex execution—didn't have Meredith's DNA on it? Sure. But he did it in perhaps the only possible way to suggest that this was in some way damning to Amanda.

AMANDA KNOX'S DNA 'WAS FOUND ON KNIFE PROSECUTORS CLAIM
WAS USED TO MURDER BRITISH EXCHANGE STUDENT'

New DNA tests on a knife allegedly used to murder British student Meredith Kercher show traces of Amanda Knox but crucially none of the victim, a leaked copy of the report has revealed.

The court-ordered findings will be revealed in full next week, when the retrial resumes against 26-year-old Knox and her ex-boyfriend Raffaele Sollecito, 29. It is already being seen by both defense teams as a boost to their cases. . . . At the original hearing against Knox and Sollecito, the court was told how Knox's DNA was found on the handle and Miss Kercher's DNA on the blade.[4]

Meanwhile, Amanda Knox sat in Perugia's Capanne prison, where she was sexually harassed by prison guard Raffaele Argiro. She said he would call her to his office and ask about her sexual experiences, and that he always attended her physical examinations. Argiro was later put on trial for sexual harassment of another female inmate.[5]

The DNA evidence against Amanda Knox was always weak. Just because someone's DNA is on a bra clasp—or a spoon or a chair—doesn't mean they put it there. With DNA evidence, there is a potential for something called cross-contamination.

Something in your home that you don't ever touch can get your DNA on it. It could be someone else's shoe, for example, or a jacket or anything that's left out that could be cross-contaminated.

If you could have seen the way the Italian police treated the crime scene, you'd wonder how anything in the house wasn't cross-contaminated. Even outside of the crime scene, the knife, aka the closest thing these bumbling cops had to a smoking gun, was transported from Raffaele's apartment in a shoe box—which probably had other people's DNA on it.

They were picking things up without gloves, rooting around in the refrigerator, scrubbing fingerprints off the walls. More than a month after they'd first been stomping around the house, they found Meredith's bra clasp. And, as the experts pointed out, they believed it had DNA from the three suspects and perhaps two other individuals on it.

So, just to be clear: there are two pieces of physical evidence that the prosecution claimed proves that Amanda killed Meredith in a ritualistic satanic sex execution. The first is a kitchen knife, which we now know doesn't have the victim's DNA on it.

The other is a bra clasp, which, after more than a month where dozens of people have trampled on and around it, is found to have the DNA of up to five different people on it. (When Conti and Vecchiotti later used proper scientific procedures, they found *no* evidence of cellular material on any of the samples taken from the bra clasp.)

Does this sound like a very convincing case to you? Even Nick Pisa got this one right:

THE 'FILTHY FORENSICS THAT TAINT THE CASE AGAINST FOXY KNOXY': INCOMPETENT POLICE 'WORE DIRTY GLOVES AND DROPPED MEREDITH'S BLOODIED BRA ON THE FLOOR'

Police scientists involved in the Amanda Knox murder case made a series of glaring errors, an appeal court heard yesterday . . . There were gasps from the public gallery as the two officers were seen picking up the clasp, passing it from hand to hand, dropping it, picking it up and then placing it on the floor again.

The two added that numerous people had been in and out of the crime scene and that objects had been moved, putting all evidence at risk of contamination.

In a damning point-by-point deconstruction the experts said that the errors made by the police during the original investigation meant the evidence should be considered inadmissible.[6]

Citing the lack of DNA or any other evidence for that matter, the court of appeals overturned the convictions of Knox and Sollecito on October 2, 2011.[7]

The whole family—mom, dad, aunts, sisters—was in the courtroom for the verdict, and everyone immediately boarded a British Airways flight home with Amanda.

The *Daily Mail* couldn't stand it. They couldn't wait for a guilty verdict, so they jumped the gun and initially reported—in an article by Nick Pisa, of course—the exact opposite of the verdict.[8]

GUILTY: AMANDA KNOX LOOKS STUNNED AS APPEAL AGAINST
MURDER CONVICTION IS REJECTED

Amanda Knox looked stunned this evening after she dramatically lost her prison appeal against her murder conviction.[9]

That should tell you everything you need to know about the way the reporters covering the case handled it day in and day out.

Upon arrival in Seattle, Amanda was greeted by supportive community members, and more family and friends. When the verdict came in, I was sitting in my car outside the Seattle studio where I usually did my broadcasts, trying to listen to news on the radio while my phone was bombarded with callers seeking comment. I broke into tears of joy and relief. Raffaele Sollecito left the country after the verdict, settled in the Italian-speaking part of Switzerland, and tried to start his life over. But the Swiss eventually expelled him, so he had to go back to Italy and take his chances.

When Amanda got back home to Seattle, she gave a speech thanking everyone for the support and said she was looking forward to spending time with her family. Alone. She asked for privacy. Surprisingly, the local press obliged.

The Seattle press, for the most part, saw Amanda for who she was: an innocent Seattle girl who, through no fault of her own, had been tossed into an Italian jail and become an international obsession. Most of the local news organizations said they wouldn't cover her. As news in her legal matters broke, sure, they'd cover it. But collectively, they agreed not to cover her like a tabloid figure.

Sadly, the foreign tabloids still stalked her. She'd be in a bakery or a favorite coffee shop, and she'd find herself staring into a long, expensive photographer's lens (usually someone from England). But at least she was home, in Seattle.

DON'T JUST BELIEVE WOMEN (OR ANYONE ELSE)

I cried the day Amanda Knox returned home, and I cried the day Clarence Thomas was confirmed by the Senate years earlier for a spot on the US Supreme Court. I was getting my car repaired in the south end of Seattle—my car was always breaking down back then in 1991. They had the radio turned way up, and I could hear the vote confirming him as a Supreme Court Justice.

He had been accused of sexually harassing Anita Hill when she was a lawyer and he was her supervisor at the US Department of Labor and the US Equal Employment Opportunity Commission. The case seemed obvious. Clearly, he had repeatedly sexually harassed her. But it felt like nobody believed her, or if they did, they didn't care. I felt like it had been a chance, a big chance to acknowledge that women should be treated equally, and to show that when they are not there should be consequences.

I don't know Anita Hill, but I saw myself in her—all of us in her. All of us women who worked around high-powered lawyers.

In fact, the behavior she endured started for me before my career even began. I had a creepy English professor in college who was always trying to come onto me. He played up all kinds of emotional stuff. "Hey baby," he'd say. "I really feel this way about you. . ."

Once, when I was sitting in his office asking about a paper, he sat on the arm of my chair and slid down on top of me, knocking me onto the ground. I got up and ran out the door as fast as I could. Then he started calling me. "Can't we just talk?" I was having none of it. But I didn't say anything either. I was worried about my grades and what would happen if I talked.

Later, after I'd established myself, I would get work when a client wanted "a skirt." It wasn't hard to see why. So many law firms at the time were what we called "pale, stale, and male." When a corporation, understandably, thought their case would be more sympathetic to a jury coming from a woman, they came looking for one.

Some jurors like women more than others. I, for example, am not typically liked by middle-aged women and suburban housewives. We've done research that's shown they keep me at arm's length. They're suspicious of me, a single, sixty-something blonde who goes on TV and who's never stayed home to raise children. They see me as a showboater, someone proud of what they do. And, oftentimes, they tend to side with men. They don't do it on purpose. Mostly, it's subconscious. But smart companies and their consultants hire the attorney who will be most appropriate for a case or jury. Sometimes, what they feel they need is a skirt.

An old dear friend of mine used to direct that kind of work to me. Once, he left me a voicemail saying: "Trust me—you'll want to call me back for this one."

A large insurer had gotten into a lot of trouble, and they'd hired him to find a skirt. So, he called me, a woman he didn't think of as a skirt. He called me Barbie. And I never minded. He respected me and treated me as an equal. In the evolution of the "pale, stale, and male" industry, this was progress.

Today there's little daylight between grandfatherly sexism—a man of another generation referring to a woman by what he thinks of as an endearing, if sexist, term—and keeping a woman down in the office or even holding her down against a desk. But it's the difference between being politically correct and being fair. I didn't mind being called a skirt by someone who respected me enough to tell me the way the world worked and that some cases could be won easier by a woman, and then he directed such work my way. I took the jobs and cashed the checks.

But I never liked the come-ons. And I never doubted Anita Hill. But that doesn't mean I think we should always believe women who make allegations. I don't always believe men, either. Sometimes, people don't tell the truth. Sometimes they no longer know the truth themselves.

Within a week of September 11, a group of researchers distributed surveys asking people about the attacks. They asked what they knew about the details of the attacks—how many planes were involved, for example—but they also asked people how they found out about the events of September 11. Where were you? What were you doing? Who was the first person you talked to about the attacks?[1]

The answers are what are known as a person's "flashbulb memory," which was mentioned earlier in this book as it related to false confessions in the West Memphis Three and Amanda Knox cases. A flashbulb memory is a recollection of a particularly important moment.[2,3] Most of us who were alive that day remember where we were, what we were doing, and who we were with when we learned that a plane had been flown into the World Trade Center, just like those of us who were alive the day John F. Kennedy was murdered remember where we were, what we were doing, and perhaps the way our teacher sobbed.[4]

The catch with this study is that researchers kept asking participants the same questions as the years went by.[5] First, a year later, then two years, and, finally, ten years after the attacks. They wanted to see how much their stories changed. And change they did. Particularly when it came to the way they found out about the attacks. The stories didn't just change a little bit. Ten years after the September 11 attacks, people were saying they were doing different things in different places when they learned about the attacks than they had reported a week after the events.

The survey found that the biggest change in memory happened in the first year. Then, over the years, that inconsistent version of the event is what was relayed. In other words: that *became* the memory. That became the version of the event that people told themselves. That became the one they believed.

The paper notes that one of the interesting aspects of flashbulb memory is that, unlike run-of-the-mill personal memories, even as their reported recollections declined over time, confidence did not decline. People are sure they're remembering it correctly, even when they are not.

A week after September 11, for example, one respondent said she was in her kitchen making breakfast when she heard about the attacks. A year later, she said she was in her dorm room folding laundry. Later, she said she was ironing in her dorm room, which ended up being the story she stuck with. A decade after the attacks, she remembered being in a very different place doing something completely different than she remembered a week after the event.[6]

This does not mean she was lying or making up her story. As the paper puts it: "Individuals are not simply 'filling in' missing details about the reception event with guesses as they recollect. Rather, when responding with an inconsistent memory, they truly believe they are 'remembering' it accurately."[7]

In other words: people aren't making things up or lying; they genuinely believe what they're saying. Even though what they're saying they remember ten years after an event is different than what they wrote down a week after the event.

"We may recollect the events of 9/11 with great confidence over an extremely long period of time," the paper notes. "That longevity might speak to the stability of the memory, but it does not ensure its accuracy."

In other words, being confident in a memory of an event is not the same as recalling an event accurately. This is because memory is not an undoctored photograph or video footage of an event. It is a living, evolving thing.

"It's not like memory is when you remember something, you're retrieving it and it remains absolutely stable and then you put it in the footlights of your consciousness," Bill Hirst, one of the paper's lead authors, told Malcolm Gladwell in his podcast, *Revisionist History*. "It's more that when you retrieve it, it is open up to the possibility of change."[8]

In 2014, Sabrina Erdely wrote an article for *Rolling Stone* magazine called "A Rape on Campus." She reported that a woman named Jackie was raped two years earlier at a frat party at the University of Virginia (UVA). It was a horrible, vicious event. Her date, a member of the fraternity and a fellow lifeguard at the school's pool, walked her up the stairs after midnight and opened the door to a bedroom. It was pitch black. She heard a noise. And then she was attacked. She and her attacker smashed into a glass table, breaking it into pieces. Then she was beaten and raped by seven men. Her date encouraged them.

Hours later, Jackie woke up in the dark, alone in the fraternity. The party was still raging, and she left, barefoot and distraught and unsure of where she was.

She called some friends and pleaded for them to pick her up. When they did, she told them what happened. One friend insisted she go to the hospital. Another disagreed: "Her reputation will be shot for the next four years."

This is the way the story was relayed by *Rolling Stone* in an article that "ultimately attracted more than 2.7 million views, more than any other feature not about a celebrity that the magazine had ever published" according to the magazine.[9]

The fallout from the story came as soon as it was published. The university launched an investigation. All Greek activities were suspended across the entire campus. The frat house was vandalized.[10]

The story unraveled nearly as quickly.

As the article's author made the media rounds discussing her piece, other journalists started to ask questions about the story. *Slate* wondered: Did you even talk to the men she's accusing of rape?[11] No, she had not.

Subsequent news reports and an investigation into the article's missteps undertaken by Steve Coll, dean of the Columbia School of Journalism, at the request of the magazine, completely discredited the story. Key details emerged: The fraternity did not hold an event the night in question and the reporter never interviewed the woman's friends—neither the one who had allegedly suggested she go to the hospital nor the one who said doing so would ruin her reputation. Crucially, it was revealed that *Rolling Stone* didn't know the name of the man—the lifeguard friend—who took Jackie to the fraternity when it published the story, because Jackie refused to tell the reporter. As such, they could not ask him for his side of the story.

"Jackie refused to provide (reporter Sabrina Erdely) the name of the lifeguard who had organized the attack on her. She said she was still afraid of him," Coll wrote in his report. "That led to tense exchanges between Erdely and Jackie, but the confrontation ended when *Rolling Stone*'s editors decided to go ahead without knowing the lifeguard's name or verifying his existence. After that concession, Jackie cooperated fully until publication."[12]

Other inconsistencies emerged.

Jackie told a university dean that she'd been forced to perform oral sex on seven men—a very different type of attack than the one she described to *Rolling Stone*. While testifying in 2016 as part of several lawsuits that grew out of the article, an attorney asked her about the discrepancy.

"My comfort level was different, and I don't remember exactly what I told Dean Eramo or *Rolling Stone*," she said.[13]

There are even questions about whether the man she says brought her to the party exists. The report notes that "the friends said that Jackie told them that her date on Sept. 28 was not a lifeguard but a student in her chemistry class named Haven Monahan. (The Charlottesville police said in March they could not identify a UVA student or any other person named Haven Monahan.)."[14] The report goes on to note that a comparison between members of the fraternity and lifeguards at the aquatic center showed no overlap.

Columbia's report said the article was a failure from top to bottom, often skipping "basic, even routine journalistic practice." The report's two most damning lines involve a detail and a fact.

The detail: "Social scientists analyzing crime records report that the rate of false rape allegations is 2 to 8 percent."

The fact: "Erdely and her editors had hoped their investigation would sound an alarm about campus sexual assault and would challenge Virginia and other universities to do better. Instead, the magazine's failure may have spread the idea that many women invent rape allegations."[15]

Rolling Stone is the Tom Sneddon (the prosecutor in the Michael Jackson case) of this story. They didn't just believe Jackie's story. They *wanted* the story she told them to be true. They wanted it so badly that, according to the Columbia report, they were willing to forgo basic journalistic practices, just like Sneddon and Mignini (and Michael Nifong, for that matter) ignored basic judicial and investigatory principles when they wanted their cases to be open and shut more than the evidence allowed. This desire to believe appears to have obscured the magazine's staff from seeing the facts of the case—or the lack of them—just like Sneddon, Mignini, and Nifong. Rather than thoroughly confirming Jackie's story, they looked for reasons it was true.

Here's another example. The West Memphis Police Department (WMPD) early on developed the idea that the murder of three young boys was the work of a satanic cult. Once they got this idea, any evidence or hearsay related to this idea was leaked to the press, enforcing the idea that the killings were the work of a satanic cult. The media went along with the idea and published the leaked information.[16]

"The problem of confirmation bias—the tendency of people to be trapped by preexisting assumptions and to select facts that support their own views while overlooking contradictory ones—is a well-established finding of social science," the report on the *Rolling Stone* article noted.[17] "It seems to have been a factor here. Erdely believed the university was obstructing justice. She felt she had been blocked. Like many other universities, UVA had a flawed record of managing sexual assault cases. Jackie's experience seemed to confirm this larger pattern. Her story seemed well established on campus, repeated and accepted."[18]

This is something we all do. We all view facts through the prism of our biases.

There are plenty of news outlets and social media accounts to support a person's confirmation bias. Far too many people gravitate toward what they want to believe, to television channels and websites that will give you the truth you want. In this tribal era, it's not about finding fact or truth; it's become more about reinforcing bias. We don't come into an event or a crime or a headline looking for facts, we come looking for reinforcement, largely because we don't want to be proved wrong. We're also looking for like-minded individuals to confirm our own confirmation biases. In the end, it becomes a community.

Four years after *Rolling Stone* published "A Rape on Campus," President Donald Trump nominated Brett Kavanaugh to sit on the United States Supreme Court. Kavanaugh was an esteemed jurist and lawyer in many people's eyes, especially in Washington, DC, where he had been serving as a federal judge in the United States Court of Appeals. But in the current politically charged climate, to liberals he was a pariah.

Soon after his nomination, a university professor named Christine Blasey Ford alleged that he had sexually assaulted her when they were in high school in suburban Maryland. In her telling, they were at a party, and Kavanaugh and a friend cornered her in a bedroom, Kavanaugh pinned her to the bed and groped and tried to pull her clothes off. When his friend jumped on the bed, all three fell to the ground and she was able to escape.

From the beginning, Kavanaugh was a divisive figure. He was nominated by Trump. He was hostile and defensive during his confirmation hearings. He's a middle-aged, privileged white guy, who was also a Catholic, so people assumed he would be against abortion. Many people didn't *want* him to be innocent. They wanted to believe Ford.

Kavanaugh and Ford obviously had different perceptions about what happened. Is it possible that their perceptions were different? Yes. Is it possible that memories for events can change over time? As outlined earlier, the answer to that is yes as well.

In the wake of the allegations and the subsequent FBI investigation and Senate hearing, "Believe Women" became Twitter dogma to the point that opinions—even conversations—to the contrary were dismissed, invalidated, considered anti-women. People couldn't understand: Why *wouldn't* you just believe women? In that sense it was the perfect bumper sticker. Like "pro-life," what is the alternative? pro-death? Like so many bumper stickers, this topic is far more complicated than a reductive catch phrase.

That is not to say there is not a historical impropriety in how these cases have been handled and how women's testimony has often been treated compared to men's. That said, women don't need separate treatment from men.

Women are just as capable as men of doing good and bad. We're just as capable of standing up to tough questioning as men; we're just as thoughtful as men; and we have a lot of qualities that are superior to men, qualities that I think are scarcely acknowledged.

I have plenty of experience with criminal rape cases that were false accusations or cases that you believe are true but know you can't win. Prosecutors have a responsibility to bring forth cases they think they will win. Bringing anything else forward doesn't do the accuser any favors.

Once, as a young prosecutor, I went to the hospital to see a woman who had jumped naked out of the window of a high rise. When I got there, she was in rough shape.

She said that a weirdo took her back to his place, tried to assault her, and she jumped out of the window to escape. She landed on a balcony a couple floors down. It was terrible. A little boy who fell asleep in front of his TV woke up to find a bloody arm reaching toward him through the balcony door.

Her story sounded credible, so I took the case and agreed to prosecute it.

Then things got complicated. It turns out she'd claimed she'd been raped previously under very similar circumstances. In this case, witnesses saw her and the man before she jumped and said they looked normal and happy. Her clothes were found in the hallway of the building, as if she'd started taking them off outside of the apartment (these were the days before ubiquitous security cameras). If I wasn't sure before that she wouldn't make a great witness, the kicker was when she came in to see me after she got out of the hospital, she showed up with caked-on makeup on her face like a clown.

What was sadly clear was that this woman was extremely unbalanced. What was not clear was whether she had been assaulted. All we had was her word. There was no evidence at the hospital or at the apartment that she had been assaulted. In the end, we decided not to pursue the case.

Does that mean she wasn't assaulted? No. Does that mean she was lying to us? Absolutely not. Deciding not to believe everything every woman (or man) says is not the same thing as treating them as liars. Does it mean that mentally unstable people are not assaulted? Of course not. It means that I didn't believe—the prosecutor's office didn't believe—we could prove guilt beyond a reasonable doubt. We passed on a case we didn't believe we could win, and that we knew would make things worse for the woman if we lost. We believed the best way to protect all the innocent parties in the case was to decline to prosecute.

In her 2016 testimony, Jackie said: "I stand by the account I gave to *Rolling Stone*. I believed it to be true at the time."[19]

When the story an accuser puts forward falls apart, as Jackie's did, it's not necessarily because they were telling a lie. As is common with human beings, what we honestly believe to be true is not always accurate, and what we remember can drastically change over time, as we discussed earlier in this chapter.

I'll admit it's tempting. You want to believe all women who make accusations. You want to believe they wouldn't lie, and most of the time they don't. You don't want to believe that a mother would kill her babies—and normally they don't. You don't want to believe that women would lie about sexual assault—and usually they don't. But sometimes, unfortunately, they do. Or they recall things that are completely different than what actually happened. We're all capable of doing these things—men and women.

But just because most people don't lie doesn't mean all of the accused are guilty. In fact, our system is set up in a way that lets some of the guilty go free.

We don't convict people based on our first impressions. We convict people we can prove are guilty beyond a reasonable doubt in a court of law. And we know that, sometimes, this means guilty men and women go free.

It's when people feel morally justified passing judgment without facts based on bias—and vilify arguments to the contrary—that we get to a situation like Knox.

Benjamin Franklin put it best: "That it is better 100 guilty persons should escape than that one innocent person should suffer, is a maxim that has been long and generally approved."[20]

22

<u>EXONERATED</u>

Given the peculiarities of the Italian judicial system, the not guilty finding of Amanda Knox and Raffaele Sollecito in the murder of Meredith Kercher was sent back to Italy's Court of Cassation. Based on an administrative review, the court overturned the appellate court's opinion, which meant that the case had to go back to another trial. This was probably a political maneuver to not show "disrespect" to the court that had rendered the original guilty verdict, which was now so obviously flawed. In the United States, we're used to this narrative: person found guilty appeals ruling, wins on appeal, is set free. And that's what happened with Amanda. But we're not used to what Italy threw at Amanda next. After spending four years in prison, after being vindicated on appeal and after she returned home to the United States, Italy decided they were going to try her and Raffaele again. A new trial began in Florence on September 30, 2013.

Italy doesn't prohibit double jeopardy the way we do in the United States. Here, if a jury of your peers finds you not guilty, that's pretty much the end of it. They can't throw you in prison again for the same crime. In Italy, double jeopardy is possible. They can try you again for the same crime. And that's exactly what happened to Amanda.

The big difference was that Amanda wouldn't be attending her third hearing. Two were quite enough, thank you. She was back home, and though the Italians asked her to come on back for the trial, she passed. She'd seen the prison and the courtrooms and had enough of it. Amanda would be tried in absentia.

Trial Three felt like a rerun of Trial One, dredging up all the prosecution's old hits: Amanda made the boys do this! Look at how she acted! This is not how innocent people act! Can you believe she went out for pizza! And bought lingerie! Oh, that Rudy guy couldn't have done this himself; there must have been more than one person there!

It was pathetic but deadly serious, especially when the prosecution got to the physical evidence that we all thought had been relegated to the dust bin of history. The judge was enamored with the original ideas and evidence—and overlooked the new DNA analysis on the knife and bra clasp—and let it all in. It would have been funny to watch had it not been so horrifying.

Before the verdict came in, Amanda talked to the BBC about what she'd do if found guilty, yet again: "I'm definitely not going back to Italy willingly. They'll have to catch me and pull me back kicking and screaming into a prison that I don't deserve to be in. I will fight for my innocence."[1]

After the jury deliberated in the third trial, on January 30, 2014, the verdict came in, and Amanda was found guilty, again, of a crime she did not commit.

The immediate question that arose was what would happen to her now? Her attorneys were going to appeal, of course, but would she be extradited? Would the United States send her back to Italy to serve a couple more decades in prison for a crime she didn't commit? That she'd previously been found not to have committed?

The prevailing theory was, yes, she would. Crying "what about double jeopardy?" isn't much of a defense in these cases. And though Italy doesn't extradite murderers to the United States on account of the death penalty, there's no equivalent going the other way. If she didn't win her next appeal, then, yeah, chances were she'd have to spend the best years of her life back in an Italian prison.

She'd have to wait another year to find out where things stood.

As horrifying as Amanda's experience was, she never lost sight of who the victim was: Meredith Kercher, her young friend. To the prosecution, however, this story was never about finding Meredith's killer. It was about finding Amanda guilty. But that is just one piece of what Amanda was truly a victim of: the Italian justice system. We can rightly make all the swipes we want at the system in the United States, but for all its faults it has its advantages over other systems.

First, had Amanda been detained for a crime back in Seattle, she could only have been held for seventy-two hours without being charged with a crime. In Italy? It's two years.

We've already talked about the fact that Italy doesn't sequester its juries. In a big press case like this, that means they're absorbing all the salacious gossip and lies about the case. The prosecution knows this. Mignini knew that even things that weren't admissible in court would be devoured by the tabloids. So, he made sure they were fed a steady diet of unsubstantiated rumors, playing up, of course, his idea that Amanda was a vixen she-devil.

The case, in other words, wasn't tried in the courtroom. It was tried in the press.

This was made all the more difficult by the questionable scheduling decisions. Bizarrely, the trial was held on weekends—with the summer off, to boot. That was for the convenience of Sollecito's lawyer, Giulia Bongiorno, so she could pop up on weekends when the parliament wasn't in session. In the United States, you have a right to a speedy trial. Not so in Italy.

One of the other differences between the American and Italian justice systems is that in this country, we find people either guilty or not guilty. In Italy, the court can exonerate people. It's a slight, but significant distinction. In the United States, you're presumed innocent until proven guilty, but you are found not guilty of something—not innocent. In Italy, the court can say you didn't do it. You're innocent.

After the second guilty verdict, the case was sent to the Italian Supreme Court. On March 27, 2015, they released their verdict. They didn't find the defendants not guilty. They found them innocent.[2]

I remember exactly where I was. It was the afternoon, and I was sitting in my car outside a TV studio, listening to the radio. When the news came that the court had exonerated Amanda, I started to cry again, just like after the original not guilty verdict. *Finally*, I thought, *someone gets it.*

I've highlighted the differences between the Italian and American judicial systems. No system is perfect. I've pointed out deficiencies in the Italian system. They would probably point to our use of capital punishment and the large number of persons incarcerated for nonviolent crimes, disproportionately young black men. Also, sometimes people literally get lost in American jails.[3] Take the example of

Randall McCrary, a forty-five-year-old mentally ill man from Atlanta, Georgia, who was arrested for disorderly conduct after he was found outside a gas station covered in excrement and screaming at the customers. Indigent, he couldn't afford the $500 bail. He sat in jail for two months. Meanwhile, the government discontinued his disability payments. Only after a lawyer for the Southern Center for Human Rights filed a petition for his release, and a Good Samaritan paid his bail, was he released.[4]

The Italian court issued its "motivation"—its explanation of its decision and how it decided that the pair was innocent of the murder. They said that the murder investigation was ultimately hindered by the fact that investigators were under pressure to come up with answers once the case was prominently covered in media around the world.[5] The judges also wrote that "the history of this trial has been characterized by a troubled and intrinsically contradictory path, around one sole certainty; the guilt of Amanda Knox for the slanderous accusation of Patrick Lumumba."[6]

This, of course, is true. But only after she was abused by the police in an overnight interrogation in which she also falsely accused herself in a classic case of coerced confession.

The judges clung to the idea that the pair had been in the house that night, although, decidedly, not in the room where the murder happened or, of course, guilty of the murder. Whatever that can possibly mean.

But on the matter of the couple's trial and treatment, the motivation was damning.

"The trial had oscillations which were the result of stunning flaws, or amnesia, in the investigation and omissions in the investigative activity," they wrote. And under these conditions "was never capable of reaching a conclusion beyond any reasonable doubt."[7]

The problems, the judges noted, started with the way the case was played out in the press: "The international spotlight on the case in fact resulted in the investigation undergoing a sudden acceleration, that, in the frantic search for one or more guilty parties to consign to international public opinion, certainly didn't help the search for substantial truth."[8]

The judges went on to blow up each of the prosecution's points one by one. The focus, rightly, was on two key pieces of the prosecution's evidence: Raffaele's kitchen knife, the alleged murder weapon, which was originally said to have had both Amanda's and Meredith's DNA on it; and the bra clasp, which was kicked around for weeks before it was recovered.

First, on the matter of collecting the DNA evidence, which the judges stated was so poorly done and ignored so many of the proper protocols for collecting evidence, that "one really cannot see how the results of the genetic analysis . . . can be considered endowed of the characteristics of seriousness and preciseness."[9]

The judges pointed out that the knife, for example, was in fact transported in a simple cardboard box "of the sort used to package Christmas gadgets." And even if the DNA was a match to Amanda's, they said that was not surprising considering how often she was staying at Raffaele's house.

The judges also pointed out that because the knife "showed no traces of Kercher's blood," it "contradicts the prosecution's hypothesis that it was the murder weapon." This is all the more damning when you consider, as the judges pointed out, that the lack of blood on the knife was not the result of rigorous cleaning.

"As noted by the defense," they wrote, "the knife showed traces of starch, a sign of ordinary domestic use and of cleaning that was anything but meticulous. Not only this, but starch is famous as a substance with a high absorbance rate, thus, it is highly likely that, in the event of a stabbing, it would have retained blood traces."[10]

Then they got to the bra clasp:

More unusual—and disturbing—is the fate of the bra clasp. Noticed during the first site inspection by the Scientific Police, the object was ignored and left there on the floor for quite some time (a good 46 days), until it was finally collected during an additional visit. It is certain that in the time period between the site inspection when it was noticed and the one when it was collected, there were other visits by the investigators, who rummaged everywhere, moving furniture and fixtures, in search of evidence that would be useful to the investigation. The clasp was perhaps trodden on or, in any case, moved (such that it was found on the floor in a different position from where it had initially been noticed). Not only this, but the photographic documentation produced by Sollecito's defense demonstrates that, at the time of the collection, the clasp was passed from hand to hand by the agents, who in addition were wearing dirty latex gloves.[11]

Ouch.

On the matter of the fact that there was no sign of Raffaele or Amanda in the room where Meredith was killed (save for such a small trace of Raffaele's DNA on the bra clasp, which they said should have been inadmissible), the judges didn't buy the prosecution's argument that this was because the pair had done such a thorough cleaning of the room.

"It has been claimed in vain that, after staging the break-in, the authors of the crime performed a 'selective' cleaning of the crime scene, in order to remove only those damning traces attributable to them, while leaving behind, instead, those attributable to others," they wrote. "This hypothesis is patently illogical."[12]

They went on:

After all, the assertion itself of a presumed carefulness in the cleaning is factually proven wrong, since in the "small bathroom" traces of blood have been found on the mat, on the bidet, on the tap, on a Q-tips box and on the light switch. And yet, had the defendants been guilty, they surely would not have lacked the time for an accurate cleaning, in the sense that there was no reason for the perpetrators to hurry up for fear of the possible arrival at home of other people.

And just to drive the point home one last time:

It is indisputably impossible that traces attributable to the appellants would not have been found at the crime scene had they taken part in Kercher's murder. No trace belonging to them was found in particular on the sweater that the victim was wearing at the time she was attacked nor on her shirt underneath, which would have been the case if they had participated in the murder.[13]

The judges wrapped up their report by noting that the only decision that had to be made was what kind of annulment to give. In other words: were they going to say that there needed to be another trial, or fully acquit Amanda and Raffaele? The evidence had been handled so poorly, they wrote, that a new trial would be difficult.

For example: "The computers of Amanda Knox and Kercher, which might have been useful to the investigation, were, incredibly, burned by the careless actions of the investigators, causing a short circuit due probably to an erroneous power supply; and they cannot give any more information, given that the damage is irreversible."[14]

In the end, the judges fully acquitted them both for Meredith's murder.

This felt like vindication, indeed. For Amanda, of course, that's the most important thing. But it also felt like vindication of the efforts our group had mounted. We always believed that when this case became an international spectacle, the chances of Amanda getting a fair trial got slimmer and slimmer. We knew the trial would be heard in the press more than it was in the courtroom, and that if Amanda was ever going to go free, we had to fight in the press.

In a statement Amanda released after the exoneration, she relayed her thanks to the Italian Supreme Court and to everyone who had supported her, and she said: "I will now begin the rest of my life with one of my goals being to help others who have been wrongfully accused."[15]

The death of my mother when I was a girl was devastating. It could have been crippling. As a girl, I looked toward stories of strong women who had overcome tragedy in their lives to triumph. That was my way of pulling myself out of the void of despair and not becoming a victim of my own tragedy. Some of them were crushed by adversity, like another woman from Seattle, Frances Farmer. Others went on to achieve important things, like Dolly Madison, Martha Washington, Sacagawea, Harriet Tubman, and the Red Cross' Clara Barton.

When I started working on behalf of Amanda Knox, I saw her as a misunderstood woman from Seattle—a place that was no stranger to misunderstood young women (something I could relate to). But as the case progressed and she distinguished herself on the other side of the prison walls, I began to admire her in a way I couldn't have anticipated when I took the case.

In the years since her release, Amanda didn't parlay her notoriety into becoming a reality TV star or a darling on the party circuit. She wrote a book about the experience,[16] she hunkered down in Seattle, and she worked with the Innocence Project and other efforts to advocate for the wrongly accused.

As the late Martin Luther King Jr. said, "Injustice anywhere is a threat to justice everywhere."

She faced tragedy head-on and overcame it.

I advocated for Amanda Knox when hardly anyone else believed her. I was a voice for Amanda Knox, the underdog.

In a way I didn't understand at the time, in speaking up for her, I was speaking up for myself.

As well as other victims. Like Susan Cox Powell.

23

JUSTICE DELAYED FOR SUSAN COX POWELL

Josh Powell killed himself and his children in 2012 when the police were closing in on him for the disappearance of his wife, Susan Cox Powell. Approached by a social worker at his Washington home, Josh barricaded himself inside the house with Charlie and Braden, his two sons. He murdered the boys with an axe and set the home on fire. They all died. By the time firefighters could neutralize the blaze, only the skeleton of the house remained.

I took on Susan's parents (and the children's grandparents) case. It took years to move Chuck and Judy Powell's matter forward. First, we had to deal with the life insurance. Josh had taken out policies on both Susan and himself. Big ones. Worth millions. The Powell family wanted Susan declared legally dead, so they could collect the money. Josh named his brother, Michael, his beneficiary. Michael, however, jumped to his death from the top of a building. It was a big, sad, mess. But all of that was small time compared to going after the state for what they did—or, rather, what they did not do—for Charlie and Braden Powell.

I took on the case with my longtime friend and colleague, Ted Buck, and with trial co-counsel Evan Bariault. They are the two finest trial lawyers I know. For the trial, which didn't get underway until February 2020, the three of us who were running point moved into a big, old house in Tacoma, Washington. This was the first time in my career that I lived with the other attorneys with whom I was working on a case—though, I felt like I was living with a bunch of attorneys during the Michael Jackson trial. But it was very productive. It immersed us in the case. And I think it helped the story come alive for the jury.

I'd get up around 4:00 a.m. just to get started. Ted would get up around 5 or 6 a.m. Our colleague Evan got up a bit later. We'd chat, make breakfast, and start to go over what was still swirling around our heads from the previous day: how we thought jurors had responded, what we might have done differently, etc. Then we'd get to work on preparing for the day.

After the trial, we were back at the house. Recapping everything. Making dinner. Going over how we were going to make the next day's arguments. We had a big table in the kitchen where we spread everything out. The guys had reams of paper and notebooks. I brought my Post-its.

In the courtroom, we told the story of Susan, Charlie, and Braden Powell—three people let down by those who were supposed to care for them. We talked about Susan, a mom who disappeared when her husband said he was taking his boys for a midnight camping trip. We talked about Charlie, four years old when his mom went missing, and Braden, just two. We talked about the house of horrors their dad raised them in with a grandfather who was, by then, a convicted sex offender, and was still obsessed with the kids' mom. And we talked about the state of Washington authorities, who still felt it prudent to let Josh have the boys over to his home.

The State of Washington, of course, tried to shirk responsibility.

"Mr. Powell is the sole cause of the murder of his sons," Assistant Attorney General Joseph Diaz told the jury. "There was not any negligence by the state of Washington."[1]

As the trial progressed, news from Wuhan, China, was making its way to America. A mysterious virus, scientists noted, was reported to have originated in bats and was spreading throughout the city. Not that I was watching the news while I was in trial.

But soon, I would have to pay attention. Beginning in March 2020, COVID-19 brought everything to a halt, including our trial. For the next five months, everything froze.

It's a tricky thing, being on a jury. You're away from your job and often absent from your family. In a case like this, you have to live with the impossibly tragic details of a man who killed his family. Few people want to be on jury duty. But nobody wants to go through *this*.

Meanwhile, on the other side of the country, a call came into the Brunswick, Georgia, 911 dispatcher.

"I'm out here at Satilla Shores," the caller said. "There's a Black male running down the street."[2]

AHMAUD ARBERY: "THERE'S A BLACK MAN RUNNING DOWN THE STREET"

911 Dispatcher: *Numbers and communications officer.*
Caller: *I'm out here at Satilla Shores. There's a guy in the house, right now. It's a house under construction.*
911 Dispatcher: *OK, do you have your address? Or that house's address?*
Caller: *Right now it's 219 or 220 Satilla Drive.*
911 Dispatcher: *And you said someone's breaking into it right now?*
Caller: *No, it's all open. It's under construction. And he's running right now. There he goes right now.*
911 Dispatcher: *Okay, what is he doing?*
Caller: *He's running down the street.*
911 Dispatcher: *OK, that's fine, I'll get them out there. I just need to know what he was doing wrong. Was he just on the premises and he's not supposed to be?*
Caller: *And he's been caught on camera a bunch. It's kind of an ongoing thing out here. The guy that's*

building the house has a heart condition. I don't think he's going to finish the house.

911 Dispatcher: *OK, that's fine. And you said he was a male in a black t-shirt.*

Caller: *A white t-shirt. He's a black guy, in a white t-shirt. And he's been back there. Been back there running through the neighborhood. In my front yard.*[1]

On February 23, 2020, a twenty-five-year-old black male set out for a jog under the Spanish moss-covered live oak trees that gracefully line the roads along the Georgia coast. Ahmaud Arbery was from Brunswick, Georgia, and a former star football player for Brunswick High School.[2] Gregory McMichael, a retired police officer for the Glynn County Police, saw him running past. Travis McMichael, his son, put in the call to the Brunswick 911 emergency line, reporting a man in the open area of a house under construction.[3] Gregory McMichael put in the second call to 911 saying "there's a black male running down the street." Shortly after he is heard calling his son and disconnecting the call.[4]

Gregory McMichael ran into the house and told Travis, to grab his gun because he saw someone "running down the street."[5, 6] They jumped into their truck and pursued Arbery, repeatedly shouting at him to stop and trying to cut him off with the truck as he tried to run away. Neighbor William Bryan followed, recording everything with his cell phone. The McMichaels cornered Arbery and Travis jumped out of the truck to confront him. The pair struggled, just out of view of the camera. Travis shot Ahmaud Arbery and killed him. The police report only involved an interview with Gregory McMichael, who was described as a witness.[7] McMichael claimed he recognized the man as someone who showed up on security footage on the property of a house under construction in the neighborhood.[8] The report said that he and his son drove up next to Arbery and that Travis got out of the truck with his gun. He and Arbery then struggled over the gun, Travis fired a shot, and a second later there was a second shot. No arrest was made at the scene, and Bryan's video was not collected.[9]

A police officer later called Arbery's mother and told her that Arbery had broken into a house to burglarize it and that the homeowner had shot him in self-defense.[10] The story was clearly inaccurate, however the McMichaels had *claimed* there had been multiple break-ins in the neighborhood, and that Arbery "fit the description" of someone seen on surveillance footage. Yet an open records request by the *Brunswick News* to the Glynn County police later revealed that the only burglary that had been committed in the neighborhood was the theft of a handgun Travis McMichael had left on the driver's seat of his unlocked truck that was parked in his driveway.[11, 12, 13]

Following Arbery's death, the Glynn County police had little to say about the circumstances around his shooting to a reporter from the *Brunswick News* named Larry Hobbs.[14] The case was assigned to Brunswick District Attorney Jackie Johnson.[15] She recused herself from the case on February 27, 2020, based on the fact that Gregory McMichael had previously worked as an investigator in her department—but not before telling two police officers not to arrest Travis McMichael.[16, 17] It was later revealed that she and Gregory McMichael had sixteen phone conversations, starting the day after the murder, and continuing long after she had supposedly recused herself.[18] The last call was on May 5, 2022, the day a video of the murder was released, when she gave him advice on how to deal with the fallout.[19]

Johnson asked for assistance from Waycross Ware County District Attorney (DA) George Barnhill, before recommending that he take over the case.[20] Ware County is the next county over from Glynn County. Thinly populated, a large part of it is made up the uninhabited Okefenokee Swamp. It was later revealed that Johnson knew in advance before referring the case to Barnhill that he would not press charges against McMichael and his son.[21]

Barnhill argued that no charges should be filed against the McMichaels because they had acted in self-defense and were legally justified to make a citizen's arrest under Georgia law.[22] This opinion was later described by Atlanta attorney Michael J. Moore as "flawed." He said, "The law does not allow a group of people to form an armed posse and chase down an unarmed person who they believe might have possibly been the perpetrator of a past crime."[23] He felt the McMichaels should be arrested. The Arbery family filed a complaint against Barnhill, accusing him of having a conflict of interest since his son was an assistant district attorney in the Brunswick office.

Up until this point, the story of the Arbery killing had been covered solely by Larry Hobbs of the *Brunswick News*. One of only four staff members for the local newspaper, they published six days a week for the 85,000 residents of Glynn County, Georgia. Hobb's reporting had kept the embers of interest in the case burning on a local level. On April 13, 2020, the case was transferred to Tom Durden, district attorney for Liberty County in Hinesville, Georgia, part of the Atlanta Judicial Circuit.[24]

Family and friends of Ahmaud Arbery continued to post about the case on social media and protest the lack of action on the part of prosecutors. This repeated pressure finally led to attention from the national media, when, on April 26, 2020, the *New York Times* ran a story titled "Two Weapons, a Chase, a Killing, and No Charges."[25] On April 29, 2020, the *Brunswick News* published a story with the 911 transcripts that seemed to show there was no probable cause for the so-called attempted citizen's arrest of Arbery.[26] On May 5, 2020, a Brunswick lawyer named Alan Tucker who was "informally consulting" with the suspects leaked the cell phone video of the shooting made by Bryan, arguing that it would show that: "it wasn't two men with a Confederate flag in the back of a truck going down the road and shooting a jogger in the back."[27] That logic turned out to be fatally flawed when, after the video went viral on social media and there were calls for the arrest of the McMichaels, DA Durden asked the Georgia Bureau of Investigation (GBI) to get involved.[28] The case was sent to a grand jury, and Travis and Gregory McMichael were arrested and charged with murder.[29]

I had time to watch all this on the news, since while these events unfolded the judge put the trial related to the family of Susan Cox Powell on hold due to the pandemic.

Glynn County Commissioner Bob Coleman said Jackie Johnson should have turned the case over to the GBI right away, not to George Barnhill, the DA in the next county.[30] William Bryan was arrested and charged with murder a few weeks later.[31]

The Arbery case again highlights a central theme of this book: the critical role of both conventional media coverage of high-profile crimes and the effects of social media on these cases. If the *New York Times* had not run a story, the case would probably have gone nowhere. Bogged down in the cronyism of the police and prosecutors in Glynn County, Georgia, and their pals over in Ware County, the three men were not even arrested, let alone charged. The story led a lawyer to (unwisely) release the cell phone footage that led to their arrest. The video spread like wildfire on Facebook and Twitter, with the social media outcry dramatically impacting the prosecution and ultimately the outcome of this case.

The national attention and GBI involvement meant that Glynn County couldn't keep things wrapped up in business as usual like before.[32] And it meant that things finally caught up with Brunswick DA Jackie Johnson. She was indicted by a Glynn County Grand Jury on September 8, 2021, for "violation of oath of a public officer" and "obstruction and hindering a law enforcement officer."[33] At the time of this writing, she was awaiting trial and facing up to five years in prison.

The Ahmaud Arbery case shined a light on the troubled history of DA Jackie Johnson and her dealings with the Glynn County police.[34] It turned out that the Arbery case wasn't the first time that Johnson's actions—combined with Glynn County police misconduct—had fatal consequences. On June 18, 2010, a thirty-five-year-old mother of two with substance abuse and mental health issues sat alone in her car. In that moment, Caroline Small was actively traumatized by the final disposition of her recent divorce. So when an officer from the Glynn County police asked her to step out of her vehicle, Small drove off, leading officers on a low-speed chase.[35] The car crashed and one of the officers got out to pull her out of the car. The dashboard recording showed that an officer said, "If she moves the car, I'm going to shoot her." That was in spite of the fact that the car had four flat tires and was pinned against a utility pole by the police car. It had no chance of escape. Small was unarmed.[36] She inched the car forward. Sergeant Robert C. ("Corey") Sasser and Officer Michael T. Simpson fired shots, hitting Small in the head. They can be heard in the video bragging about their aim. Small later died.[37]

The Glynn County Police Department tampered with the crime scene and created misleading evidence to the grand jury that resulted in no indictment of the police officers for the murder of Caroline Small. Jackie Johnson was district attorney at the time and shared state's evidence with the police officers[38, 39] Glynn County Commissioner Bob Coleman later said about the case: "There was no question in my mind that was cold blooded murder on that girl that day."[40] Sasser, one of the police officers that shot and killed Caroline Small, subsequently had a number of complaints and disciplinary hearings related to excessive use of force but remained a member of the police.[41] In 2018, while out on bond after being arrested for threatening his estranged wife, he shot and killed her and her boyfriend, then turned the gun on himself.[42] Small's attorney said, "The Glynn County Police Department has been protecting Corey Sasser for 20 years, and they did it again here."[43]

Shortly after the arrests of the McMichaels and Bryan, there was another high-profile death that set the nation on fire. On the streets of Minneapolis, Minnesota, cell phone footage captured the last minutes of George Floyd's life, pinned beneath the knee of a police officer. And just like in the Arbery case, a video that spread like wildfire across the internet and social media changed the course of justice.

"I CAN'T BREATHE": THE DEATH OF GEORGE FLOYD

On May 25, 2020, sometime around 8:00 pm, a forty-six-year-old Black man named George Floyd bought a pack of cigarettes with a twenty-dollar bill at Cup Foods, a store in Minneapolis, Minnesota. A store employee thought that the bill was fake and followed Floyd out to his car. He asked for the cigarettes back, and Floyd refused. The employee called the police, and reported that Floyd had passed a counterfeit bill. He added that Floyd seemed "awfully drunk" and was "acting erratically."[1]

Minneapolis police officers Alexander Kueng and Thomas Lane arrived at the scene first. Lane tapped on the window of Floyd's car and told him to show him his hands. When he didn't comply right away, Lane pulled his gun on Floyd, who complied and showed his hands. A brief struggle followed. Lane pulled Floyd from the car, handcuffed him, and placed him sitting on the curb. He told Floyd that he was acting erratically and asked if he had been using drugs. Floyd replied that he had been "hooping."[2] Kueng and Lane then told Floyd he was under arrest, walked him across the street, and leaned him against the door of a police car. Floyd said that he wasn't resisting arrest, but that he had claustrophobia and anxiety and that he didn't want to get into the police car. Kueng and Lane placed Floyd in the car and struggled with him in the back seat as Floyd said, "I can't breathe."[3]

Police officers Derek Chauvin and Tou Thao arrived in another car and Chauvin took command of the situation. Chauvin pulled Floyd from the car, placed him face down on the ground, and put his knee on his neck, while Floyd repeatedly said, "I can't breathe." Bystanders gathered and began videotaping the scene on their phones, while others told the officers to get off of Floyd and put him in the car. After six minutes with Chauvin's knee on his neck, Floyd lost consciousness. Chauvin took out a can of mace to spray at the crowd, while continuing to kneel on Floyd. The crowd yelled at the officers that Floyd was not responsive and to check his pulse. Lane checked his wrist but could not find a pulse. Chauvin continued to kneel on Floyd for another minute after an ambulance arrived. He kneeled on Floyd's neck for a total of nine minutes and twenty-nine seconds.[4] Floyd was taken by the ambulance to a hospital, during which cardiopulmonary resuscitation was attempted without success. He was declared dead at the hospital due to cardiopulmonary arrest.[5]

A statement from the Minneapolis Police Department initially said that George Floyd had resisted arrest and suffered medical distress, but did not mention Chauvin kneeling on his neck.[6] After video circulated on the internet showing Chauvin kneeling on Floyd's neck, the situation exploded. There were national calls for the arrest and prosecution of Chauvin, and for justice for George Floyd.[7, 8] Thousands of protestors quickly gathered at the site of his death, and later marched to the Minneapolis 3rd Precinct headquarters with signs that said BLACK LIVES MATTER and I CAN'T BREATHE.[9] Most of the protestors eventually left but a smaller group breached the fence around the police headquarters and began vandalizing property and throwing rocks and bottles at the police.[10] The police retreated to the rooftop and fired tear gas and rubber bullets at the crowd. The crowd burned a building across the street, vandalized property, and broke business store windows.[11] Over the next few days protests continued with the breaking of glass windows, vandalizing of property, and burning of businesses. A six-story apartment building under construction across the street from the police headquarters as well as the 3rd Precinct police headquarters itself were burned to the ground.[12] Over the coming weeks, protests spread throughout the United States and the world, making common cause with protests related to the death of Ahmaud Arbery in Brunswick, Georgia, and promoting the slogan "Black Lives Matter."[13] The protests broke out in 140 cities in the United States, and the National Guard was activated in twenty-one states. At least six people were killed during protests.[14]

As the situation in Minneapolis worsened, then President Trump delivered an ultimatum to protestors on May 29, 2020, stating that he would send in the military if they didn't stop.[15] He called the protestors "thugs" and said, "When the looting starts, the shooting starts." He further commented, "I can't stand back [and] watch this happen to a great American city."[16] He went on to criticize the Democratic mayor of the city. The same day, protests broke out in Atlanta, Georgia. The windows of multiple downtown businesses were broken, and protestors spray-painted graffiti on the CNN sign.[17] Protests broke out simultaneously in New York City, and after a crowd gathered outside the White House, President Trump retreated to an underground bunker.[18]

Meanwhile, violent incidents involving police occurred in several other American cities, further stoking the tension. In Buffalo, New York, on June 6, 2020, two police officers were shown on video shoving a seventy-five-year-old male protestor backward. He fell forcefully onto the concrete and appeared motionless on the ground with blood pouring out of his head. He was hospitalized with a head injury and the police officers were charged with felony assault. A grand jury later voted not to indict them.[19]

On June 12, 2020, a twenty-seven-year-old Black man named Rayshard Brooks fell asleep in his car while waiting in line in the drive-thru at a Wendy's restaurant in the Peoplestown neighborhood of Atlanta, Georgia.[20] Police were called, and they engaged in forty minutes of questioning and sobriety tests. When police went to make an arrest, Brooks hit the officer, grabbed a Taser, discharged it, and ran away. One of the officers discharged his Taser. Brooks turned back to fire his Taser, and then turned to run. The officer shot Brooks twice in the back, killing him.[21]

Just like in the Arbery and Floyd cases, bystanders took video footage of the whole thing. It was uploaded on social media, went viral, and everything exploded. An angry crowd gathered and burned down the Wendy's. A group of protestors took over the site and held it for several days. There were cries for justice for Brooks and calls to defund the police. Protests erupted throughout the city, and the mayor was reluctant to use force to close down the Wendy's site.[22] The air in Atlanta was filled with the sounds of sirens and helicopters overhead.

During this time, we were still mired in the pandemic, waiting for our return to the courts in the civil trial for the family of Susan Cox Powell while we watched what was going on in the news. Everything had changed since that trial had ground to a halt, what with school closings, businesses shutting down, calls to defund the police, and widespread protests in the streets.

Finally that summer, things moved forward. The judge was calling us back to resume the civil trial for the family of Susan Cox Powell.

JUSTICE ACHIEVED FOR SUSAN COX POWELL

On July 16, 2020, the trial for the family of Susan Cox Powell resumed. It was then that I learned that through everything that had gone on in the past five months, through the pandemic and its associated disruptions of their lives, not a single member of the jury had lost sight of the case.

Every single member of the jury—eleven men and one woman, our foreperson—returned to the trial when it resumed, albeit socially distanced and occasionally via Zoom. They were Black and white, in their forties and fifties, twenty-one, and pregnant. They were nurses, grandparents, and former members of the military. It was a mix of men and one woman who, I would later learn, had been united by a cause. Who had become a part of something bigger than themselves: justice.

On Friday, July 31, 2020, more than ten years after Susan Powell went missing and eight since Charlie and Braden were killed, the jury stepped into the socially distanced courtroom and handed in a $98.5 million judgment, finding the state liable for Charlie and Braden's deaths.[1] It was a shocking judgment, the likes of which had never been awarded by a jury in the state before.

Of course, during the trial, the team and I had no contact at all with the jury outside of our work in the courtroom, but afterward, we started to get to know them. We learned, as is common, that they'd more or less made up their minds early and perhaps during or shortly after opening statements.

Like I said earlier, the opening statement is the most important part of any trial.

I think that's one reason we got this verdict. Their minds were never changed. The jury immediately knew they had a mission. And that's why, after five months away, every one of them came back to finish their job.

We held a luncheon for the jury in Tacoma after the verdict. And it was amazing to get to know them, to hear their thoughts on the case, and how they wanted to work together in the future. They want to be part of the solution. They want to change laws so that kids are not put in this situation again.

The state has to care. The state has to take responsibility. The state needs to understand that they have a duty to these kids. Somebody needed to tell them: if you remove a child from his parents' home to keep him safe, you have a duty to keep him safe. And that's what this jury did.

We had never had a jury like this.

I originally called this book *Amanda Knox and Justice in the Age of Judgment*. I wanted to explain the true story of what happened to Amanda Knox and how she was hung out to dry by the tabloids, social media, and a public that treated her case like a reality TV series. But as I began to tell the story, as the years went by and cases came into my life and I relived others, I realized the story was a lot bigger than just Amanda.

When people think of justice today, they often think of injustice. They think about innocent people killed at the hands of people on the front lines of the criminal justice system. They think about the wrongfully convicted. And they think about the difference between how a white man and a Black man are treated by the justice system.

The jury in this case knew they were asked to rise to the occasion. They knew they had a unique opportunity. Not just to get justice to Susan, Charlie, or Braden. No amount of money can bring them back. They weren't even fighting for justice for Chuck or Judy Cox, my clients, who know that no matter the size of the judgment, it won't bring their grandsons back to their house or let them see their daughter again.

But the jury knew there was still hope that justice could be served for the thousands of other families who find themselves caught in the same system as were

Charlie and Braden. They knew they couldn't right every wrong. But they knew they had a chance, this time, to do something. And they did.

In a world of chaos, mistrust, sadness, divisiveness, and loss, they proved that while justice is complicated, takes time, and is rarely satisfying, it is still possible. While our jury labored away sequestered from the media, the storm continued to rage across the nation in the aftermath of the George Floyd killing. Black Lives Matter (BLM) protestors clashed with police and right-wing militia members. Shortly after our jury returned its verdict, things came to a head on a fateful night in Kenosha, Wisconsin, when a seventeen-year-old boy answered a post on Facebook calling people to protect businesses from rioting BLM protestors.

KYLE RITTENHOUSE

On the evening of August 25, 2020, a third night of angry, destructive protests raged on in Kenosha, Wisconsin. Jacob Blake, a young Black man, had been shot by a white police officer days earlier. He was left permanently paralyzed.[1] As was the case in George Floyd's and Ahmad Arbery's deaths, bystanders captured the shooting on cellphone video.

Protestors flooded the streets of Kenosha. Peaceful protests were the norm during the day, but riots and arson took place when night fell. In response, authorities brought in hundreds of National Guard troops while right-wing militia members and others flocked to the city's core to combat the protesters. Kyle Rittenhouse was among them.[2]

The seventeen-year-old white male from just across the border in Antioch, Illinois, had spent the previous night staying with a friend. The same friend had previously purchased the teen a semi-automatic, AR-15 style assault rifle, which Rittenhouse could not buy due to the fact that he was underage, as "a favor." The pair drove to the site of the ongoing riots, joining a group of armed men who had organized on Facebook and claimed they had gathered to protect businesses from rioters. Rittenhouse and others would later assert they had been asked to defend a particular car dealership that had suffered heavy damage the night before, although the dealership would later deny that they had asked for Rittenhouse and others to help.[3]

That night, demonstrators clashed with police and National Guard members amidst a barrage of fireworks, tear gas, and rubber bullets. Self-appointed militia members and protestors squared off in several skirmishes as the evening wore on.[4]

Rittenhouse was captured on multiple videos, including several where he was interviewed as he stood guard outside the car dealership. Throughout the evening he was seen talking to police officers and offering medical aid, and told a reporter: "People are getting injured and our job is to protect this business, [. . .] [a]nd part of my job is to also help people. If there is somebody hurt, I'm running into harm's way. That's why I have my rifle—because I can protect myself, obviously. But I also have my med kit."[5]

Rittenhouse left the dealership and claimed he was looking for people to help, then tried returning to the dealership but was blocked by police vehicles. Moments later, video captured a thirty-six-year-old unarmed Kenosha man named Joseph Rosenbaum chasing Rittenhouse across a parking lot as the teen tried to leave the area. Rittenhouse later testified he heard another man shout to Rosenbaum to "get him and kill him." Another person fired a shot in the air, prompting Rittenhouse to stop running and aim his gun at Rosenbaum. Rittenhouse claimed he hoped to deter him.[6]

Rosenbaum had a lengthy criminal record, a troubled past, and bipolar disorder, and had been discharged earlier that day from an inpatient psychiatric hospital after a manic episode. Witnesses reported he was acting erratically. Earlier that evening he told Rittenhouse that if he found him alone he would kill him.[7, 8]

Rosenbaum advanced toward Rittenhouse, throwing a plastic bag filled with socks, underwear, and deodorant at him and attempting to take his rifle. Rittenhouse fired four shots and killed Rosenbaum.[9] After standing in shock over the lifeless body, Rittenhouse ran toward nearby police cars as a small group chased him.

A scuffle ensued as protestors accosted Rittenhouse. The teen tripped and fell to the ground. One protestor kicked him, and Rittenhouse fired several shots but missed. Twenty-six-year-old Anthony Huber tried to disarm him with his skateboard, swinging at his head and neck while grabbing for the assault rifle. Rittenhouse fired one shot, killing Huber.[10]

A third man, twenty-six-year-old Gaige Grosskreutz, had been videotaping the protests for the ACLU and was carrying a handgun. When he pointed it at Rittenhouse, the teen shot him in the arm. Grosskreutz survived.[11]

All three victims were white and were frequent protestors around the Milwaukee, Wisconsin, area in the aftermath of the death of George Floyd.[12]

Rittenhouse, like the McMichaels in the Arbery case, claimed self-defense.

Rittenhouse was charged with multiple counts of murder for the deaths of Rosenbaum and Huber. The story was everywhere in the news and on social media. He immediately became a lightning rod for political speech. He was hailed as a hero by gun advocates and conservatives, who saw his actions as justified in pushing back against protestors who were rioting and destroying American cities and defending himself. Many others saw him as a vigilante and were horrified to see a seventeen-year-old openly carrying a semi-automatic rifle in the streets and killing protestors.[13] Lin Wood, a well-known attorney from Atlanta, Georgia, offered to represent him. It came as no surprise as Wood had come to specialize in defamation cases, and in recent years, had become a champion of right-wing causes. Wood believed in QAnon and was one of several attorneys advocating that the 2020 election had been stolen from President Trump. He also claimed that he was God.[14] Rittenhouse later called him "insane" in an interview and dropped him for alternative counsel.[15]

Conflicting reports on the news and social media further fanned the flames and added to the national division surrounding the Rittenhouse case. Many rushed to judgment and spread inaccurate reports about what happened before all the evidence could be presented in court.

The falsehoods ranged from early reports that Rittenhouse had killed two Black men, that his mother had driven him to Kenosha and dropped him off with his gun, that he had been the aggressor, and that he was a white supremacist.

Journalist Glenn Greenwald lambasted mainstream media outlets for reporting incomplete information, misinformation, or outright falsehood about the case in an interview with Fox News:

If you relied on the media, you should feel betrayed. You know, I'm somebody, before I was a journalist, who worked as a lawyer inside courtrooms for more than a decade . . . So I waited before forming a judgment, and when I did sit down to watch the trial, I was infuriated that everything I had been taught to believe by the media was radically different than the facts of the case as they developed.[16]

As I covered the case and provided analysis for several networks, it was clear what was being reported diverged a fair bit from many of the facts. All the noise around Rittenhouse as a political symbol obscured the real issues involved in his case. The key element was the legal question of whether Rittenhouse was acting in self-defense. Once again, a controversial case found itself in the spotlight, and I tried regularly to encourage viewers to focus on the evidence. Thankfully, the trial was televised and if people took the time to watch, they could see our justice system in action, and separate fact from fiction.

To many who didn't watch closely, the Rittenhouse case looked a lot like Arbery's: vigilantes taking the law into their own hands with deadly results. But the two cases were in fact very different.

That would become clear when the evidence was presented in the two cases that proceeded almost in tandem. But that would have to wait, as another trial would come before them. That was the prosecution of Derek Chauvin for the murder of George Floyd.

JUSTICE FOR GEORGE FLOYD

As the Rittenhouse case moved through the system, the legal process surrounding the death of George Floyd moved ahead in parallel in Minneapolis. An autopsy had concluded that Floyd's heart stopped while he was being restrained and that his death was a homicide caused by cardiopulmonary arrest "complicating law enforcement subdual, restraint and neck compression."[1] The autopsy had further revealed that Floyd had fentanyl and methamphetamine in his system, and that he suffered from coronary artery disease, with a 90 percent narrowing of one of his coronary arteries.[2] Derek Chauvin attempted to make a plea bargain but the deal was overruled by then US Attorney General William Barr. Chauvin was charged with second-degree murder and manslaughter and the other officers with aiding and abetting murder and manslaughter. The family of George Floyd filed a civil lawsuit against the city of Minneapolis and later settled for $27 million dollars.

Derek Chauvin's televised trial in Minneapolis, Minnesota, went from March 8 to April 19, 2021, and I covered it for Court TV. There had been intense public outcry over his initial arrest, and just as much for his conviction.

I had seen the video. It was clear Chauvin was at least in part responsible for Floyd's death. But as an attorney and legal analyst, my colleagues and I debated whether Chauvin could get a fair trial.

I saw two potentially major flaws in the way the trial was handled that could have had significant impacts on the jury. First, the jury was only partially sequestered. They got to go home at night until they were sequestered in a hotel for their deliberations. Although the judge ordered them to avoid reading or watching anything about the trial outside of the courtroom, there was no way to guarantee that.

The defense argued that given the massive media coverage, it's highly improbable they hadn't heard details about the case and formed opinions prior to their deliberations. But the judge sided with prosecutors, who successfully argued that in this day and age, there's no way to avoid all media.

The other potential issue I saw was the announcement of the $27 million settlement between the city and Floyd's family during the trial. If any of the jurors heard about it, they could have easily perceived it as an admission of guilt, which could have biased their verdict.

While Chauvin was convicted in the court of public opinion before the trial even started, the jury convicted him of all charges on April 20, 2021, and he was sentenced to twenty-two and a half years in prison.[3]

In the end, I was satisfied the trial was as fair as possible. There was no realistic way to find an entire jury of people who'd never heard anything about the case, even if you moved the trial to another jurisdiction. Yes, there were medical reasons that could have contributed to Floyd's death. But the evidence was overwhelming (most notably the video) and proved Chauvin was guilty of murder beyond a reasonable doubt. We could all see that.

But we had two more major trials looming on the horizon. The cases of Arbery and Rittenhouse looked similar to most of the public. Armed vigilantes striking out in self-defense. The public was confused about what differentiated them. In my opinion these were in fact two very different cases. It would take presenting the evidence in a court of law to make that clear.

TWO DIFFERENT JURY TRIALS, TWO DIFFERENT OUTCOMES

The Rittenhouse and Arbery trials played out in tandem at almost the same time with two very different results, one verdict coming right after the other.

I covered both trials for CNN, MSNBC, and Dan Abrams's Law and Crime Network. The Rittenhouse trial for murder got started in Kenosha, Wisconsin, on November 1, 2021. Rittenhouse came under further fire for his behavior prior to the trial, with video emerging of Rittenhouse drinking beer in a bar with members of the Proud Boys, a right-wing group that participated in the assault on the United States Capitol on January 6, 2021.[1] The defense was able to suppress that video as unduly prejudicial to their client. The judge also ruled that calling Rosenbaum and Huber "victims" would be unduly prejudicial because it would imply he was guilty and responsible for the deaths before the evidence was fully presented.[2]

During the trial the prosecutors tried to portray Rittenhouse as a reckless instigator who had inserted himself in the protests and shot people without provocation.[3] The defense argued that Rittenhouse's actions were in self-defense and were consistent with Wisconsin law which states that if someone "reasonably believes that such force is necessary to prevent imminent death or great bodily harm to himself," then they are justified in their actions and have no duty to retreat.[4] Crucial to the defense were witnesses who testified that Rosenbaum threatened to kill Rittenhouse, and grabbed for his gun shortly before being shot. Huber also hit Rittenhouse with his skateboard, and Grosskreutz aimed a gun at Rittenhouse.[5] The trial was televised, and the nation got to watch Judge Bruce Schroeder speculate on legal matters, Roman history, and the Bible, show personal text messages from friends and family complaining about his rulings, and encourage the court-room to applaud a defense witness who was a veteran because it was Veterans Day.[6] The judge came under fire on social media and in the press, with critics accusing him of bias and favoring the defense. Social and traditional media highlighted the judge's poor demeanor in the court, highlighting several racist or xenophobic comments Schroeder made during the course of the trial. While the critiques were likely valid, the influence the media held continued to add to the general mael-strom of chaos about the proceeding.

After twenty-six hours of deliberation, on November 19, 2021, the jury found Rittenhouse not guilty on all counts.[7] The reaction to the verdict seemed to bend the justice system to the breaking point. Critics argued the case demonstrated a failing justice system including an activist judge who tipped the scales in favor of the defense. Like many, Democratic strategist Max Burns called the verdict "wrong" and questioned whether the jury system stilled "worked," without offer-ing any specific legal points to back up his statements.[8] He pointed to polls show-ing declining confidence of Americans in the judicial system, especially the Supreme Court.[9] California Governor Gavin Newsom said that the verdict sent the signal that "armed vigilantes" could do whatever they wanted.[10] Republican Senator Ron Johnson of Wisconsin, echoing the view of many on the right that his actions were justified in the face of rioting that had gotten out of control in American cities, said "justice had been served."[11] As prosecutor Thomas Binger told the jury before their deliberations, "people look at this case and see what they want to see."[12]

While the Rittenhouse trial was still going on, the trial of Travis and Gregory McMichael and William Bryan for the killing of Ahmaud Arbery got underway in Brunswick, Georgia. The trial started on November 5, 2021, but since the time of the killing the Georgia State Legislature had largely gutted the citizen's arrest law dating back to the Civil War that the defendants had invoked.[13] During jury selec-tion, many of the black potential jurors were excluded based on their stated belief that the trial would not be fair, and the final jury consisted of only one black man, two white men, and nine white women.[14] There were fears the racial imbalance would prejudice the jury. The trial certainly had plenty of racial overtones. It was attended by many prominent Black figures, including the Reverend Jesse Jackson, prompting a defense attorney to state in court: "I don't want any Black pastors in this courtroom." The judge found that it was a public trial and all could attend, and the attorney's comments caused an uproar resulting in other prominent black pastors, including the Reverend Al Sharpton, to travel to Brunswick to attend the trial.[15]

The lawyers for the defense argued that their clients suspected Arbery of committing a crime and therefore were justified in making a citizen's arrest and acted in self-defense in shooting him. Their problem was that Arbery was only seen on security footage at an open construction site, not committing any crime, and later just running down the street,[16] which witnesses testified he did for exercise. Their argument for a citizen's arrest was undermined by the fact that the only crime that had occurred in the neighborhood recently was the theft of Travis McMichael's gun, which he had unwisely left in an unlocked truck in his driveway.[17, 18] The footage taken by Bryan showed the McMichaels pursuing Arbery and cornering him with their truck, with Travis McMichael saying he had pinned him "like a rat," before shooting him.[19] The prosecution argued that "it's not self-defense if you started it."[20] Although many called it a racially motivated killing, the prosecution did not bring up race as a factor until late in the trial, possibly due to the mostly white makeup of the jury.[21]

After eleven hours of deliberation, the jury came back with a verdict on November 24, 2021. They found Travis McMichael guilty on all charges: malice murder, four counts of felony murder, two counts of aggravated assault, false imprisonment, and criminal attempt to commit a felony. Gregory McMichael was found guilty on all charges but malice murder.[22] William Bryan was found guilty of three counts of felony murder, one count of aggravated assault, false imprisonment, and criminal attempt to commit a felony. Bryan was cleared on the charge of malice murder, felony murder involving aggravated assault with a firearm, and the count of aggravated assault with a firearm. Following the verdict, Rev. Al Sharpton introduced Arbery's parents to the crowd outside the courtroom and led the crowd in prayer, with many praising the outcome as a victory for justice.[23]

Media attention was intense for both the Rittenhouse and Arbery cases, as it was for the George Floyd case. Opinions were sharply divided, especially for the Rittenhouse case. Once again social media played an outsized role, shaping public opinion and ultimately the outcomes, with cell phone footage presenting a different reality of what happened than that of the Minneapolis police report or the report of retired policeman Gregory McMichael in Arbery's shooting. With Rittenhouse, widespread video supported defense arguments that he had been threatened and acted in self-defense.

The Rittenhouse and Arbery verdicts on the surface both looked like cases of vigilantism. They came one right after the other in a tense atmosphere threatening possible civil unrest depending on the outcomes, so it was difficult for many to focus on and absorb what was going on in the legal arena. Public opinion was putting intense pressure on the judicial system. I had first seen this dynamic start to have an outsized impact in the Amanda Knox cases and other cases covered in this book, and these more recent cases showed the exponential impact on justice in the age of judgement with so many more outlets online and on the air, where people make snap judgements about guilt based on what they see on social media, and have far more channels to amplify their opinions. We've talked about what's called confirmation bias and other cognitive distortions throughout the book. And as I've mentioned several times, this rush to judgement regardless of facts undermines our judicial system.

Regardless of people's opinions, the law is the law. In the Rittenhouse case, the jury determined Rittenhouse had a right to self-defense under Wisconsin law. As I repeatedly reminded viewers, the state had to prove the absence of self-defense beyond a reasonable doubt. The defense convinced the jury Rittenhouse had a legal right to be there, was threatened with potentially deadly force, had a right to return deadly force to protect himself, and had no duty to retreat. The state simply couldn't disprove that beyond a reasonable doubt. The verdict was the right one based on the evidence.

In Arbery, the facts were much different. The defendants did not have a right to chase down Arbery and accost him. They argued they had a right to make a citizen's arrest, but the law prohibited that. Arbery had committed no crime. They pinned him "like a rat" and murdered him with a shotgun. The law clearly stated the McMichaels didn't have the right to use deadly force because they acted as the first aggressor. And the law made clear they couldn't claim self-defense. The McMichaels lynched Ahmaud Arbery.

In the end, justice was served in both cases.

The evidence and the law were on Rittenhouse's side. The evidence and the law were against the McMichaels.

If you're angry with the outcome, don't blame the justice system. It worked. You should focus on changing the law. But the facts are the facts, and the law is the law. The Rittenhouse verdict wasn't wrong. The McMichaels verdict wasn't wrong.

Here, the media didn't manage to usurp the power of the courts. Perhaps it was a testament to good lawyering; perhaps it was a fluke. In any event, social media shone a light on each proceeding. In the Rittenhouse case, politics ran amok online, but the verdict was fair. In the McMichaels' case, social media put pressure on a corrupt prosecutor's office—the net positive resulted, again, in a fair verdict.

These two cases are a testament to the idea that new media can exist alongside justice; judgment online or in the media need not touch the law. Opinions were amplified, but they did not drown out the voice of the courts.

JUSTICE, EVEN IN THE AGE OF JUDGMENT

It took a while, but ultimately Amanda Knox and Raffaele Sollecito got justice.

If there is a moral to be gleaned from their story, it's that when prosecutors run off the rails, no system, no matter how solid, can totally prevent the damage they cause. We saw that with the Italian prosecutor Giuliano Mignini, with his bizarre right-wing Catholic beliefs and conspiracy theories about Masons and satanic cults. But we saw that in America as well, with Michael Nifong, who threw justice out the window in his ambition to be elected district attorney of Durham County, North Carolina. That ambition that would see him exploit preconceived biases about race, class, and privilege. We saw that with Jackie Johnson, the district attorney of Brunswick, Georgia, who engaged in small town cronyism and covered for dangerous police until it led to tragedy—and with the stories about satanic killings leaked to the press in the case of the West Memphis Three.

Prosecutors' missteps, misconceptions, and misconduct—when coupled with an information-hungry media—can be devastating. For Amanda, it was.

In the end, it was the first two guilty verdicts that sealed Amanda's fate in the court of public opinion. When you talk to the average person in Italy, England, or the United States, they typically think of Amanda as a killer. Some think she's wanted back in Italy, others think she got off for murder. She's been free every day since she got out of prison, but she'll forever be looked at with skepticism because of the recklessness of the Italian police and prosecutors and the international media eagerly spreading their lies to the entire world.

As Amanda said in the latest Netflix documentary about the case, you are either innocent or you are guilty. You either killed your roommate and friend with a knife in cold blood, or you didn't. You can't be "sort of guilty" or someone who "probably did it." You either committed the crime or you didn't.[1]

We all have fears that we've carried along from childhood. The bogeyman who is hiding under the bed, or the thing lurking in the forest just beyond our parents' home. Nightmares that wake us up in the night and make us afraid to fall asleep again. It's easy to put the source of our fears on someone else—the movie we watched too close to bedtime, the storybook read to us in primary school, the tales our older friends told us on the playground.

That same inclination—to pass blame, to find an outlet for discomfort or uncertainty—is why people pass judgment in the court of public opinion. That's why they flock to Twitter, blogs, and Facebook groups about the terrifying cases outlined in this book. When we find an online community that shares our biases and prejudices, it brings a sense of relief. Suddenly judgments about horrible crimes, our political beliefs, our fears are legitimized. Of course, it's nothing more than a feedback loop—it's based on confirmation biases and preconceived notions. It's called scapegoating.

But that's not how this country is supposed to work. It's not how our courts are supposed to work. Yet, the court of public opinion continues to encroach on the American justice system.

Believing what we want to believe, making determinations based on what we want to be true—rather than what we can prove to be true—that's not the system we want. It won't affirm the principle of innocence; it cannot prove guilt—not in the way our system is designed to demand it.

That's what Amanda Knox got in Italy: a belief of guilt. A public condemnation—a verdict by the press. It's what the West Memphis Three got in West Memphis, Arkansas, and the Duke lacrosse players got in Durham, North Carolina. And it's what, too often, the rest of us are doing in the courtroom of public opinion. When we click, tape, tap, tweet, and listen, we consume and, in part, consent to the manner and method by which media constructs belief. We turn away from the courts; we chip away at the structures built, in theory, to deliver just judgment. We replace the court with our own normative, moral frameworks.

We don't want angry mobs to administer justice. Blood feuds never work. Nothing is resolved in trials by fire. We need to stop fanning the flames.

True justice is not administered by the court of public opinion. It's administered by properly conducted courts of law with judges, prosecutors, and defense counsels with a strong sense of service, who believe in the integrity of the laws and have a moral commitment to uphold these ideals.

In this age of judgment, the preservation of justice is imperative. I've had one foot in each arena for decades; I know the media, know courtrooms. As I saw media—social and traditional—bleed into the justice system, I knew I had to gain a sense of control. I had been down before: men tried to elbow me out of court, others refused to envision a woman in positions I sought to hold. I had survived my mother's death; I had pivoted on a lark to welcome new and difficult people, places, and career paths.

Thirty-eight years of practice lends perspective. Judgment is best left for the courts—but I know how frequently judgment is moved by the vagaries of life. Social media is a lightning rod for traditional media stories; without a clear and assertive approach to get out in front of an issue, judgment will follow without regard for the boundaries the law sets.

We need lawyers who are familiar with this new era of justice—more so, we need lawyers who are willing and able to adapt. If I've been one thing, I've been flexible; I've been willing to change shape to fit in (or stand out) when I realized it was the best option. I withstood the discomfort—and managed the pride—of being one of the few female trial lawyers on the job in the '80s. I rallied support for Amanda Knox despite the media storm and online bloggers and forum posters hell-bent on battering her. I found justice for Susan Cox, for her late children—fought the State all through the years the family spent in darkness.

I wasn't afraid of a challenge. I wasn't afraid to start again and again: I booked TV slots in the 1980s and 1990s, showed up and showed out. I got uncomfortable until I was comfortable. When social media began its rise to prominence, I plugged in there, too. It's what's necessary. To know the environment where misconceptions can take root, we must immerse ourselves in the mediums that spread them. Attorneys must be prepared to guide the narratives—to act as arbiters for the truth, to speak out and give voice to the voiceless, to preserve, at the very least, the possibility of just judgment in the courts. Your honor, ladies and gentlemen of the jury, I rest my case.

POSTSCRIPT

STILLWATER

I got a call from my father in the summer of 2021. Didn't ask how I was doing. Just jumped straight to the point.

"Did you see *Stillwater*?"

"No. What's that?" I asked.

"It's a movie. It's about Amanda Knox. You should watch it."

That interchange should tell you everything you need to know about the film released in July 2021. It's about an American woman who goes to Italy to study, and gets accused of killing her roommate. The story is supposedly fictional, and stars Matt Damon.

But the fictional part doesn't pass the smell test. Everyone who hears the story outline says, "Hey, that's about the Amanda Knox case." Even the filmmaker admits it was inspired by Amanda's story.

But here's the kicker. In the movie version, she's guilty. And once again Amanda was vilified despite her long-ago exoneration.

Amanda was understandably upset. As she once said, "You can't be sort of guilty. You're either innocent, or guilty." She took to social media and published an essay in *The Atlantic* ("Who Owns Amanda Knox?")[1] angrily stating that the film's producers had not consulted her or got any input on what, by rights, was her story:

Does my name belong to me? Does my face? What about my life? My story? Why is my name used to refer to events I had no hand in? I return to these questions again and again because others continue to profit off my identity, and my trauma, without my consent. [2]

Stillwater was directed by Tom McCarthy and, in addition to Damon, stars Abigail Breslin in, heck, the role of Amanda, since the director said the film was "directly inspired by the Amanda Knox saga."[3] In the movie, she has a sexual relationship with her roommate, echoing the sex crazed orgy story that originally surrounded the death of Meredith Kercher. Then she tells someone to get rid of her, and he kills her instead of just chasing her away.

Even after she wrote the essay, the producers didn't bother to call her up and say, "Hey, sorry we didn't run it by you." Somebody in Hollywood thought it would be a good idea to make a film about that case involving the American girl accused of murder in Italy, they threw a script together, and made her guilty in the end.

> *By fictionalizing away my innocence, by erasing the role of the authorities in my wrongful conviction, McCarthy reinforces an image of me as guilty. And with Damon's star power, both are sure to profit handsomely off this imagined version of "the Amanda Knox saga" that will leave plenty of viewers wondering, "Maybe the real-life Amanda was involved somehow" and Googling whether the film's story is true.*[4]

Stillwater is yet another example of judgment in the court of public opinion. In this case the executioner was Hollywood. More troubling, perhaps, is that Amanda's access to the same type of media that once ridiculed and accused her—print journalism—wasn't enough to offset the allure of a star-studded film. Popular culture won out, proving the truth in Amanda's words: who owns her?

But we don't have to put up with that. What felt to Amanda like a total loss of agency and belonging is, in theory, avoidable. We can take back control, and send "judgment" back to where it belongs, the courts. Our courts are built to act rationally and without corruption or bias. They are designed to view the accused as innocent unless proven guilty using evidence that shows guilt beyond a reasonable doubt.

Of course, it is not possible to avoid the media entirely. I know that acutely. Still, its power can be harnessed before it is capable of doing harm. Imagine if Amanda or Frances Farmer had access to a megaphone, a press bullpen, before their stories went live: their lives might not have been so dramatically and irreversibly misrepresented.

When I think back on my career, I am unable to avoid the realities of my status. I remember people who tried to change the course of my story: the professor whose unwelcome advances chased me from campus, the men who tried to reduce me to nothing but a skirt. Unlike Amanda, Frances, and Susan Cox, I didn't experience a traumatic flashpoint where the media co-opted my story. As a result, I sought out situations where I could use media to shape not only my own narrative—but to reshape the stories lobbed at women who seemed fixed in a troubling situation.

To know command of a courtroom is but one iteration of empowerment. To understand how to wield—or avoid—the clutches of modern media is another. Coupling the two together is essential in this age of judgment—one where everything is a stage, one where everyone has a microphone.

Belief, as I've mentioned, is a mutable thing. It can and does change from person to person; it is a poor barometer for innocence or guilt. Because the nexus between belief and judgment is often what the public reads, listens to, or scrolls through on their morning commute, a keen understanding of the court of public opinion is the only way to reserve justice for the courts.

My story is my own: from the little girl with windswept hair running down Fishtrap Road to the young woman fishing burning cigarettes out of the trash can in a judge's chambers to the advocate in a pressed black suit before the court. Everyone deserves that agency, that autonomy. Judgment should be left to the courts—but until then, I'll continue my fight for clients' earnest representation in the press. The story is half the battle.

I rest my case.

APPENDIX

WELCOME TO THE FREAK SHOW—
ANALYZING AMANDA'S ORDEAL

This is Doug Bremner, Anne's brother. I am a doctor, like our dad, and a professor at Emory University in Atlanta, Georgia. I'm actually a psychiatrist, like my dad. I first started paying attention to the Amanda Knox case during Christmas of 2008, when I was at my parents' home with my wife and two kids. They had made white sweaters with Christmas trees on them for everyone in the extended family to wear, and we were having brunch at their house in Olympia, Washington, which is right on the water of the southern Puget Sound.

I had just written a book called *Before You Take That Pill: Why the Drug Industry May Be Bad For Your Health: Risks and Side Effects You Won't Find on the Label of Commonly Prescribed Prescription Medications, Vitamins, and Supplements.*[1] It derived from my work as an expert witness in legal cases involving drug safety—specifically an acne drug called Accutane—and how it was associated with suicide and depression.[2] My publishers urged me to start a blog in order to publicize the book. Initially I blogged about scandals in the pharmaceutical industry, but later, for reasons I describe soon, I started blogging about the Amanda Knox case.[3]

At the Christmas brunch with the extended family, we got to meet John Henry Browne, my sister's fiancé. Browne was the famous and flamboyant lawyer from Seattle who had defended Ted Bundy, among other famous clients. At the time, he had long flowing hair and granite good looks that made quite an impression at the brunch. John's client, Ted Bundy, murdered dozens of women by pretending to have broken limbs and using other duplicitous means to lure them into his car, and then to their death. John later wrote a book about his experiences as a lawyer defending clients in high-profile cases. The book is called *The Devil's Defender: My Odyssey Through American Criminal Justice from Ted Bundy to the Kandahar Massacre.*[4]

Although John Henry was the celebrity headliner of the day, what struck me was listening to my sister, Anne, talk about the Amanda Knox case, which had been in the Seattle newspapers. She was talking about how the police had totally screwed up the investigation, how the collection of evidence was a joke, that it was probably contaminated, that there was no evidence against Amanda, and that the Italian police were wrong. My instinctive reaction was: "Why do you have to assume the cops were screwups just because they were Italian? And if the cops said someone was guilty, why shouldn't we believe them?"

Shortly after that, I heard my sister on KIRO Radio in Seattle in a "debate" with Barbie Latza Nadeau, a woman who had written a book about the Knox case, *Angel Face: Sex, Murder, and the Inside Story of Amanda Knox.*[5] They got into a shouting match about the facts of the case and certain things Barbie had done that my sister was upset about, so I decided I needed to read the book, assuming that the author knew what she was talking about and had the smoking gun proving Amanda's guilt. The story was of interest to me for a number of reasons, including the fact that it was a Seattle story, and for reasons I explain later, because it included Italy.

As I read the book, I made a list of facts that were presented as evidence of Amanda's guilt. However, I soon began to notice these "facts" lacked any corroborating evidence.

Internet warriors quickly divided themselves into two camps, the innocentisti—those who thought Amanda was innocent—and the colpevisti—those who thought she was guilty. At least that's what they called themselves. Calling yourself "colpevisti" seemed a little pretentious, so we just called them "guilters."

Two main websites for the guilters were quickly established, *Perugia Murder Files*, or PMF. The other website was *True Justice for Meredith Kercher*, or TJFMK.

One of the main themes of the Amanda Knox case was the divisions between different groups, whether it was different nationalities, ethnicities, or linguistic groups.

My wife, Viola, is a native-born Italian citizen, and both our children, Sabina and Dylan, are citizens as well. Sabina spent a year in Verbania, Lombardia, Italy, as part of the American Foreign Service (AFS) foreign exchange program, and Dylan spent a year going to high school in Bolzano, Trentino-Alto Adige, Italy, while living with his host family in the nearby town of Appiano sulla Strada del Vino. At the time, I was practicing Italian in order to apply for Italian citizenship, which requires proficiency in the language. To that purpose, I had hired an Italian tutor, and initially we studied Dante's *Inferno* together. No offense to fans of Italian culture, but I found that task a little boring, and was having trouble following what was going on down there in Dante's hellhole. The Massei report had recently come out summarizing the motivations behind the initial judgments on the Amanda Knox case, and since it was in Italian, I thought it would be a useful service to translate it into English, which was something I could do with my Italian tutor to improve my language skills. At that time, I was still under the impression that my sister Anne was nuts and that if the Perugia police thought Amanda was guilty, she probably was.

In the spring of 2009, I started my translation and applied for access to the TJFMK website so I could post my translations of the report. What a surprise when I wasn't granted access! I was convinced I must have done something wrong. It turns out that the site controllers had little interest in letting me post my translations. As a scientist, whenever someone obstructs the free flow of information, that raises your suspicions.

I made a list of questions I had about what had been written about the case and then followed it up with research. Most of the "facts" created by the prosecutor and police and leaked to the press were molded to fit the narrative they were trying to make for Amanda's guilt. Everything I write here was published in the media at one point or another as fact.

Raffaele Sollecito and Amanda Knox said they were at home the night of the murder watching the movie *Amelié* that he had downloaded on his computer. The police said he was lying because they didn't find a download on his computer. The fact is that the police took several computer hard drives from Raffaele's apartment and then destroyed them when they plugged them into the wrong power source. So there is no way they would have been able to see what was downloaded, and therefore no way to verify this statement.

Much was made of several witnesses who should have been discarded from the outset as unreliable. A homeless man named Antonio Curatolo supposedly saw Amanda and Raffaele walking through Piazza Grimana where he lived on a park bench at 10:30 p.m. the night of the murder.[6] He said he saw people in Halloween costumes and disco buses that night. A woman named Nara Capezzali who lived in a nearby apartment said she heard a scream at around 11:00 or 11:30 p.m. and then heard three or four people running.[7] She said she was upset all night.

The police and prosecutor needed a timeline of 11:30 p.m. for the murder to fit with the time when Amanda and Raffaele didn't have an alibi, other than each other. The night of the murder was November 1, which is the day after Halloween. In spite of the fact that the police were aware that discos are closed on November 1 (All Souls Day, a somber holiday) they let this testimony go forward. Curatolo was also using heroin at the time, had been arrested for drug-related charges, and was trying to plea bargain. He had already offered false testimony in other cases in order to get himself out of trouble. Like the key witness in the West Memphis Three case, Curatolo was clearly lying to keep himself out of jail. It worked, but he later died of a drug overdose.

The Italian magazine *Oggi* reported that Nara was hard of hearing and had recently been in a psychiatric hospital.[8] If Nara stayed up because she was upset, why didn't she hear the rock hit the window (as part of the supposed "staged break-in") after the scream? Also, there were hundreds of people in the area but no one else heard a scream. Medical evidence I discuss in more detail later also proved that Meredith was deceased by 11:00 p.m. This evidence, however, was simply ignored, while Mignini produced a doctor who provided false medical testimony to support his timeline.

The police and prosecutor and/or media made various claims related to Amanda and Raffaele attempting to cover their tracks. The police were said to have found Amanda and Raffaele standing outside the house with a mop and bucket when they arrived, implying that they had cleaned up the crime scene. There were also claims, leaked to the press, that a receipt for bleach was found. A store owner claimed he saw Amanda buying cleaning supplies. The mixed DNA of Amanda and Meredith was found on the sink. Luminol is a chemical that reveals the residue of blood, even after cleaning. Luminol testing would later reveal that there was no clean-up at the scene, and no bleach or blood was found on the knife that the prosecution claimed was the murder weapon. The famous receipt for bleach was later shown to be a receipt for pizza. There was no evidence that Amanda and Raffaele were found standing outside with a mop and bucket; this proved to be a lie generated on the internet. The store owner was paid by a tabloid for his story, which he reported a month later. Another store employee said that Amanda was not there buying cleaning supplies. It is normal for mixed DNA to occur when people live in the same house.

The prosecutor, Giuliano Mignini, had several pet theories that had no basis in scientific fact, but which unfortunately continue to be reiterated in the Italian press to this day. The body was discovered covered by a blanket. He said this showed that a woman committed the murder. But there is no scientific evidence that women are more likely than men to cover the bodies of their victims.

He also said that Amanda's DNA was on a knife they claimed was the murder weapon and that a bloody footprint at the murder scene matched Raffaele. After he was embarrassed by a TV station showing a photo that demonstrated the bloody footprint did not belong to Raffaele, he rushed back to the murder scene forty-six days later and "found" a bra clasp in a different location from where it had originally been photographed.[9] The bra clasp contained a very small amount of DNA, which Mignini claimed was Sollecito's, but which was later determined by outside experts to be there due to contamination.[10] Based on video footage, the bra clasp was literally kicked around the crime scene for the forty-six days before it was "discovered," and in the course of that time, it went from white to black.[11]

The police also claimed there was no evidence of rape on the autopsy, although there had been recent sexual contact, which led to the theory of the sex game gone awry. They supported this with the idea that Guede could not have killed Meredith alone. They also said a broken window was evidence that Amanda had staged a break-in, because broken glass was found on top of clothes on the floor, which meant that the breaking of the window was staged and was done after the room was "tossed." Since the other house members had their rooms disturbed, this meant that the perpetrators knew each other. The Italians have continued to hold onto these myths, even as recently as 2020, when a psychologist and self-styled "criminologist" named Roberta Bruzzone opined that Guede could not act alone, and the fact that the break-in was staged proved that he was working with others he knew.[12] She also offered the opinion that the fact the body was covered shows Meredith was killed by someone who knew her.

None of these assertions, however, are true. The DNA of Rudy Guede was found inside the victim, proving that he had sex with Meredith. Since she barely knew Rudy and already had a boyfriend, it is extremely improbable that she had consensual sex. As for the "staged break-in," Rudy had recently broken into a house after throwing a rock through a second-floor window. He knew that most people went home for the holiday and the flat was likely empty. There was glass all the way across the room and in the murder victim's room. There was glass embedded in an inside shutter. This could only have been caused by a rock thrown from the outside, not from the inside as the police and Bruzzone have theorized. Since the occupants of the house were all young women, who sometimes leave their clothes on the floor, the most probable explanation is that he threw a rock through the window, the glass broke, projected through the house, and landed in pieces on the clothes, and then he climbed in through the second story window in order to burglarize the house, as he had recently done at other houses for which he was arrested.

Shortly after that, Meredith came home, and then he stabbed her and raped her. He was an athletic man who most likely was stronger than Meredith. This wouldn't be the first time a man killed a woman by himself. The fixation on the idea that he couldn't have worked alone is absurd. As for the idea that the body was covered because the murderer knew her, fair enough, Guede had met her previously, when he was playing basketball with her boyfriend, and earlier that evening. That doesn't mean Sollecito and Knox were involved. The Italian press continuously return to the idea that Guede acted with *ignoti* or other unidentified persons, based on some of the judgments of the case. Knox and Sollecito were found by the Italian courts to not be involved. There is no evidence that other "unknown" persons had to be involved.

Following my review of the case and my realization of the enormity of the factual errors in Barbie's book, I translated some of the *motivazioni* (motivations) with the help of my Italian tutor and wrote blog posts in Italian about the case. Suddenly all the "guilters" obsessed with the case, who were sharing their confirmation-biased information, flocked onto my internet postings.

Earlier in this book, a research study was described where the perception of test takers on how well they had done on the test persisted even after they were told that the test results were faked. Those who were told they did better than average continued to think they were above average and the "failures" thought they were below average. Outside observers of the testing held the same belief, even after they were told that this was an experiment on the persistence of beliefs.[13] These same researchers did another study where they separated people into those who were for or against capital punishment. They presented both groups with unbiased neutral information about the topic. What they found is that individuals viewed information as "biased" that they interpreted as not supporting their opinion, and they gravitated toward information that supported their opinion.[14] Presenting the material made the groups more polarized, not less. The researchers concluded that the results were due to affirmation bias, or the tendency to seek information that will reinforce one's beliefs.

In the case of Amanda Knox, people went onto the internet and held discussions on internet forums with others who held their beliefs about guilt or innocence. This led to some forums being "pro-guilt" and others "pro-innocence." These people found a sense of community, and support and reassurance for their opinions, thus strengthening their bias. Changing their minds meant losing a community, which could be traumatic for socially isolated persons. This case was a classic example of confirmation bias, and foreshadowed what would happen with the 2020 presidential elections in the United States.

After the arrest of Amanda and Raffaele, misinformation continued to leak out from the sealed inquiries. English tabloid journalists and American freelance-abroad-cherry-pickers descended on the case like a flock of vultures who had finally been invited to a grand feast. It didn't help that the father of the murder victim, John Kercher, was an English tabloid writer himself, thus garnering sympathy from the other tabloid writers. Her brother also worked for the British Broadcasting Corporation (BBC), which is probably why they televised the blatantly pro-guilt documentary done by Andrea Vogt.[15]

Meanwhile, Amanda and Raffaele were rotting in jail awaiting the outcome of the trial, with Raffaele spending weeks in solitary confinement. The Knox family was overwhelmed by the media and had hired a public relations consultant from Seattle named David Marriott. A group of people working on publicity related to the case formed and called themselves the Friends of Amanda Knox (FOAK). In addition to my sister, the group included Mark Waterbury, Michael Heavey (the judge), screenwriter Tom Wright, and novelist Douglas Preston, who had lived in Italy and wrote *The Monster of Florence*,[16] which outlined the botched investigation of a serial killer in Florence by Giuliano Mignini, whose conspiracy theories also led to injustice in the Knox case.[17]

Waterbury was a scientific expert on DNA evidence. He later wrote a book about the case[18] that would debunk the DNA evidence claimed by the Perugia forensic examiners. Peggy Ganong (of the PMF blog), Peter Quennell (the TJFMK website owner), and their fans claimed that David Marriott had created a "supertanker" of lies and disinformation to gloss over the crimes of Amanda Knox. They sneered about the "FOAKers" as they called them and likened them to a sinister cabal. After that I wrote a blog post where I had Marriott, Preston, and the "lolcat" (whom I used as a mascot of the ongoing controversy) on a supertanker sailing into battle against Ganong and Quennell on a pirate ship.

During the time Andrea Vogt, Barbie Nadeau, and Nick Pisa were writing various fake news articles from their perches in Italy while presenting themselves as above the fray, they implied that they had superior linguistic talents and therefore had an inside scoop on the Knox story. I posted on my blog a photo shopped image of Vogt and Nadeau as birds of prey or vultures hovering over Knox as a fish with no flesh left on her bones for them to pick at.

The Amanda Knox case was fueling a media feeding frenzy. It had the voyeuristic aspects of sadism, sex, privilege gone awry, drugs, and licentiousness. English newspapers like the *Daily Mail* and *News of the World* exploited the sensationalism of the story and tapped into the anti-American and generally xenophobic tendencies of the English. It was like the Middle Ages, where the townspeople would turn out to watch a public hanging, or a lynch mob, where the villagers would shout their opinions regarding guilt or innocence based on the expressions on the faces of the detained. Except now, instead of gathering in the town square, they gathered in chat rooms on the internet.

A star guest of the "guilter" websites TJFMK and PMF was a woman named Ellie Davies who posted online under the moniker "Miss Represented." She was a self-proclaimed "handwriting expert" who claimed that she was a clinical psychologist with a doctorate in psychology and that she could tell Knox was guilty just by viewing how she looped her d's and p's in her handwritten notes. It turns out she wasn't a psychologist and wasn't an expert in anything and didn't even actually have a degree. In fact, her only work experience was working in a spa in Bath, England, and as a social media consultant. Susan M. Kovalinsky, a freelance journalist from the United States, wrote a post about her on the pro-innocence website *Injustice in Perugia*, where she described how she had initially believed it but later decided she was dealing with a psychopath.[19]

Fox News commentator Ann Coulter weighed in on the Amanda Knox case by saying "she just looks guilty." Showing no evidence of political bias in opinions on the case, as mentioned above, future Republican President Donald Trump publicly sided with Amanda in 2010, saying America should retaliate against the Italians and stop buying Parmigiano-Reggiano cheese. The case was a literal cauldron of fake news, confirmation bias, and conspiracy theories, with partisan websites squaring off against each other and their members spending hours scouring the internet for tidbits of information that confirmed their previously held notions. The #amandaknox hashtag on Twitter was in overdrive, and Facebook groups for and against her cause proliferated. In many ways, the Amanda Knox case was a forerunner of the 2020 presidential election.[20]

An imprisoned Mafioso named Luciano Aviello, whom Barbie Nadeau elsewhere said looked like a ten-year-old, claimed on the witness stand that Meredith was not murdered by Amanda, but by his brother and an accomplice.[21] He claimed that Raffaele's attorney, Giulia Bongiorno, had offered to pay him off to give testimony favorable to her client, and that he was trying to raise money to get a sex change operation, so he could look like Vladimir Luxuria, a transgender member of the Italian parliament. A child killer named Mario Alessi, who shared a prison cell with Rudy Guede, testified that Rudy had confessed to him that he was guilty of the crime.[22]

I wrote several blog posts that I thought contributed scientific evidence establishing Amanda Knox's innocence. First, I called on my background in neuroscience and cognitive research, including studies I had done on false memory, to point out that memories are fallible, especially under stress, and up to one quarter of confessions obtained under police interrogation are later determined to be false.[23] That is what happened with the West Memphis Three, who were convicted based on a false confession obtained under false pretenses, with extended interrogation times and brutal tactics (similar to the Amanda Knox interrogation in Perugia). Our own research showed that memories are fallible and false memories can be implanted. In one of our studies, we read a list of words that were highly associated with a word like *needle* (e.g. sharp, prick) but didn't include the word itself. When people were asked to recall the words they had viewed, three-fourths of them falsely recalled seeing the word *needle*. Often people are absolutely convinced of these false memories. We also found that people who had undergone stress such as childhood abuse were more likely to falsely recall seeing the words.[24]

Another blog post I wrote drew on my medical knowledge to comment on several of the "motivations" (written descriptions of the basis of a judge's decisions that are part of the Italian judicial system) that came from the hearings and court decisions. What was at issue was the homeless man, Curatolo, claiming to see Knox leaving the area of the crime scene at about 11:00 p.m. on the night of the murder, and the report of a neighbor hearing a scream at about that time. However, it was clearly established that Meredith was with friends and had eaten some food at about 6:00 p.m., and then watched a movie that was 123 minutes long, after which she left. She arrived home shortly before 9:00 p.m., based on closed caption television (CCTV) footage and a dropped call as she walked through a garage on her way back to her house. The autopsy showed no stomach contents at the time of death. Several Italian doctors were reported to have claimed that stomach transit was highly variable and could take hours; however, in my review of the medical and experimental scientific literature, it was clearly established that food transits the stomach and enters the small intestine within two to three hours (in the absence of medical conditions like diabetic gastroparesis, which Meredith did not have).[25] This, in my opinion, was definitive proof that the 11:00 p.m. timeline for the murder was false, disqualifying the prosecution's main witnesses. I concluded that the only evidence the prosecution had was "cartwheels and kisses," and that was not adequate to convict someone in a court of law.

As 2011 rolled around, and the new trial approached, the internet frenzy continued. The internet sleuths, including Bruce Fisher and Steve and Michelle Moore, were writing on the Injustice in Perugia website, and Paul Ciolino was reporting for CBS's *20/20*, documenting the many errors in the evidence collection and faults with the prosecution's case. Piers Morgan, formerly of the English tabloid *News of the World*—the newspaper that hacked into a young girl's cell phone to get the scoop (a crime for which editor Andy Coulson went to jail) after she was kidnapped and possibly dead—chimed in to say he also thought she was guilty. Meanwhile, John Kercher Sr. wrote a book about the case that was full of false information that made Amanda out to be a murderous she-devil who didn't deserve a retrial.[26] I criticized him on twitter for wanting to send her to jail with no evidence to support her guilt, and a BBC newscaster named Daniel Sanford responded to my tweet by saying I should be ashamed, and I should delete it. I responded by saying that the family wanted her to go to jail without a trial and based on no evidence, so why should I apologize for pointing out the injustice of that? After that I had about five hundred British people tweeting at me that I was vile, I should be ashamed, I supported murderers, etc. I literally had to spend time every day blocking people.

Eventually, on October 3, 2011, Twitter banned me,[27] saying I had made violent threats. It just happened to be the day Amanda Knox's first murder conviction was overturned. I asked to see where I had made threats. They just said I violated their policy but didn't say where. I assumed there were pro-guilt employees of Twitter working in England who did it, but I had no way of finding out, short of suing them.

On July 9, 2017, my wife and I, together with our daughter, Sabina, and son, Dylan, traveled to Prague, Czech Republic, where I presented in a panel with my sister, Anne, at the annual meeting of the International Academy of Law and Mental Health (IALMH). The title of the presentation was, "Exonerated: Amanda Knox and Raffaele Sollecito, Ten Years and Many Insights Later."[28] We followed up with another panel at the Rome meeting of the IALMH in 2019 focusing on media distortions of high-profile cases and highlighting the Knox case.[29] Joining us on the panel in Prague were a child psychiatrist and a forensics expert, as well as Raffaele himself, who had Sabina translate and read a statement from the court: "It appears clear that if Mr. Sollecito would have stated immediately, without subsequent contradictions, that the girl had remained far away from him in the hours of the crime … his position in the trial would certainly have been different." In other words, he had been punished for refusing to lie about what happened.

My own presentation was "The Role of Medical Science: Physiology and False Memories." I talked about the role of doctors, including myself, in analyzing the medical evidence, such as the lack of stomach contents, which disproved the prosecution's timeline of the murder happening at about 11:00 p.m., as witnessed by the heroin addict, Curatolo, who claimed he saw Amanda and Raffaele in the piazza together near the house. I also outlined the scientific evidence regarding false memory[30, 31, 32] and the effects of harsh police interrogation tactics on creating coerced and false confessions, as had happened in this case, and the role of the media and the internet in perpetuating misinformation and creating conspiracy theories that impede the pursuit of justice.

I discussed a paper[33] I had written about a case in the International War Crimes Tribunal in The Hague, which prosecuted one of the militia members accused of war crimes in Bosnia, where the witness was a Muslim woman who was the victim of rape. Her disjointed testimony was in fact likely the effects of the stress of the attack on the encoding of the memory, and not on her reliability. Some memories for stressful events are strongly engraved, while others can be distorted. When under stress, there is an outpouring of hormones and brain chemicals like cortisol and norepinephrine that can make some aspects very clear and others not so much.[34] I discussed a study we published when I was at Yale University, where we asked soldiers from the Persian Gulf War in 1990 to fill out a questionnaire about what type of combat experiences they had in Iraq.[35] We followed up with them two years later to see if they had symptoms of posttraumatic stress disorder (PTSD), and if so, whether their symptoms were getting better or worse. We also gave them the same questionnaire about their war experiences, which we thought was a mistake, since we had already asked them those questions and didn't need to repeat it. But interestingly, when we looked at their answers, we found that the responses often changed. Sometimes, something as dramatic as having been shot and wounded was not reported at the two- or six-year follow-up, and vice versa. When we showed them the different responses, they were usually convinced that whatever they most recently reported was what actually occurred. They were convinced that it was the reality. And we couldn't find any motivation, such as seeking benefits for war-related problems, to explain our results, which we published in 1995 in the *American Journal of Psychiatry*.[36]

We all assume that our memories are infallible, but scientific research does not support this assumption. I presented a study conducted by Ira Hyman of Western Washington University in Bellingham, Washington.[37] The researchers brought in volunteers at periodic intervals and asked them questions about their memories of past experiences. The researchers introduced a story about how the volunteer had spilled a punch bowl at a wedding when they were small children, something that had never happened. At first the participants had no memory of the event (obviously, since it never happened). But with time, they started to "remember" details of the event, and with time and repeated interviews some of the participants had launched into full-fledged elaborations of details related to the spilling of the punch bowl that went beyond the original fabricated story. ("I spilled the punch on Uncle Edward, and he became very angry at me.") This study, and many more like it, showed that memory could be distorted. This had important implications for the effects of coercive police interrogations on false confessions, which have been shown to occur in as many as a quarter of cases where these coercive interrogations occur.

After I had shown evidence of false memory effects, I went on to illustrate them to my audience. I showed a list of words, then read them out loud, and asked the audience to remember them for later.[38, 39]

thread
pin
eye
sewing
sharp
point
prick

thimble
haystack
thorn
hurt
injection
syringe
cloth
knitting

I then showed a new list of words, and repeated them one by one, asking the audience to raise their hands if they had seen them before.

sharp
wallet
prick
needle
thimble
knitting

"Sharp?" yes, pretty much everyone raised their hand. "Wallet?" Nope. "Prick?" Hands raised. And then, demonstrating a parlor trick I had performed a dozen times before for audiences at scientific conferences and in lectures to professional groups in the past, I said "needle." About 80 percent of the audience raised their hands. I then put up the original list of words.

"Do you see 'needle' anywhere on that list?" The audience looked at each other, dumbfounded. "The interesting thing is that you have the feeling of knowledge, like you're sure you've seen the word before. But you haven't." I went on to explain that this was an example of false memory and showed how an accused person who is interrogated for twelve hours at a time and hit on the head and told to "Remember!" or to "Imagine the scene as if you had been there, and describe it" or lied to about "proof" that they were at the scene of the crime, would become confused and then make false confessions. And justice is not served.

NOTES

CHAPTER 1

1. Nina Burleigh, "How Amanda Knox's Trial Was the Dawn of the Fake News Era," *Rolling Stone*, June 13, 2019. Retrieved from https://www.rollingstone.com/culture/culture-features/amanda-knox-nina-burleigh-fake-news-italy-murder-847731, September 3, 2021.
2. Graig Graziosi, "Amanda Knox publicly Shames Alt-Right Blogger for Attacking Her as a 'Greedy Leech' and 'Murderer'," *The Independent*, February 10, 2020. Retrieved from https://www.independent.co.uk/news/world/americas/amanda-knox-alt-right-a9328381.html, October 7, 2021.
3. Natasha Bertrand, "'A Model for Civilization': Putin's Russia Has Emerged as a 'Beacon for Nationalists' and the American Alt-Right," *Business Insider*, December 10, 2016. Retrieved from https://www.businessinsider.com/russia-connections-to-the-alt-right-2016-11, October 7, 2021.
4. "Labyrinths: With Amanda Knox and Christopher Robinson," November 20, 2020. Retrieved from https://podcasts.apple.com/us/podcast/plato-the-primate-pooped-tim-tandice-urban/id1494368441?i=1000499554623.
5. Ibid.
6. Nina Burleigh, *The Fatal Gift of Beauty: The Trial of Amanda Knox* (New York: Crown, 2011).
7. Peter Gill, "Analysis and Implications of the Miscarriages of Justice of Amanda Knox and Raffaele Sollecito," *Forensic Science International: Genetics* 23, (2016): 9–18. Retrieved from https://www.sciencedirect.com/science/article/pii/S1872497316300333.
8. Benjamin Franklin, *Letter to Benjamin Vaughan*.
9. Douglas Preston and Mario Spezi, *The Monster of Florence* (New York: Grand Central Publishing, 2013).
10. Alix Kirsta, "'I thought—I'm in Serious Trouble Here'," *The Guardian*, December 14, 2006. Retrieved from https://www.theguardian.com/world/2006/dec/14/italy.ukcrime, September 7, 2021.
11. Burleigh, *The Fatal Gift*.
12. Daniele Mastrogiacomo, "Come funziona la giuria e in caso di parità . . ." *La Reppublica*, June 1, 1999. Retrieved from https://www.repubblica.it/online/fatti/martarusso/giudici/giudici.html, September 12, 2021.
13. "La giuria popolare in Italia e nel Common law," *studentigiurisprudenza.it*, November 15, 2018. Retrieved from https://studentigiurisprudenza.it/2018/11/15/la-giuria-popolare-in-italia-e-nel-common-law/, September 12, 2021.

14. "La giuria popolare in Italia e nel Common law," *studentigiurisprudenza.it*, November 15, 2018. Retrieved from https://studentigiurisprudenza.it/2018/11/15/la-giuria -popolare-in-italia-e-nel-common-law/, September 12, 2021.

15. Liz Robbins, "An American in the Italian Wheels of Justice," *New York Times*, December 5, 2009. Retrieved from https://thelede.blogs.nytimes.com/2009/12/05/an -american-in-the-italian-wheels-of-justice, September 12, 2021.

16. Beppe Severgnini, "I verdetti fai-da-te e quel tifo Usa sbagliato," *Corriere della Sera*, December 8, 2009. Retrieved from https://www.corriere.it/cronache/09_dicembre _08/caso-amanda-knox-tifo-america-commento-severgnini_0619fc9c-e3f1-11de -8eb6-00144f02aabc.shtml, September 12, 2021.

CHAPTER 2

1. "Meredith 'Took Two Painful Hours to Die after Refusing to Take Part In Extreme Sexual Experiences'," *Daily Mail*, November 10, 2007. Retrieved from https://www .dailymail.co.uk/news/article-492695/Meredith-took-painful-hours-die-refusing -extreme-sexual-experiences.html.

2. Amanda Knox. "European Court of Human Rights," *Amanda Knox* 2019. Retrieved from *Amanda Knox, European Court of Human Rights* Amandaknox.com (2019), http://www.amandaknox.com/2019/01/24/european-court-of-human-rights-2 / August 30, 2021.

3. William F. Buckley, Jr. and Dr. Giovanni Costigan Debate, University of Washington, Seattle. [audio] In A. A. O. P. Broadcasting (Producer). Retrieved from https: //americanarchive.org/catalog/cpb-aacip-27-m901z42b2w, September 7, 2021.

CHAPTER 3

1. Washington Pattern Instructions Committee. (2021). *Advance Oral Instruction-Beginning of Proceedings*, In Washington Courts (Ed.), (Vol. 1.01). Olympia, Washington: State of Washington.

2. Ibid.

3. Ibid.

4. Ibid.

5. Ibid.

6. Ibid.

7. Ibid.

8. Ibid.

9. Ibid.

10. Ibid.

CHAPTER 4

1. Lee Ross, Mark R. Lepper, and Michael Hubbard, "Perseverance in Self-Perception and Social Perception: Biased Attributional Processes in the Debriefing Paradigm," *Journal of Personality and Social Psychology*, 32, no. 5 (November 1975): 880–892.

2. Ibid.

3. Ibid.
4. Ibid.
5. Charles G. Lord, Lee Ross, and Mark R. Lepper, "Biased Assimilation and Attitude Polarization: The Effects of Prior Theories on Subsequently Considered Evidence," *Journal of Personality and Social Psychology*, 37, no. 11 (November 1979): 2098–2109.

CHAPTER 5

1. Cassandra Tate. "God Dies: An Essay by Frances Farmer," *HistoryLink.org*. Retrieved from https://www.historylink.org/file/4008 August 30, 2021.
2. Ibid.
3. Ibid.
4. Ibid.
5. "Frances Farmer to Get Hearing," *Spokane Chronicle*, January 15, 1943, p. 5. Retrieved from newspapers.com, August 30, 2021.

CHAPTER 6

1. Amy Wallace, "Till Murder Do Us Part: Dan and Betty Broderick's Divorce Played Out over five Vicious Years," *Los Angeles Times*, June 3, 1990. Retrieved from https://www.latimes.com/la-me-broderick3jun0390-story.html, August 30, 2021.
2. Julie Tamaki and Lisa R. Omphroy, "Public Reacts: Broderick Got What She Deserved: Opinion: In Wake of the Verdict, Most People Interviewed Agreed with Conviction. Some would Have Even Voted for First-Degree Murder," *Los Angeles Times*, December 11, 1991. Retrieved from https://www.latimes.com/archives/la-xpm-1991-12-11-me-369-story.html, May 27, 2022.
3. Ibid.
4. Personal communication, Betty Broderick to Anne Bremner, June 6, 2015.

CHAPTER 7

1. Michael Newton, *The Encyclopedia of Unsolved Crimes*. Infobase Publishing (New York: Checkmark Books, 2009).
2. Mara Leveritt, *Devil's Knot: The True Story of the West Memphis Three* (New York: Atria Books, 2003).
3. Ibid.
4. Ibid.
5. "Three Teens Are Arrested in Murder of Eight-Year-Olds.," *Baxter Bulletin*, June 5, 1993, p. 1.
6. Leveritt, *Devil's Knot*.
7. Ibid.
8. "Three Teens Are Arrested," *Baxter Bulletin*.
9. Ibid.
10. Leveritt, *Devil's Knot*.
11. Ibid.
12. Ibid.

13. Ibid.
14. Tim Hackler, "Complete Fabrication," *Arkansas Times*, October 7, 2004. Retrieved from https://arktimes.com/news/cover-stories/2004/10/07/complete-fabrication?oid=1886107, September 6, 2021.
15. Hackler, "Complete Fabrication."
16. Ibid.
17. Ibid.
18. Roger Brown and James Kulik, "Flashbulb Memories," *Cognition* 5, (1977): 73–99.
19. John Neil Bohannon III and Victoria Louise Symons, "Flashbulb Memories: Confidence, Consistency and Quantity," in Eugene Winograd and Ulrich Neisser (eds.), *Affect and Accuracy in Recall: Studies in "Flashbulb" Memories.* (New York: Cambridge University Press, 1992), 65–94.
20. David B. Pillemer, "Flashbulb Memories of the Assassination Attempt on President Reagan," *Cognition* 16, (February 1984): 63–80.
21. Ulric Neisser and Nicole Harsch, "Phantom Flashbulbs: False Recollections of Hearing the News about Challenger," in Eugene Winograd and Ulrich Neisser eds., *Affect and Accuracy in Recall: Studies in "Flashbulb" Memories.* (New York: Cambridge University Press, 1992), 9–31.
22. Brown and Kulik, "Flashbulb Memories," *Cognition* 5, (1977): 73–99.
23. Neisser and Harsch, "Phantom Flashbulbs."
24. Tim Hackler, "Complete Fabrication."
25. Ibid.
26. Leveritt, *Devil's Knot.*
27. Neal Earley, "Echols' Attorney Files Motion In Wake of Missing Evidence," arkansasonline.com. Retrieved from https://www.arkansasonline.com/news/2021/jul/17/echols-attorney-files-motion-in-wake-of-missing/, September 6, 2021.
28. Ibid.

CHAPTER 8

1. Cydney Adams, "June 17, 1994: O.J. Simpson White Bronco Chase Mesmerizes Nation," CBS News, June 17, 2016. Retrieved from https://www.cbsnews.com/news/june-17-1994-o-j-simpson-car-chase-mesmerizes-nation/, August 30, 2021.
2. Joel Achenbach, "Ito Blinks in Spotlight," *Washington Post*, November 19, 1994. Retrieved from https://www.washingtonpost.com/archive/politics/1994/11/19/ito-blinks-in-spotlight/b0a3f3d5-eab5-46e1-994b-ddf1a8b6222e/, October 7, 2021.
3. Elizabeth Chuck, "Susan Smith, Mother Who Killed Kids: 'Something Went Very Wrong That Night,'" NBC News, July 13, 2015. Retrieved from https://www.nbcnews.com/news/us-news/susan-smith-mother-who-killed-kids-something-went-very-wrong-n397051, October 8, 2021.
4. Ibid.
5. Jeffrey Toobin, "An Incendiary Defense," *New Yorker*, July 25, 1994. Retrieved from https://www.newyorker.com/magazine/1994/07/25/an-incendiary-defense, August 30, 2021.
6. Ibid.
7. Ibid.
8. Ibid.

9. Ibid.
10. "Detective Grilled about Bloody Glove at Estate, Past Testimony," *Baltimore Sun*, March 15, 1995. Retrieved from https://www.baltimoresun.com/news/bs-xpm-1995-03-15-1995074023-story.html, September 3, 2021.
11. "Frances Farmer to Get Hearing," *Spokane Chronicle*.

CHAPTER 9

1. "LeTourneau Found in Car with Former Student," *Kitsap Sun*, February 4, 1998. Retrieved from https://products.kitsapsun.com/archive/1998/02–04/0011_letourneau_found_in_car_with_form.html, September 1, 2021.
2. Pamela Warrick, "The Fall from Spyglass Hill," *Los Angeles Times*, April 29, 1998. Retrieved from https://www.latimes.com/archives/la-xpm-1998-apr-29-ls-45407-story.html, October 8, 2021.
3. Ibid.
4. Ibid.

CHAPTER 10

1. Nick Madigan, "Modesto Police Seek to Identify Bodies on Shore," *New York Times*, April 16, 2003. Retrieved from https://www.nytimes.com/2003/04/16/us/modesto-police-seek-to-identify-bodies-on-shore.html.
2. Kate Sheehy, "Sweet Laci's Journey from Love Study to Tale of Horror," *New York Post*, November 13, 2004. Retrieved from https://nypost.com/2004/11/13/sweet-lacis-journey-from-love-story-to-tale-of-horror/, September 2, 2021.
3. "Scott Peterson Talks to ABC News," Diane Sawyer. ABC News, January 28, 2003. Retrieved from https://abcnews.go.com/GMA/story?id=124563, September 2, 2021.
4. Ibid., Video."/Interviewer: D. Sawyer. *ABC News*. Retrieved from https://abcnews.go.com/US/video/april-24-2003-scott-peterson-speaks-49711850 September 2, 2021. "Scott Peterson Jailed In Wife's Death," *CNN*, April 19, 2003. Retrieved from https://www.cnn.com/2003/US/West/04/19/peterson.case/index.html, October 8, 2021.
5. "Laci Peterson Case: Defense: Two-Timer, Yes, but No Murderer," *CNN*, December 31, 2007. Retrieved from http://www.cnn.com/2007/US/law/12/11/court.archive.peterson3/index.html May 27, 2022.

CHAPTER 11

1. Duncan Campbell, "Police Raid Jackson Ranch Following Fresh Allegations from Boy, 13," *The Guardian*, 18 Nov 2003. Retrieved from https://www.theguardian.com/world/2003/nov/19/usa.michaeljacksontrial, September 2, 2021.
2. Charles G. Lord, Lee Ross, and Mark R. Lepper, "Biased Assimilation and Attitude Polarization: The Effects of Prior Theories on Subsequently Considered Evidence," *Journal of Personality and Social Psychology*, 37, no. 11 (November 1979): 2098–2109.
3. John M. Broder, "Jackson's Ex-Wife Depicts Him as Victim," *New York Times*, April 29, 2005. Retrieved from https://www.nytimes.com/2005/04/29/us/jacksons-exwife-depicts-him-as-a-victim.html?searchResultPosition=1, September 2, 2021.

4. Roger Friedman, "Jacko's Mom Had $20K Deal for Story," FOX News May 19, 2015. Retrieved from https://www.foxnews.com/story/jacko-accusers-mom-had-20k-deal -for-story, May 31, 2022.

5. Ibid.

6. Ibid.

7. Ibid.

8. "Transcripts from the Superior Court of the State of California-Santa Barbara THE PEOPLE OF THE STATE OF CALIFORNIA, (Plaintiff,)-vs-MICHAEL JOE JACKSON, (Defendant.) No. 1133603," *The Michael Jackson Allegations.* Retrieved from https://themichaeljacksonallegations.com/2017/05/14/general-credibility-problems -with-the-arvizo-family/, May 31, 2022.

9. *The Michael Jackson Allegations,* Retrieved from https://themichaeljacksonallega-tions.com/2017/05/14/general-credibility-problems-with-the-arvizo-family/ May 31, 2022.

CHAPTER 12

1. S. L. Price, "The Damage Done," *Sports Illustrated*, June 26, 2006. Retrieved from https://vault.si.com/vault/2006/06/26/the-damage-done, September 2, 2021

2. William D. Cohan, "The Duke Lacrosse Player Still Outrunning His Past," *Vanity Fair*, March 24, 2014. Retrieved from https://www.vanityfair.com/style/2014/03/duke -lacrosse-rape-scandal-ryan-mcfadyen, September 2, 2021.

3. "Judge Sentences Ex-Durham County District Attorney Nifong to Jail for a Day," Fox News, August 31, 2007. Retrieved from https://www.foxnews.com/story/judge -sentences-ex-durham-county-district-attorney-nifong-to-jail-for-a-day, September 3, 2021.

4. William D. Cohan, "Duke Lacrosse Player."

5. Ibid.

6. Ibid.

7. Selena Roberts, *A-Rod: The Many Lives of Alex Rodriguez* (New York: Harper, 2009).

8. Selena Roberts, "Sports of The Times—When Peer Pressure, Not a Conscience, Is Your Guide," *New York Times*, March 31, 2006. Retrieved from https://www.nytimes.com /2006/03/31/sports/when-peer-pressure-not-a-conscience-is-your-guide.html, September 3, 2021.

9. Ibid.

10. "Judge Sentences," Fox News, August 31, 2007.

11. Cohan, "Duke Lacrosse Player."

12. Ibid.

13. "Judge Sentences," Fox News, August 31, 2007.

14. Cohan, "Duke Lacrosse Player."

15. John Koblin, "The Sportswriter Who Left Her Job after Finding a Million Dollars," deadspin.com, July 15, 2013. Retrieved from https://deadspin.com/the-sportswriter -who-left-her-job-after-finding-a-milli-731176557, September 3, 2021

CHAPTER 13

1. Nick Pisa, "Foxy Knoxy Singing and Smiling at Murder Trial," *Express,* September 18, 2008. Retrieved from https://www.express.co.uk/news/world/62019/Foxy-Knoxy-singing-and-smiling-at-murder-trial, September 7, 2021
2. "Amanda Knox Framed: Picture Hung in Italian Police 'Hall of Shame' BEFORE She Was Charged with Murder," CBS News, April 15, 2010. Retrieved from https://www.cbsnews.com/news/amanda-knox-framed-picture-hung-in-italian-police-hall-of-shame-before-she-was-charged-with-murder/, September 3, 2021.
3. Pisa, "Foxy Knoxy."
4. Andrew Malone, "The Wild, Raunchy Past of Foxy Knoxy," *Daily Mail*, December 3, 2007. Retrieved from https://www.dailymail.co.uk/femail/article-498853/The-wild-raunchy-past-Foxy-Knoxy.html#:~:text=Amanda%20Knox%20%2D%20accused%20of%20killing,%2C%20drugs%20and%20sex%20.
5. "Secret Diary Reveals Foxy Knoxy Was 'Always Thinking about Sex'," *Daily Mail*, November 30, 2008. Retrieved from https://www.dailymail.co.uk/news/article-1090608/Secret-diary-reveals-Foxy-Knoxy-thinking-sex.html, September 3, 2021.
6. Rod Blackhurst and Brian McGinn (writers). *Amanda Knox*, Netflix, 2016.
7. Gordon Rayner, "Meredith Kercher Trial: How Angelic Student Orchestrated 'Satanic' Murder," *The Telegraph*, December 4, 2009. Retrieved from https://www.telegraph.co.uk/news/worldnews/europe/italy/6727259/Meredith-Kercher-trial-how-angelic-student-orchestrated-satanic-murder.html.
8. Frances D'Emilio, "Italy Top Court: Amanda Knox Conviction Based on Poor Case," AP News, September 7, 2015. Retrieved from https://apnews.com/article/9b31c8e321064b2e83094602d152f46a, September 4, 2021.
9. Nina Burleigh, "How Amanda Knox's Trial Was the Dawn of the Fake News Era," *Rolling Stone*, June 13, 2019. Retrieved from https://www.rollingstone.com/culture/culture-features/amanda-knox-nina-burleigh-fake-news-italy-murder-847731, September 3, 2021.

CHAPTER 14

1. Elisabetta Povoledo, "Italian Experts Question Evidence in Knox Case," *New York Times*, June 29, 2011. Retrieved from https://www.nytimes.com/2011/06/30/world/europe/30knox.html September 3, 2021.
2. "Amanda Knox: A Complete Timeline of Her Italian Murder Case and Trial," biography.com Retrieved from https://www.biography.com/news/amanda-knox-murder-trial-timeline-facts.
3. Mark C. Waterbury, *The Monster of Perugia: The Framing of Amanda Knox* (New York: Perception Development, 2011).

CHAPTER 15

1. "Court Documents: Susan Powell's Blood, Hand-Written Note Expressing Fear Were Found in Utah Home," NBC News, March 30, 2012. Retrieved from https://www

.nbcnews.com/news/world/court-documents-susan-powells-blood-hand-written
-note-expressing-fear-flna611568.

2.   Nancy Ramsey and Kevin Dolak, "Susan Powell's Blood Found at Josh Powells's Utah
Home," ABC News, March 30, 2012. Retrieved from https://abcnews.go.com/US
/susan-powells-blood-found-josh-powells-utah-home/story?id=16042493, September
5, 2021.

3.   "Court Documents," NBC News, March 30, 2012.

4.   Ramsey and Dolak, "Susan Powell's Blood."

5.   "DSHS Documents Reveal Disturbing Information about Powell Family," www
.king5.com, February 17, 2012. Retrieved from https://www.king5.com/article/news
/local/dshs-documents-reveal-disturbing-information-about-powell-family
/330902365, September 5, 2021.

6.   Ibid.

7.   Kevin McCarty, "Caseworker Describes Last Moments of Susan Cox Powell's
Children's Lives," www.KIRO7.com, March 11, 2020. Retrieved from https://www
.kiro7.com/news/local/caseworker-describes-last-moments-susan-cox-powells
-childrens-lives/IA23JW5K6ZGPHEXQG6KX2OPDSI/.

8.   Ibid.

CHAPTER 16

1.   Ellen Killoran, "Mysterious Deaths at Spreckels Mansion: 'Loud Party' the Day after
Max Shacknai's Accident," *International Business Times*, July 18, 2011. Retrieved
from https://www.ibtimes.com/mysterious-deaths-spreckels-mansion-loud-party-day
-after-max-shacknais-accident-299779, September 10, 2021.

2.   Ibid.

CHAPTER 17

1.   "Island County Behavioral Health Impact Report," Island County, Washington.
Retrieved at https://www.islandcountywa.gov/Health/COVIDDOCS/August%20BH%20
Report.pdf, May 27, 2022.

2.   Eric Stevick, "Teen Fugitive Colton Harris-Moore Becomes a National Celebrity,"
Herald*Net*, October 9, 2009. Retrieved from https://www.heraldnet.com/news/front
-porch-54/, September 6, 2021.

3.   Eric Stevick, "Teen fugitive Colton Harris-Moore becomes a national celebrity,"
Herald.net, October 9, 2009. Retrieved from https://www.heraldnet.com/news/front
-porch-54/ September 6, 2021.

4.   Ibid.

5.   Ed Grossweiler, "Hijacker Bails Out with Loot," *Free Lance-Star*, November 26, 1971,
p. 1. Retrieved from https://news.google.com/newspapers?id=vuVNAAAAIBAJ&pg
=6384%2C3320413, September 10, 2021.

6.   "'Barefoot Bandit' Leaves Note, $100 at Raymond Clinic," KIROTV.com, June 17,
2010. Retrieved from http://www.kirotv.com/news/23939095/detail.html, September 6,
2021.

CHAPTER 18

1. "Cindy Anthony Breaks Down in Court at 911 Tapes," CNN.com—Transcripts, May 31, 2011. Retrieved from https://transcripts.cnn.com/show/ng/date/2011-05-31/segment /01.
2. Tim Ott, "Casey Anthony: A Complete Timeline of Her Murder Case and Trial," biography.com, Dec 2, 2020. Retrieved from https://www.biography.com/news/casey -anthony-muder-trial-timeline-facts, October 3, 2021.
3. "Anthony Trial: Internet Searches Focus of the Day," www.CBS8.com, June 8, 2011. Retrieved from https://www.cbs8.com/article/news/anthony-trial-internet-searches -focus-of-the-day/509-f06bacb3-024a-4c1e-845d-2f2cc7f1f390, September 6, 2021.
4. "Casey Anthony Insists She's a Victim in Jailhouse Interview," Associated Press, January 16, 2009. Retrieved from https://www.youtube.com/watch?v=ii2Okf1xpwE, September 6, 2021.
5. "Sex-abuse Claim May Force Casey Anthony to Take the Stand," *Florida Times-Union: Jacksonville.com*, May 27, 2011. Retrieved from https://www.jacksonville.com /article/20110527/NEWS/801250884.
6. "Hackers Finally Post Stolen Ashley Madison Data," wired.com, August 18, 2015. Retrieved from https://www.wired.com/2015/08/happened-hackers-posted-stolen -ashley-madison-data/, September 6, 2021.
7. Steven Lemongello, "Jeff Ashton Scandal: Former Casey Anthony Prosecutor Admits Using Ashley Madison," *Orlando Sentinel*, August 23, 2015. Retrieved from https: //www.orlandosentinel.com/news/breaking-news/os-jeff-ashton-ashley-madison -20150823-story.html, October 11, 2021.
8. "The Casey Anthony Murder Trial," CNN.com transcripts. Retrieved from http: //www.cnn.com/TRANSCRIPTS/1107/03/cnr.06.html, May 27,2022.

CHAPTER 19

1. Sharon Churcher, "Foxy Knoxy, the Girl Who Had to Compete with Her Own Mother for Men," *Daily Mail*, November 11, 2007. Retrieved from https://www.pressreader .com/uk/the-mail-on-sunday/20071111/281814279510863, September 4, 2021.
2. "Amanda Knox News: Donald Trump Says Convicted Murderer Innocent, Calls for Boycott of Italy," KOMO4 News, March 4, 2010. Retrieved from https://www.youtube .com/watch?v=jCIa5WUbTr4, September 6, 2021.
3. Ibid.
4. Ibid.

CHAPTER 20

1. Povoledo, "Italian Experts."
2. Stefano Conti and Carla Vecchiotti, "The Conti-Vecchiotti Report," Retrieved from http://amandaknoxcase.com/files/2011/07/translation-of-the-conti-vecchiotti-report2 .pdf, October 3, 2021.
3. Ibid.
4. Nick Pisa, "Amanda Knox's DNA 'WAS found on knife prosecutors claim was used to murder British exchange student'," *Daily Mail*, November 1, 2013. Retrieved from

https://www.dailymail.co.uk/news/article-2483410/Amanda-Knoxs-DNA-knife-used-murder-Meredith-Kercher.html, September 3, 2021.

5. Nick Pisa, "'I can't wait for the moment we are freed': Amanda Knox Bares Her Soul to Raffaele Sollecito in Never-Before-Seen Prison Letter," *Daily Mail*, November 4, 2013, Retrieved from https://www.dailymail.co.uk/news/article-2487148/Amanda-Knox-bares-soul-Raffaele-Sollecito-seen-prison-letter.html, September 3, 2021.

6. Nick Pisa, "Experts Slam Forensics Used to Convict Amanda Knox, Ex-Boyfriend," CNN, July 25, 2011, Retrieved from http://edition.cnn.com/2011/WORLD/europe/07/25/italy.knox.appeal/index.html, September 3, 2021.

7. "Amanda Knox: A Complete Timeline."

8. Stuart Kemp, "Amanda Knox Verdict: Daily Mail's Website Posts Wrong Decision: Mailonline Mistakenly Published a Report Stating That the 2009 Murder Conviction Upheld," *Hollywood Reporter*, October 3, 2011. Retrieved from https://www.hollywoodreporter.com/news/general-news/amanda-knox-verdict-daily-mail-243191/, September 4, 2021.

9. Stuart Kemp, "Amanda Knox Verdict."

CHAPTER 21

1. William Hirst et al., "A Ten-Year Follow-Up of a Study of Memory for the Attack of September 11, 2001: Flashbulb Memories and Memories for Flashbulb Events," *Journal of Experimental Psychology: General* 144, no. 3 (June 2015): 604–623. Retrieved from https://www.academia.edu/22013572/A_Ten_Year_Follow_Up_of_a_Study_of_Memory_for_the_Attack_of_September_11_2001_Flashbulb_Memories_and_Memories_for_Flashbulb_Events, September 8, 2021.

2. Brown and Kulik, "Flashbulb Memories."

3. David C. Rubin and Marc Kozin, "Vivid Memories," *Cognition* 16, no. 1 (February 1984): 81–95.

4. Ibid.

5. William Hirst et al., "Ten-Year Follow-Up."

6. Ibid.

7. Ibid.

8. Malcolm Gladwell, "Free Brian Williams," *Revisionist History* (podcast), June 7, 2018. Retrieved from https://www.pushkin.fm/episode/free-brian-williams/ May 27, 2022. Transcript retrieved at https://www.happyscribe.com/public/revisionist-history/revisionist-revisited-free-brian-williams, May 27, 2022.

9. Sheila Coronel, Steve Coll, and Derek Kravitz, "Rolling Stone and UVA: The Columbia University Graduate School of Journalism Report," *Rolling Stone*. Retrieved from https://www.rollingstone.com/culture/culture-news/rolling-stone-and-uva-the-columbia-university-graduate-school-of-journalism-report-44930/, September 7, 2021.

10. Molly Greenberg, "UVA Fraternity House Vandalized in Response to Rolling Stone Article," Bizjournals.com, November 20, 2014. Retrieved from https://www.bizjournals.com/washington/inno/stories/news/2014/11/20/uva-fraternity-house-vandalized-in-response-to.html, May 27, 2022.

11. Allison Benedikt and Hannah Rosin, "The Missing Men," *Slate*, December 2, 2014. Retrieved from http://www.slate.com/articles/double_x/doublex/2014/12/sabrina

_rubin_erdely_uva_why_didn_t_a_rolling_stone_writer_talk_to_the_alleged.html, September 7, 2021.

12. Ibid.
13. "'Jackie' Testifies: Rolling Stone Story Was 'What I Believed to Be True At The Time'," *The Guardian*, October 24, 2016. Retrieved from https://www.theguardian.com /media/2016/oct/24/rolling-stone-defamation-trial-uva-jackie-testifies, September 7, 2021.
14. Coronel, Coll, and Kravitz, "Rolling Stone and UVA."
15. Ibid.
16. Mara Leveritt, *Devil's Knot*.
17. "'Jackie' Testifies," *The Guardian*, October 24, 2016.
18. Ibid.
19. Ibid.
20. Franklin, *Letter to Benjamin Vaughan*.

CHAPTER 22

1. Simon Hattenstone, "Amanda Knox: 'They'll Have to Pull Me Back Kicking and Screaming to Prison'," *The Guardian*, January 30, 2014. Retrieved from https://www .theguardian.com/world/2014/jan/30/amanda-knox-prison-meredith-kercher-murder, September 4, 2021.
2. Conti and Vecchiotti, "The Conti-Vecchiotti Report."
3. Richard Fausett, "Bail Was $500, Money He Didn't Have. Atlanta Faces Calls for Change," *New York Times*, January 11, 2018. Retrieved from https://www.nytimes .com/2018/01/11/us/atlanta-bail-courts-reform.html, September 5, 2021.
4. Ibid.
5. Gennaro Marasca et al. "RULING On the Appeals Filed by SOLLECITO Raffaele, Born in Bari on 26/03/1984 KNOX Amanda Marie, Born in Seattle (USA) on 09/07/1987," September 24, 2015, Retrieved from http://amandaknoxcase.com/files /wp-content/uploads/2015/09/marasca-bruno-motivations-report.pdf, September 4, 2021.
6. Ibid.
7. Ibid.
8. Ibid.
9. Ibid.
10. Ibid.
11. Ibid.
12. Ibid.
13. Ibid.
14. Ibid.
15. D'Emilio, "Italy Top Court."
16. Amanda Knox, *Waiting to Be Heard: A Memoir* (New York: Harper, 2015).

CHAPTER 23

1. "Jury: Washington State Liable in Powell Boys' Deaths," ABC News, July 31, 2020. Retrieved from https://abcnews.go.com/Politics/wireStory/jury-washington-state -liable-powell-boys-deaths-72113884, September 5, 2021.

2. Larry Hobbs, "Dispatcher: 'What Was He Doing Wrong?'," *Brunswick News*, April 29, 2020. Retrieved from https://thebrunswicknews.com/news/local_news/dispatcher -what-was-he-doing-wrong/article_fe51cdd4-3bb6-5815-9dec-ddcdc8f879f8.html, December 19, 2021.

CHAPTER 24

1. Jade Abdul-Malik, "LISTEN: 911 Dispatcher Doesn't Understand What Arbery Is 'Doing Wrong'," Georgia Public Broadcasting, Retrieved from https://www.gpb.org /news/2020/05/08/listen-911-dispatcher-doesnt-understand-what-arbery-doing -wrong May 27, 2022. "Brunswick 911 Call 1:08 pm," *NPR*, February 23, 2020. Retrieved from https://cpa.ds.npr.org/wjsp/audio/2020/05/1_GCPD_Position_Line_2020 _02_23_13_08_14_by_Start_Time_desc.mp3, January 10, 2022.
2. Hobbs, "Dispatcher."
3. Ibid.
4. Abdul-Malik, "911 Dispatcher."
5. Hobbs, "Dispatcher."
6. Larry Hobbs, "Liberty County DA to Probe Glynn Shooting," *Brunswick News*, April 14, 2020. Retrieved from https://thebrunswicknews.com/breaking/liberty-county -da-to-probe-glynn-shooting/article_eae2baa1-07be-5ded-b742-758a8732ff58.html, December 19, 2021.
7. Richard Fausset, "Two Weapons, a Chase, a Killing and No Charges," *New York Times*, April 26, 2020. Retrieved from https://www.nytimes.com/2020/04/26/us /ahmed-arbery-shooting-georgia.html?action=click&module=RelatedLinks&pg type=Article, December 18, 2021.
8. Ibid.
9. Ibid.
10. Rick Rojas, Richard Fausset, and Serge F. Kovaleski, "Georgia Killing Puts Spotlight on a Police Force's Troubled History," *New York Times*, May 8, 2020. Retrieved from https://www.nytimes.com/2020/05/08/us/glynn-county-police-ahmaud-arbery.html, December 18, 2021.
11. Hobbs, "Liberty County DA."
12. Fausset, "Two Weapons."
13. "Ahmaud Arbery Shooting: A Timeline of the Case," *New York Times*, November 24, 2021. Retrieved from https://www.nytimes.com/article/ahmaud-arbery-timeline.html, May 27, 2022.
14. Larry Hobbs, "Police Mum on Circumstances Behind Satilla Shores Shooting," *Brunswick News*, February 26, 2020. Retrieved from https://thebrunswicknews.com /news/local_news/police-mum-on-circumstances-behind-satilla-shores-shooting /article_d06f0b36-04ea-51d5-ab7b-3ea858918ec5.html, May 27, 2022.
15. Rojas, Fausset, and Kovaleski, "Georgia Killing."
16. Eliott C. McLaughlin, Devon M. Sayers, Aita Spells, and Steve Almasy, "Ahmaud Arbery Killing: Three Men Found Guilty of Murder," CNN, November 24, 2021, Retrieved from https://www.cnn.com/2021/11/24/us/ahmaud-arbery-killing-trial -wednesday-jury-deliberations/index.html.

17. Nicole Carr, "Troubled Officer Shot and Killed Estranged Wife, Boyfriend," WSB-TV, June 29, 2018. Retrieved from https://www.wsbtv.com/news/local/georgia-officer-in-caroline-small-death-fatally-shoots-wife-male-friend-sources-say/779563495/, December 20, 2021.

18. "Gregory McMichael Had 16 Calls with Then-DA Jackie Johnson in the Weeks after Ahmaud Arbery's Death, Court Document Says," CBS News, May 5, 2022 Retrieved from https://www.cbsnews.com/news/ahmaud-arbery-death-gregory-mcmichael-district-attorney-jackie-johnson-spoke-16-times-document-says/, May 31, 2022.

19. Ibid.

20. Hobbs, "Liberty County DA."

21. "Gregory McMichael Had 16 Calls," CBS News, May 5, 2022.

22. Hobbs, "Liberty County DA."

23. Fausset, "Two Weapons."

24. Hobbs, "Liberty County DA."

25. Fausset, "Two Weapons."

26. Hobbs, "Dispatcher."

27. "Ahmaud Arbery Shooting," *New York Times*, November 24, 2021.

28. Hobbs, "Liberty County DA."

29. McLaughlin, Sayers, Spells, and Almasy, "Ahmaud Arbery killing."

30. Rojas, Fausset, and Kovaleski, "Georgia Killing."

31. "Ahmaud Arbery Shooting," *New York Times*, November 24, 2021.

32. Rojas, Fausset, and Kovaleski, "Georgia Killing."

33. LZ Granderson, "Column: Who Else Has Been Terrorized and Killed by Police Where Ahmaud Arbery Was Murdered?," *Los Angeles Times*, November 27, 2021. Retrieved from https://www.latimes.com/opinion/story/2021-11-27/jackie-johnson-prosecutor-caroline-small-ahmaud-arbery, December 20, 2021.

34. Rojas, Fausset, and Kovaleski, "Georgia Killing."

35. Granderson, "Column."

36. Nicole Carr, "Troubled Officer Shot and Killed Estranged Wife, Boyfriend.," WSB-TV, June 29, 2018. Retrieved from https://www.wsbtv.com/news/local/georgia-officer-in-caroline-small-death-fatally-shoots-wife-male-friend-sources-say/779563495/, December 20, 2021.

37. Granderson, "Column."

38. Carr, "Troubled Officer."

39. Granderson, "Column."

40. Ibid.

41. Carr, "Troubled Officer."

42. Ibid.

43. Ibid.

CHAPTER 25

1. Dalton Bennett, Joyce Sohyunn Lee, and Sarah Cahlan, "The Death of George Floyd: What Video and Other Records Show about His Final Minutes," *Washington Post*, May 30, 2020. Retrieved from https://www.washingtonpost.com/nation/2020/05/30/video-timeline-george-floyd-death/, December 20, 2021.

2. Josh Glancy, "George Floyd: Murder Conviction Is Far From Certain, Warn Legal Experts," *The Times*, August 9, 2020. Retrieved from https://www.thetimes.co.uk /article/george-floyd-murder-conviction-is-far-from-certain-warn-legal-experts -pg6dmrqw7, December 31, 2021.

3. Evan Hill, Ainara Tiefenthaler, Christiaan Triebert, Drew Jordan, Haley Willis, and Robin Stein, "How George Floyd Was Killed in Police Custody," *The New York Times*, May 31, 2020. Retrieved from https://www.nytimes.com/2020/05/31/us/george-floyd -investigation.html, December 20, 2021.

4. Eric Levenson, "Former Officer Knelt on George Floyd for 9 Minutes and 29 Seconds— Not the Infamous 8:46," CNN, March 30, 2021. Retrieved from https://www.cnn.com /2021/03/29/us/george-floyd-timing-929-846/index.html May 27, 2022.

5. Hill, Tiefenthaler, Triebert, Jordan, Willis, and Robin Stein, "How George Floyd Was Killed."

6. Derrick Bryson Taylor, "George Floyd Protests: A Timeline," *New York Times*, Nov 5, 2021. Retrieved from https://www.nytimes.com/article/george-floyd-protests-timeline.html, December 21, 2021.

7. Ibid.

8. Liz Navratil and Libor Jany, "As Mayor Frey Calls for Officer's Arrest, Violence Intensifies in Minneapolis," *Minneapolis Star Tribune*, May 28, 2020. Retrieved from https://www.startribune.com/as-mayor-frey-calls-for-officer-s-arrest-violence -intensifies-in-minneapolis/570804062/, May 27, 2022.

9. Liz Navratil and Jany, "Mayor Frey."

10. Ibid.

11. Ibid.

12. Ibid.

13. Bryson Taylor, "George Floyd Protests."

14. Ibid.

15. Ibid.

16. Ibid.

17. Ibid.

18. Ibid.

19. Ibid.

20. Aimee Ortiz, "What to Know About the Death of Rayshard Brooks," *New York Times*, May 6, 2021. Retrieved from https://www.nytimes.com/article/rayshard-brooks-what -we-know.html, December 22, 2021.

21. Ibid.

22. Ibid.

CHAPTER 26

1. "Jury Delivers Verdict In Wrongful Death Trial on Behalf of Susan Cox Powells's Sons," *News Tribune*, July 31, 2020. Retrieved from https://www.thenewstribune.com /news/local/article244647422.html, September 6, 2021.

CHAPTER 27

1. "Victims of Shooting During Kenosha Protests Engaged Gunman," Associated Press, August 28, 2020. Retrieved from https://apnews.com/article/ap-top-news-racial-injustice-il-state-wire-shootings-wi-state-wire-0994e25654d255e552aaa-d8a15e16c84, May 27, 2022.
2. Ibid.
3. Julie Bosman, "What to Know About the Trial of Kyle Rittenhouse," *New York Times*, Nov 19, 2021. Retrieved from https://www.nytimes.com/article/kyle-rittenhouse-trial.html, December 22, 2021.
4. Ibid.
5. "Shootings, Arrest, Trial, and More: The Kyle Rittenhouse Case Explained," NBC Chicago, November 15, 2021. Retrieved from https://www.nbcchicago.com/news/local/shootings-arrest-trial-and-more-the-kyle-rittenhouse-story-explained/2684756/, December 31, 2021.
6. Bosman, "What to Know."
7. "Victims of Shooting," Associated Press, August 28, 2020.
8. Julie Bosman, "Kyle Rittenhouse Acquitted on All Counts," *New York Times*, November 19, 2021. Retrieved from https://www.nytimes.com/live/2021/11/19/us/kyle-rittenhouse-trial, December 22, 2021.
9. "Victims of shooting," Associated Press, August 28, 2020.
10. Ibid.
11. Ibid.
12. Ibid.
13. Bosman, "What to Know."
14. Aila Slisco, "Pro-Trump Lawyer Lin Wood Said He 'Might Actually Be' Second Coming of Christ: Lawsuit," *Newsweek*, Dec 31, 2020. Retrieved from https://www.newsweek.com/pro-trump-lawyer-lin-wood-said-he-might-actually-second-coming-christ-lawsuit-1558400, December 22, 2021.
15. Mary Papenfus, "QAnon Believers Rattled After Kyle Rittenhouse Calls Extremist Lawyer Lin Wood 'Insane'," yahoo! news, November 27, 2021. Retrieved from https://news.yahoo.com/qanon-believers-rattled-kyle-rittenhouse-141259289.html May 27, 2022.
16. "US Media's Inaccurate Reporting on Rittenhouse Had Real Consequences Internationally: Greenwald," Fox News, November 20, 2020. Retrieved from https://www.foxnews.com/media/kyle-rittenhouse-glenn-greenwald-media-consequences December 31, 2021.

CHAPTER 28

1. "George Floyd Death Homicide, Official Post-Mortem Declares," BBC News, June 2, 2020. Retrieved from https://www.bbc.com/news/world-us-canada-52886593 December 20, 2021.
2. Ibid.
3. Tim Arango, Shaila Dewan, John Eligon, and Nicholas Bogel-Burroughs, "Derek Chauvin Is Found Guilty of Murdering George Floyd," *New York Times*, April 20, 2021. Retrieved from https://www.nytimes.com/2021/04/20/us/chauvin-guilty-murder-george-floyd.html, December 21, 2021.

CHAPTER 29

1. Julie Bosman, "What to Know."
2. Ibid.
3. Bosman, "Kyle Rittenhouse Acquitted."
4. Ibid.
5. Ibid.
6. Ibid.
7. Ibid.
8. Max Burns, "After Kyle Rittenhouse Trial, Biden Still Thinks the Jury System Works. He's wrong," NBC News, Nov 20, 2021. Retrieved from https://www.nbcnews.com /think/opinion/after-kyle-rittenhouse-trial-biden-still-thinks-jury-system-works -ncna1284295 December 22, 2021.
9. Ibid.
10. Bosman, "Kyle Rittenhouse Acquitted."
11. Ibid.
12. Ibid.
13. McLaughlin, Sayers, Spells, and Almasy, "Ahmaud Arbery Killing."
14. Ibid.
15. Ibid.
16. Hobbs, "Dispatcher."
17. Ibid.
18. Hobbs, "Liberty County DA."
19. Russ Bynum, "Defendant: Ahmaud Arbery 'Trapped Like a Rat' Before Slaying," ABC News, 10 November 2021. Retrieved from https://abcnews.go.com/US/wireStory /defendant-ahmaud-arbery-trapped-rat-slaying-81085944 December 31, 2021.
20. McLaughlin, Sayers, Spells, and Almasy, "Ahmaud Arbery Killing."
21. Ibid.
22. Ibid.
23. Ibid.

CHAPTER 30

1. Blackhurst and McGinn (writers). *Amanda Knox.*

POSTSCRIPT

1. Amanda Knox, "Who Owns Amanda Knox?," *The Atlantic*, July 31, 2021. Retrieved from https://www.theatlantic.com/ideas/archive/2021/07/amanda-knox-stillwater -matt-damon/619628/, October 11, 2021.
2. Ibid.
3. Ibid.
4. Ibid.

APPENDIX

1. J. Douglas Bremner, *Before You Take That Pill: Why the Drug Industry May Be Bad For Your Health: Risks and Side Effects You Won't Find on the Label of Commonly Prescribed Drugs, Vitamins, and Supplements* (New York: Penguin/Avery, 2008).
2. Doug Bremner, *The Goose That Laid the Golden Egg: Accutane, the Truth That Had to Be Told* (Atlanta, Georgia: Laughing Cow Books, 2011).
3. Doug Bremner, "Amanda Knox," Retrieved from https://beforeyoutakethatpill.com /blog/category/amanda-knox/, September 7, 2021
4. John Henry Browne, *The Devil's Defender: My Odyssey Through American Criminal Justice from Ted Bundy to the Kandahar Massacre* (Chicago, Illinois: Chicago Review Press, 2016).
5. Barbie Latza Nadeau, *Angel Face: Sex, Murder, and the Inside Story of Amanda Knox* (New York: Beast Books, 2010).
6. Burleigh, *Fatal Gift*.
7. Richard Owen, "Witness Tells of Meredith Kercher's Final 'Terrifying' Scream," *The Times*, March 27, 2009. Retrieved from https://www.thetimes.co.uk/article/witness -tells-of-meredith-kerchers-final-terrifying-scream-k8pdv7hd3k9, October 3, 2021.
8. "Murder Suspect 'Heard Meredith's Screams'," *Metro*, November 6, 2007. Retrieved from https://metro.co.uk/2007/11/06/murder-suspect-heard-merediths-screams -471409/, August 30, 2021.
9. Peter Gill, "Analysis and Implications of the Miscarriages of Justice of Amanda Knox and Raffaele Sollecito," *Forensic Science International: Genetics* 23 (July 2016): 9–18. Retrieved from https://www.sciencedirect.com/science/article/pii/S1872497316300333.
10. Johnny Brayson, "Why the DNA Evidence Against Amanda Knox Failed," *Bustle*, September 30, 2016. Retrieved from https://www.bustle.com/articles/186393-what- was-the-dna-evidence-in-the-amanda-knox-case-crime-scene-findings-raised-many -questions, October 3, 2021.
11. Ibid.
12. Rosa Scognamiglio, ""Guede non può aver agito da solo": tutti i dubbi sul delittl Kercher," *Il Giornale*, November 2, 2020. Retrieved from https://www.ilgiornale.it /news/cronache/omicidio-meredith-guede-non-ha-agito-solo-troppi-dubbi -sulla-1899881.html?fbclid=IwAR16qDFxs5zTe53HMVgZAojNy72-iSNJ-E5q Uxz9EOGZ3Z7URGyHN3oOqDU, May 27, 2022.
13. Lee Ross, Mark R. Lepper, and Michael Hubbard, "Perseverance In Self-Perception and Social Perception: Biased Attributional Processes in the Debriefing Paradigm," *Journal of Personality and Social Psychology* 32, no. 5 (November 1975): 880–892.
14. Charles G. Lord, Lee Ross, and Mark R. Lepper, "Biased Assimilation and Attitude Polarization: The Effects of Prior Theories on Subsequently Considered Evidence," *Journal of Personality and Social Psychology*, 37, no. 11 (November 1979): 2098–2109. doi:10.1037/0022–3514.37.11.2098.
15. Andrea Vogt (director), *Is Amanda Knox Guilty?* (BBC, 2005). Retrieved from https:// www.imdb.com/title/tt3549490/ September 7, 2021
16. Douglas Preston and Mario Spezi, *The Monster of Florence* (New York: Grand Central Publishing, 2013).
17. Ibid.

18. Mark C. Waterbury, *The Monster of Perugia: The Framing of Amanda Knox* (New York: Perception Development, 2011).

19. Susan M. Kovalinsky, "When the Blogger Misrepresents," *Musings in Obama's America*. Retrieved from https://musingsinobamasamerica.blogspot.com/2011/09/when-blogger-misrepresents.html, September 7, 2021

20. Nina Burleigh, "Fake News Era."

21. Krissy Allen, "Luciano Aviello: Star Witness for Amanda Knox and Raffaele Sollecito, Cleared," *Blasting News*, January 30, 2018. Retrieved from https://uk.blastingnews.com/world/2018/01/luciano-aviello-star-witness-for-amanda-knox-and-raffaele-sollecito-cleared-002325513.html, September 4, 2021.

22. Nick Pisa, "Convicted Child Killer Tells Italian Court Amanda Knox Did Not Kill British Student Meredith Kercher," *Daily Mail*, June 18, 2011. Retrieved from https://www.dailymail.co.uk/news/article-2005151/Amanda-Knox-did-kill-Meredith-Kercher-Mario-Alessi-tells-Italian-court.html, September 4, 2021.

23. J. Douglas Bremner, "The Neurobiology of Trauma and Memory in Children," in *Stress, Trauma, and Children's Memory Development: Neurobiological, Cognitive, Clinical, and Legal Perspectives*, Mark L. Howe, Gail S. Goodman, and Dante Cicchetti eds. (New York: Oxford University Press, 2008): 11–49.

24. J. Douglas Bremner, Katie K. Shobe, and John F. Kihlstrom, "False Memories In Women with Self-Reported Childhood Sexual Abuse: An Empirical Study," *Psychological Sciences* 11 (July 2000): 333–337.

25. Stephan Hellmig et al., "Gastric Emptying Time of Fluids and Solids In Healthy Subjects Determined By C-13 Breath Tests: Influence of Age, Sex and Body Mass Index.," *Gastroenterology* 21 (December 2006): 1832–1838.

26. John Kercher, *Meredith* (London, U.K.: Hodding, 2013).

27. Doug Bremner. "Banished from Twitter." in *Before You Take That Pill*, May 1, 2016. Retrieved from https://beforeyoutakethatpill.com/blog/2016/05/01/banished-from-twitter/, September 6, 2021

28. Doug Bremner. "Live Blogging from the XXXVth IALMH Meeting in Prague: Panel on the Amanda Knox & Raffaele Sollecito Case: Exonerated: Ten Years and Many Insights Later," *Before You Take That Pill*, July 13, 2017. Retrieved from https://beforeyoutakethatpill.com/blog/2017/07/13/live-blogging-from-the-xxxvth-ialmh-in-prague-panel-on-the-amanda-knox-raffaele-sollecito-caseexonerated-ten-years-and-many-insights-later/.

29. Doug Bremner. "Live Blogging from the International Academy of Law and Mental Health (IALMH) in Rome: The True Story of Amanda Knox, an Innocent Abroad," *Before You Take That Pill*, September 3, 2019. Retrieved from https://beforeyoutakethatpill.com/blog/2019/09/03/live-blogging-from-the-international-academy-of-law-and-mental-health-ialmh-in-rome-the-true-story-of-amanda-knox-an-innocent-abroad/, September 7, 2021

30. Bremner, Shobe, and Kihlstrom, "False memories."

31. J. Douglas Bremner, John H. Krystal, Dennis S. Charney, and Steven M. Southwick, "Neural Mechanisms In Dissociative Amnesia for Childhood Abuse: Relevance to the Current Controversy Surrounding the 'False Memory Syndrome.'" *American Journal of Psychiatry* 153, no. 7 (July 1996): 71–82.

32. Ira E. Hyman, Troy H. Husband, and F. James Billings, "False Memories of Childhood Experiences," *Applied Cognitive Psychology* 9 (June 1995): 181–197.
33. Landy Sparr and J. Douglas Bremner, "Posttraumatic Stress Disorder and Memory: Prescient Medicolegal Debate at the International War Crimes Tribunal?," *Law and Psychiatry* 10 (March 2005): 147–159.
34. Bernet M. Elzinga and J. Douglas Bremner, "Are the Neural Substrates of Memory the Final Common Pathway in Posttraumatic Stress Disorder (PTSD)?," *Journal of Affective Disorders* 70, no. 1 (June 2002): 1–17.
35. Steven M. Southwick, Charles A. Morgan, Linda M. Nagy, J. Douglas Bremner, Andreas L. Nicolaou, Dennis R. Johnson, Robert Rosenheck, and Dennis S. Charney, "Trauma-Related Symptoms In Veterans of Operation Desert Storm: A Preliminary Report," *American Journal of Psychiatry* 150, no. 10 (October 1993): 1524–1528.
36. Steven M. Southwick, Charles A. Morgan, Adam Darnell, J. Douglas Bremner, Andreas L. Nicolaou, Linda M. Nagy, and Dennis S. Charney, "Trauma Related Symptoms In Veterans of Operation Desert Storm: A Two-Year Followup," *American Journal of Psychiatry* 59 (August 1995): 97–107.
37. Hyman, Husband, and Billings, "Childhood Experiences."
38. Bremner, Shobe, and Kihlstrom, "False Memories."
39. Susan A. Clancy, Daniel L. Schacter, Richard J. McNally, and Roger K. Pitman, "False Recognition In Women Reporting Recovered Memories of Sexual Abuse.," *Psychological Sciences* 11 (January 2000): 26–31.

INDEX